Praise for *Progress in the Pulpit*

Biblical preaching is the urgent need of the contemporary church. In *Progress in the Pulpit*, Jerry Vines and Jim Shaddix explain why expositional preaching matters and how to do it. Rookie preachers and seasoned preachers will benefit from the counsel of these wise and faithful preachers.

H.B. CHARLES JR.
Shiloh Metropolitan Baptist Church, Jacksonville, FL

Power in the Pulpit, published years ago, remains today one of the most effective books in history for teaching the art and science of expository preaching. In *Progress in the Pulpit*, Shaddix and Vines have drawn from their vast knowledge and experience, not only on preaching, but from living lives of godly character. This book encourages pastors and preachers to continue to progress and grow in their preparation, delivery, and evaluation. I highly recommend this book to anyone who serves in the ministry of teaching and preaching.

MATT CARTER
Pastor of Preaching, The Austin Stone Community Church

Preaching is at the heart of Christianity. Biblical, Christ-centered preaching brings salvation to non-Christians (1 Cor. 1:21). Such preaching also matures and equips those who are already followers of Jesus Christ (2 Tim. 3:16–4:5). No wonder the apostle Paul stated that preachers that "work hard at preaching" are "to be considered worthy of double honor" (1 Tim. 5:17). If a preacher ought to prioritize anything, it should be preaching. In *Progress in the Pulpit*, veteran pastors and homileticians, Jerry Vines and Jim Shaddix, give beneficial insights that will help any Christian preacher improve. I enthusiastically recommend this helpful work.

STEVE GAINES
Pastor, Bellevue Baptist Church, Memphis, TN
President of the Southern Baptist Convention

Progress in the Pulpit is not just another preaching resource. It's a clarion call for men of God to resist the temptation to be parrots, puppets, or pirates of others' sermons to being prophets of God's Word. Readers will walk through a step-by-step process for moving from a blank screen to a Spirit-empowered sermon. Each chapter contains a treasure trove of applicable insights, which can be incorporated into one's preaching immediately. Whether you're the lead preaching pastor or fill-in Bible study teacher, everyone will walk away from the book with the confidence to grow as a better communicator of God's Word.

ROBBY GALLATY
Senior Pastor, Long Hollow Baptist
Author, *Growing Up* and *The Forgotten Jesus*

Jerry Vines and Jim Shaddix have once again written a book that every preacher could benefit from. As a follow up to their incredible book *Power in the Pulpit*, you now hold in your hand their new inspirational book *Progress in the Pulpit*. Both of these men of God have a desire to see every preacher grow in their preaching. Many preachers unfortunately have pressed the cruise control button when they stand in the pulpit on Sunday mornings and yet wonder why the ministry is not growing. Well, I assure you that you will not see growth in the pew until you see growth in the pulpit. Thank you Vines and Shaddix for understanding that if our churches desire to have growth in the pews we must first see progress in our pulpits!

FRED LUTER JR
Pastor, Franklin Avenue Baptist Church, New Orleans, LA
Former President, Southern Baptist Convention

When Vines and Shaddix wrote *Power in the Pulpit*, they gave preachers and teachers of preaching a sound, practical guide that has become a standard text for teaching expository preaching in many seminaries, including my own. That they have followed up with a new volume, *Progress in the Pulpit*, is welcome news to all students of good preaching. This book will prove valuable both to seasoned preachers who desire to continue their progress, and to seminary students who are eager to tackle additional topics of study beyond the basics.

BARRY McCARTY
Professor of Preaching and Rhetoric, Southwestern Baptist Theological Seminary

PROGRESS IN THE PULPIT

HOW TO GROW IN YOUR PREACHING

JERRY VINES AND
JIM SHADDIX

MOODY PUBLISHERS

CHICAGO

Unless otherwise indicated, Scripture quotations are from the ESV® Bible (The Holy Bible, English Standard Version®), copyright © 2001 by Crossway, a publishing ministry of Good News Publishers. Used by permission. All rights reserved.

Scripture quotations marked KJV are taken from the King James Version.

Scripture quotations marked NKJV are taken from the New King James Version. Copyright © 1982 by Thomas Nelson. Used by permission. All rights reserved.

Scripture quotations marked NASB are taken from the New American Standard Bible®, Copyright © 1960, 1962, 1963, 1968, 1971, 1972, 1973, 1975, 1977, 1995 by The Lockman Foundation. Used by permission. (www.Lockman.org)

Scripture quotations marked THE MESSAGE are from The Message, copyright © by Eugene H. Peterson 1993, 1994, 1995, 1996, 2000, 2001, 2002. Used by permission of Tyndale House Publishers, Inc.

All websites listed herein are accurate at the time of publication but may change in the future or cease to exist. The listing of website references and resources does not imply publisher endorsement of the site's entire contents.

Edited by: Jim Vincent
Interior design: Erik M. Peterson
Cover design: Smartt Guys design
Cover image of grapes copyright © 2017 by Vitaly Korovin/Adobe Stock (78324663).
All rights reserved.

Library of Congress Cataloging-in-Publication Data

Names: Vines, Jerry, author.
Title: Progress in the pulpit : how to grow in your preaching / Jerry Vines and Jim Shaddix.
Description: Chicago : Moody Publishers, 2017. | Includes bibliographical references and index.
Identifiers: LCCN 2017009775 (print) | LCCN 2017016854 (ebook) | ISBN 9780802495372 | ISBN 9780802415301
Subjects: LCSH: Preaching.
Classification: LCC BV4211.3 (ebook) | LCC BV4211.3 .V56 2017 (print) | DDC 251--dc23
LC record available at https://lccn.loc.gov/2017009775

We hope you enjoy this book from Moody Publishers. Our goal is to provide high-quality, thought-provoking books and products that connect truth to your real needs and challenges. For more information on other books and products written and produced from a biblical perspective, go to www.moodypublishers.com or write to:

Moody Publishers
820 N. LaSalle Boulevard
Chicago, IL 60610

1 3 5 7 9 10 8 6 4 2

Printed in the United States of America

To all the faithful pastors who have modeled

for us sanctification in the pulpit

by continuing to make progress in their preaching.

CONTENTS

FOREWORD

This powerful book is predicated upon a rather radical notion—that preachers should make progress in their preaching. While hardly a new idea, this is surely an idea whose time has come. Far too many preachers are like ants embedded in amber. Their preaching is the same as it was when they began their ministries. This fact is not only a tragedy; it is unfaithfulness.

There is no higher calling than the preaching of the Word of God. The preacher is not a mere professional, for he must be called of God and commissioned by the church. At the same time, the preacher is surely not held to less than we expect of one who represents a profession. None of us would want to undergo surgery at the hands of a surgeon who has made no progress since completion of his residency. We expect physicians to learn with every surgical procedure and we entrust our lives to their expertise and knowledge. Most professions formalize this expectation with requirements for continuing education.

Congregations entrust the stewardship of the Word—the proclamation of the Word of God—to preachers. This is the mandate of the New Testament, and the church calls out men who are gifted and qualified by knowledge and spiritual maturity to preach and teach the Holy Scriptures. That is where the task of preaching begins, and it only ends when the preacher, after years and years of preaching "in season and out of season," lays that burden down. For most preachers, committed with heart and mind and soul to this calling, that means as close to the grave as possible.

Along the way, the preacher is a devoted student of the Bible. If truly faithful, the preacher is also a devoted student of preaching.

This is why I am so eager for you to read *Progress in the Pulpit*. The book's very title testifies to its importance. In this book you will find a most remarkable combination of encouragement, practical advice, and thoughtful reflection on preaching. Every preacher needs this assistance.

Furthermore, Progress in the Pulpit is a master class in preaching, written by two most-qualified authors. Dr. Jerry Vines is truly a Prince of the Pulpit. To hear him preach is to hear almost sixty-five years of faithfulness in preaching and expertise in exposition distilled into every single message. But Dr. Vines also represents something even more rare—the model of a preacher who simply will not stop learning about preaching. He is a master preacher, but he increases his mastery with every passing year. Just read his chapters in this book and you will know exactly what it means for a man to devote himself to the joy and burden of preaching until the race is finally run.

Dr. James Shaddix combines academic experience in the teaching of preaching with years of ministry in the local church. Rare is the man who has been both pastor of leading churches and a writing professor of preaching. Jim Shaddix is as respected in the pulpit as he is in the classroom. His wisdom from the pulpit and the classroom are brought together in this volume.

Together, Vines and Shaddix cover an amazing range of issues in preaching and they do so in a style that is as free from nonsense as it is filled with wisdom. Every page is practical and every page is biblical. This is their second major book on preaching, written together. Let's hope it is not their last.

If you know all you need to know about preaching, or if you have stopped growing in your preaching and you are content with that state, then this book is not for you. If you are a preacher committed to growing in every dimension of your preaching, then get ready to grow as you read every chapter in this book. So get to it.

R. Albert Mohler Jr.
President, The Southern Baptist Theological Seminary

INTRODUCTION

"HE WILL HAVE TO DO BETTER THAN THAT!"

Jerry Vines and Jim Shaddix

John and Mary were returning home from prayer meeting in a pouring rain. They had driven to church in a similar drenching rain. Active members of Shady Grove Baptist Church in Villa Rica, Georgia, John was deacon chairman and Mary was president of the Women's Missionary Union. The bad weather kept the crowd small—only eight people, plus the young preacher and the song leader who came with him.

"What did you say the boy's name is?" John asked.

"Jerry Vines."

"Didn't they say he was only sixteen?"

"Yes. He's Clarence's boy."

"Oh, I know Clarence well. Used to deliver bread to our store. Good people. But I'm not sure this boy will ever make a preacher."

"Why do you say that, John?"

"He was scared to death. Didn't have much to say. Preached only twenty minutes. Hardly raised his voice. He was so nervous he could barely get his words out."

"Now, John, he's only sixteen. And it was his first sermon ever."

"And he used notes. How can that be preaching in the Spirit? And he kept looking down and up, like a chicken drinking water."

"John!!"

"I guess I am too hard on the boy. But he will have to do better than that."

The above conversation is imaginary, and I did not know a John and Mary at Shady Grove Baptist Church. I am unsure what those who were listening actually said then, but such a conversation could well have occurred on a rainy night in Georgia sixty-four years ago. Now, I look back on eight pastorates and thousands of sermons preached all over America and several foreign countries. I've even written some books on preaching. Have I done "better than that?" Have I made any progress in the pulpit?

I (Jim) remember my first sermon painfully well. It was during a Sunday night service at Alexandria Baptist Church in Alexandria, Alabama, in the early 1980s. "Ready, Aim, Fire!" was the title. It was a stellar (not so much!) exposition on spiritual warfare from Ephesians 6:10–20. I cringe every time I run across that half sheet of paper with the outline on it that's still tucked away in a box in my attic.

I also remember the first time my dad ever came to hear me preach. While I'm sure he had some encouraging things to say afterward, one particular observation he made was seared in my mind: "Jim, you preach with a scowl on your face." And he was right. Now I too look back with the same question. After thirty-five years of preaching experience, two postgraduate degrees in preaching, four senior pastorates, and a couple of books on preaching under my belt—have I made any progress in the pulpit?

Although my father's words were real, those of the "John" and "Mary" about Jerry's earliest preaching efforts were imaginary (though they could have said that, based on his efforts). Now let's listen in on another imaginary conversation that could have taken place as well—this one in Ephesus in the first century. Brother and sister Onesiphorus are returning from services at First Church of Ephesus. Their young pastor, Timothy, had preached his heart out. "I really like Paul's young protégé but—in his preaching—he's no Paul," says Mr. Onesiphorous. "I doubt he will ever preach as well as Paul does. He has great potential. But, he's so young. He is preaching in a difficult day."

Did Timothy make progress in the pulpit?

We should never be content with where we are in our Christian journey. Indeed, sanctification is a progressive growth in righteousness. Nor should we who preach be satisfied in our preaching. All preachers, young and old, need to make sermonic improvement, both in content and in delivery. The people who listen to us should see we are growing in our Christian life, our calling, and our preaching. Both of us believe we have improved some (though certainly not enough) in almost a century of combined preaching experience. We pray we're not like the pastor who had a member say to him after his message, "Oh, pastor, every sermon you preach is better than the next one!"

The need for improvement in one's preaching has been recognized throughout the history of the Christian church. In his classic volume *Lectures to My Students,* Charles H. Spurgeon included a chapter entitled "The Necessity of Ministerial Progress." In a manner unique to Spurgeon he said, "Serve God with such education as you have, and thank Him for blowing through you if you are a ram's horn, but if there be a possibility of your becoming a silver trumpet, choose it rather."[1] Later he added, "I am certain that he who thinks he has gained perfection in oratory mistakes volubility for eloquence, and verbiage for argument."[2]

Paul understood the need for young Timothy to grow in his preaching ability. In his first letter to him, Paul wrote, "Meditate upon these things; give thyself wholly to them; that thy profiting may appear to all" (1 Tim. 4:15 KJV). Most of the newer translations have "progress" rather than "profiting." The ESV renders the verse: "Practice these things, immerse yourself in them, so that all may see your progress." The word is interesting and informative. The verb form in the Greek is *prokóptō*, occurring six times in the New Testament (see Luke 2:52; Rom. 13:12; Gal. 1:14; 2 Tim. 2:16; 3:9, 13). The noun form is *prokóptā*, which occurs three times in the New Testament (here and Phil. 1:12, 25). The word is a compound of the preposition *pro*, meaning "forward" and the verb *kóptō*, meaning "to cut" or "to lengthen out by hammering." The word pictures a smith stressing a piece of metal with his hammer and extending it to new lengths. This is the idea when Luke says, "And Jesus increased [*prokóptō*] in wisdom and in stature and in favor with God and man" (Luke 2:52).

Paul used the verb form in Philippians 1:12 with the further idea of advancement and progress. The root idea is to cut forward or move forward to an improved state. In military use it conveyed the idea of soldiers who went ahead of an army, cutting down trees and removing obstacles, building bridges and preparing roads for the army to follow. They were the Seabees of the ancient world. This seems to be what Paul has in mind when he uses the noun form to urge young Timothy to make progress, which will be apparent to all. The noun conveys the ideas of movement forward, advancement, progress. Spiritual Seabees, you might say.

But what kind of progress does Paul have in mind? The context around his admonition is instructive. First Timothy 4:1–5 places Timothy's ministry in an atmosphere of apostasy. These were times of departure from the faith (apostasy), of seducing spirits and doctrines of demons, and the like. Paul recognizes those were tough times to be a young pastor just starting out. So he begins by giving the young preacher some general encouragement and prohibition. Paul charges him to be a "good servant of Jesus Christ." He is to refuse unhelpful fables, to seek godliness, and to place his trust in the "living God" who desires to save all men.

Then, in the immediate context (1 Tim. 4:12–16), Paul calls the young man of God to a life of personal spiritual growth and to progress in his ministerial life. God's answer to days of apostasy is the faithful preaching of the Word of God. Timothy was not to let his youth be a hindrance, but rather set an example of progress "in speech, in conduct, in love, in faith, in purity" (v. 12). By most estimates Timothy is between thirty and thirty-five years of age at the time. Paul encourages him to grow in the whole gamut of graces he would need as a pastor. He can cause older saints to overlook how young he is by showing how godly he is!

Paul goes on to admonish Timothy to demonstrate advancement in his ministerial duties as well, especially in preaching. He was to "devote [himself] to the public reading of Scripture, to exhortation, to teaching" (v. 13). The public worship service is the setting here. The reading of Scripture is to be followed by exposition. John Stott writes, "It was taken for granted from the beginning that Christian preaching would be expository preaching, that is that all Christian instruction and exhortation would be drawn out of the passage which had been read."[3] He is also to make progress in the exercise of his spiritual gift, divinely bestowed at his ordination service. As Paul and the other elders laid trembling hands upon him, promises of God's blessings upon his life and ministry were uttered (1 Tim. 4:14). He received a special touch for a specific task.

Summing it all up, Paul says to Timothy, "Keep a close watch on yourself and on the teaching" (1 Tim. 4:16). In so doing he will "save [himself] and [his] hearers." He's not talking about soul salvation. Rather, he's talking about a life that's worthy of our salvation. Paul wants young Timothy to have a life that's not wasted, but fruitful. Stott summarizes the need for progress on the part of young ministers by saying, "People should be able to observe not only what they are but what they are becoming."[4]

The thrust of this entire passage is that in life and ministry the youthful preacher was to make progress. Those who saw and heard him should notice that he was making progress out of the pulpit, as well as in the pulpit. And because we regard Paul's words to be those of the Holy Spirit to our hearts as well, we hear God's admonition to us that we should make *progress in the pulpit*.

In the summer of 1984—at the urging of Dr. Paige Patterson—I (Jerry) wrote two volumes on preaching out of my own ministry experience, *A Practical Guide to Sermon Preparation* (1985) and *A Guide to Effective Sermon Delivery* 1986), both published by Moody Press. After about fifteen years of very positive reception by many colleges, seminaries, and pastors, Jim Shaddix and I partnered to combine the two books into one volume, *Power in the Pulpit* (Moody, 1999). God continued to bless this single volume as part of the curriculum in many schools and in the libraries of thousands of pastors. In June 2017, Moody Publishers published a revised edition of *Power in the Pulpit* to extend its usefulness in God's kingdom.

For several years now Jim and I have considered a second book on preaching to accompany *Power*. Although both of us are in the second half of our ministries, we're constantly trying to improve in our preaching and stay current in the fields that relate to its practice. We're not content to stop making progress as preachers. So we are delighted that the good folks at Moody graciously agreed to publish this volume in an effort to help other preachers make *Progress in the Pulpit*. This book is being released the same month as the revised edition of *Power in the Pulpit*.

Today's ministers preach in a far different world than the one of the 1980s. Current cultural, church, and homiletical trends are sweeping across the landscape like a warming El Niño. Things are not the same. The culture outside the church house is a challenge. Inside the church house professing Christians compose a different kind of audience than those who once attended on a rainy Wednesday night in rural Georgia or a sleepy Sunday night in northeast Alabama. Faithful preachers want to know how to get the message across in today's culture. They desire to communicate the gospel in a clear, simple, and effective manner.

A considerable amount of new information is available to the preacher. Linguistic studies of Hebrew and Greek texts give promise of helpful insights into Scripture. New help in understanding how to preach the various genres of Scripture is useful. The emphasis on text-driven and Christ-centered preaching assists the preacher in conveying the meaning of the Bible, not only through books and various theological journals, but also blogs and other valuable Internet resources. Studies in rhetoric, which take into consideration the latest in communication theory, attention spans, verbal and visual communication, are a storehouse of tools to keep the preacher current in his preaching. Advances exist in how to do better sermon planning and evaluation. This book will deal with these and many other areas to assist those who would preach to our culture.

The format of the book is simple. Part 1 on *defining the sermon* isn't intended to convey that one ever "masters" preaching sermons, but simply to suggest that an understanding of the theology of preaching, the spiritual development of the preacher, and a plan for preaching are foundational areas for progressing as preachers. Part 2 on *developing the sermon* attempts to address some current topics that can help the preacher do a better job of "manufacturing his product," so to speak. Such themes as language and literature, the use of the imagination, and the centrality of Christ in our preaching are considered. Part 3 on *delivering the sermon* looks at "marketing the product" through our delivery. Using communication theory and technology, we will highlight our message to the "consumers" and we will consider achieving a response, evaluating our sermons, and extending preaching education.

At the end of each chapter we have included some suggestions for "Reading for Progress." Here we will suggest additional reading in recent books dealing with the subject of the respective chapter. The book concludes with a challenge and plan for preachers to continue to make progress in their preaching so that "the people will all see you mature right before their eyes!" (1 Tim. 4:15 THE MESSAGE). Our desire is to enhance the preaching ministry so the message of the gospel continues in America and even to the ends of the earth.

One final word regarding the development of this book. While each of us has written six of the twelve chapters that make up this book, we've reviewed one another's work and added insights as we've felt inclined. And while we may have slight disagreements with one another on a very few minor points, both of us consider our writing relationship on both *Pulpit* projects to have been a real joy. And we're honored to share our journey with other pastors and preachers. Whether or not you use the term *pulpit* as a metaphor for preaching like we do, our desire is that we all grow and mature in our practice of this high calling.

So, here we go. Decades from our humble beginnings, let us apply the words of an old hymn to preaching:

> I'm pressing on the upward way, New heights I'm gaining every day;
> Still praying as I'm onward bound, "Lord, plant my feet on higher ground."[5]

In our preaching let us ever be onward and upward. May the Lord be able to say of all of us who preach, "He has indeed made progress in the pulpit."

PART I

DEFINING
THE
SERMON

I

"GENTLEMEN, THIS IS A SERMON!"

REVISITING THE ROOTS OF EXPOSITORY PREACHING

Jim Shaddix

Any self-respecting sports fan (and even some who aren't!) has heard the stories of the motivational prowess of Vince Lombardi, the legendary coach of the Green Bay Packers. He started every season the same way—gathering his players together and giving them what became one of his famous speeches.

With a football in hand, the feared and revered coach would walk to the front of the meeting room, take a moment to gaze over the group of assembled players, hold out the pigskin in front of him, and say, "Gentlemen, this is a football." After describing the importance of the football as if no one on his team had ever seen one, he then would lead the team outside and show them the field. He would explain the out-of-bounds lines and the end zones, and then remind the players that the football was intended to go across the end zone line.[1]

Lombardi knew the importance of stressing fundamentals—even to seasoned athletes. No doubt that emphasis played a huge role in him winning five National Football League championships, including Super Bowls I and II, during his tenure with the Packers. It shouldn't be any different for preachers. While it may seem strange to begin a book on progressing in your preaching with the fundamentals, nothing is more important to our growth as preachers than returning to the basics. It would do us all well to periodically have someone with a Bible in their hand say to us, "Gentlemen, this is a sermon!"

Jerry and I both are unapologetic in our conviction that biblical exposition should serve as the foundational approach to preaching. In exposition, the preacher lays open a biblical text in such a way that the Holy Spirit's intended meaning and attending power are brought to bear on the lives of contemporary listeners. The word *expose* means to lay open or uncover, and it includes the totality of the preacher's study, interpretation, and proclamation. So before we venture too far into some new territory of making progress in our preaching, let's take a trip down Memory Lane and revisit the basic nature of our preaching "football"—the expository sermon.

As we begin to think about making progress in the pulpit, we want to summarize, consolidate, and briefly comment on some of the theological moorings we have discussed in our previous works. Hopefully doing so will give us a solid foundation on which to build the rest of the help we offer in this book. True expository preaching is rooted in five basic theological convictions about the Bible that make it a faithful stewardship as opposed to a sermon form, a sacred obligation instead of a sermonic option. See if your sermons are driven by these things.

THE INSPIRATION OF THE BIBLE

The expository sermon is first and foremost shaped by a high view of Scripture.[2] V. L. Stanfield, a giant among teachers of preaching, helps us at this point by describing preaching as "giving the Bible a voice,"[3] which coincides with John Broadus's simple and accurate definition of preaching as "letting God speak out of his Word."[4] In other words, these preaching forefathers saw the Bible as the written record of God's voice, and preaching as the act of giving God His voice in the hearing of people. That's huge when it comes to determining what a sermon ought to look like! Why? Because expository preaching of the Bible provides the only chance we have to preserve God's voice and reveal it to listeners correctly. God has spoken and the Bible is the accurate record of His speech. So we're compelled to communicate it accurately so that we represent Him rightly.

Representing God rightly depends on a certain conviction about biblical inspiration. By "inspiration" we are referring to "the supernatural work of the Holy Spirit that enabled and motivated the human authors of Scripture to produce an accurate record and revelation of God's redemptive will, purpose, and activity."[5] Preaching has to be driven by an understanding that the text of Scripture accurately records God's voice. If you believe the Bible merely *contains* the Word of God, rather than actually *is* the Word of God, you won't be as driven to study it carefully, to organize its theology, or to proclaim it authoritatively and uncompromisingly.[6] The conviction that the Bible is God's Word will dictate everything in the preparation and delivery of your sermons.

The Bible itself makes its own claims about its divine origin. Paul asserted that "all Scripture is breathed out by God" (2 Tim. 3:16), suggesting the divine source of the words we have in our Bible. Peter wrote that "prophecy never came by the will of man, but holy men of God spoke as they were moved by the Holy Spirit" (2 Peter 1:21 NKJV). Essentially, these men were carried along by the Holy Spirit much like a sailboat is carried along by the wind. They were superintended by the Holy Spirit, giving Scripture a dual authorship—the Holy Spirit as the sole divine Author and a company of divinely chosen men as human authors. We refer to this process as verbal plenary inspiration. God let us hear His voice through the unique personalities of individual writers, each one being fashioned by the circumstances of his own life and the genetic combination of his own personality, yet all the while being filled by the breath of the divine Spirit.

If the Bible is inspired by God, and preaching gives the Bible a voice, there's an essential relationship between inspiration and the way one's sermons are crafted. Sermons necessarily have to rightly reflect the very voice of God. Consequently, your sermon journey must begin with finding out what God has said. You can't expect to stand up and say "Thus saith the Lord" if you don't know what the Lord saith! So the basic question both you and your listeners have to ask about the sermon is: who said it, the preacher or the Bible? The answer to that question determines whether your sermon came from the Bible or from your own experience and opinion.[7] Whenever you reveal God's eternal truth found in the Bible, you can be confident that your people are hearing the very voice of God instead of your voice.

So how does this happen? How do you go about rightly reflecting what God has said? After all, regarding the preaching and teaching gifts, Peter said, "If anyone speaks, let him speak as the oracles of God" (1 Peter 4:11 NKJV). So how can you ensure that you're speaking the oracles of God in such a way that His words rightly reflect what the Holy Spirit gave to us? The only logical answer to this question is the exposition of biblical texts, or expository preaching. This process alone maintains the integrity of the Holy Spirit's intended meaning in any given text of Scripture. Consequently, exposition is the natural outgrowth of what the Spirit has inspired the text to say and mean.

THE REVELATION OF THE BIBLE

The expository sermon not only grows out of *how* God spoke, but also *when* He spoke. Where contemporary preachers stand in relation to the time in which God revealed His Word says a lot about how we preach. I've heard more than once the seemingly spiritual call for contemporary preachers to preach more like the prophets, Jesus, and the apostles. Certainly, the quest to preach like the Bible preachers preached is a noble one—unless we fail to realize we haven't been called to preach like they did! Here's what I mean. An important difference exists between preaching *now* and preaching *then*. In fact, the role of every preacher after the apostolic age has been fundamentally different than that of preachers before them. And that difference actually provides one of the strongest rationales for biblical exposition.

During the biblical period, preachers like Old Testament prophets and New Testament prophets—Jesus, and the apostles—often were giving *revelation* in their preaching. They communicated things God said that people had never heard before. It was new information because God had never said it before. But those preachers also did a lot of *explanation* in the sermons they preached. Sometimes they weren't giving new information, but simply providing explanation of stuff that had already been revealed. Additionally, they did a lot of *persuasion* in their preaching based both on what had been revealed as well as on what they had explained. Under the leadership of God's Spirit they pleaded with people to say "yes" to what they said.[8]

As the sun set on the biblical period, however, some things changed. First, God's voice was funneled into the Christ event, and God's words were fulfilled totally and completely in His Son. The author of Hebrews summarizes, "Long ago, at many times and in many ways, God spoke to our fathers by the prophets, but in these last days he has spoken to us by his Son, whom he appointed the heir of all things, through whom also he created the world" (Heb. 1:1–2). About this astounding declaration, David Allen writes,

> Amazingly, the author viewed the revelation of the Son as God's "speech" to us, and thus it is an appropriate metaphor for all that

God does through Christ in the world and not just in reference to the words of Christ. Additionally, when Scripture speaks of the "word of the Lord" addressed to and through Old Testament prophets, the Son, as the second Person of the Trinity, is always involved as well.[9]

Second, God's special revelation—which the early church understood to be the accurate record of God's revelatory works and words[10]—was canonized to form the Old and New Testaments that comprise our Bible.[11] Chapell writes, "Each verse, each recorded event, and each passing epoch of biblical history God uses to build a single, comprehensive understanding of who he is."[12] Thus, the voice of God that reveals who He is and the mission He is on became contained in the Bible.

Now do the math. One of the natural results of the canonization of Scripture was that preaching simplified. Instead of involving the revelation, explanation, and persuasion that characterized the biblical period, preaching evolved to only include explanation and persuasion. The closing of the biblical canon, so to speak, marked the end of God's revelation of new material, at least as far as what He determined was necessary to be passed on through the ages to accomplish His purpose. And every preacher since that time has enjoyed the blessing of not living under the pressure of being responsible to introduce new information from God. Why? Because God stopped giving new revelation about "all things that pertain to life and godliness" (2 Peter 1:3) and encapsulated them in the person of Jesus Christ. Since that time preachers have been charged only with the responsibility of explaining what God has already revealed in Christ and persuading people to act on it.

That reality magnifies the characteristic that is at the very heart of biblical exposition—explanation of the biblical text. Broadus identifies four functional elements in preaching: explanation, argumentation (proof), illustration, and application. Of these four, he says explanation is "among the primary functions of the preacher."[13] And it's not difficult to understand why. Essentially, the other three elements are servants to explanation. Although some of these functional elements at times overlap, explanation fundamentally drives the train. We don't just do application; we apply something. We don't just use illustrations; we illustrate something. We don't just do argumentation; we argue something. And that something is the truth of God's Word rightly explained and understood. The text has to be explained in order for us to do the other elements of good preaching. Steven Smith insightfully describes preaching as "re-presenting the Word of God."[14] He writes:

This is a theology of preaching in one sentence: we speak for God because he has already revealed himself in his Son and his Son has revealed himself in his Word. This book is God's communication with us. . . . We have an obligation to re-present what God has already said. So, we have to get at the meaning.[15]

So the default approach to preaching must be—by necessity—to explain what God has already revealed in His Word and persuasively apply it to people's lives so they can obey it.

Your responsibility, then, is to peel back the layers of language, culture, background, worldview, literary genre, and more that characterize the differences between then and now. You do this in order to expose God's revelation and all of its relevance. This makes an expository sermon more than a homiletical form defined by the length of a given text, a particular rhetorical design, or even a Bible book series. An expository sermon is the result of a journey that begins long before your sermon is developed or preached. Essentially, exposition describes the manner of treatment with which you handle Scripture, a process by which you discover and encounter the true voice of God. And in the sermon that you birth from this process, you explain enough of your journey to your listeners to enhance their understanding of the truth and its relevance for their lives.

THE NATURE OF THE BIBLE

Another theological mooring that grounds the expository sermon is the nature of the Holy Scriptures, which contain God's inspired and revealed voice. Contemporary Christian culture has a tendency to view the Bible as nothing more than a practical manual for daily living. We demand relevance, we long for practical application, and we gravitate toward what works. This earthly view of the Bible, while not totally without merit, has serious ramifications. It causes us to overlook some of the Bible's most important qualities. For example, the Bible is much more than just a book *about* God. It is a book *from* God. When the apostle Paul told the Corinthians he had come to them declaring "the testimony of God" (1 Cor. 2:1), he used the possessive "of God" to convey his understanding of the nature of Scripture. Paul considered his message to be the testimony that God gave inasmuch as it had God as its content. It was both from God and about God.

As a message both from God and about God, the Bible's specific content was intended to be delivered to people in a way that accurately represents what God has to say to them. Let's be honest. As a preacher, you can take just about any subject under the sun and somehow relate it to something about God from some place in Scripture. But just because a message is about God doesn't mean that it's the message God intended people to hear. This is a subtle yet significant qualification for biblical exposition. Your preaching isn't validated on the basis of its relational proximity to the idea of God. You've been given a very specific message to deliver, and that message doesn't always include all things God-related. It's a specific message that God dictated and intended for a specific purpose (a subject that we'll take up shortly).

The Bible's God-centered and God-dictated nature creates a tension in preaching. Preachers—especially pastors—rightly want to meet people's needs and heal their hurts. But what are we to do when the Bible's God-centered and God-dictated message doesn't offer any specific and practical help for certain life situations? When that happens we naturally feel the temptation to run down to the local Christian bookstore and take our content from sources other than the Bible. After all, if it's written by the most popular Christian author, then surely it's sermon worthy. Surely if it's not heretical in principle, then it's allowable in preaching. And it makes great fodder for life application, felt needs, and topical sermons that provide helpful wisdom for anyone to follow.

But just because something isn't heresy doesn't mean it faithfully represents the inspired Word of God, especially when it involves subjects God didn't directly address. Jerry and I previously identified this subtlety as the distinction between *God's stuff* and *good stuff*.[16] God's stuff is the body of truth that is revealed in the Bible, given for the purpose of accomplishing God's agenda. It's the true nature of the Bible. Good stuff, on the other hand, is all the helpful advice and practical information we get in life that isn't necessarily drawn directly from biblical teaching, but instead from information or principles that we glean from simple observation and research.

To illustrate the difference, consider some topics that God clearly addresses in the Bible. The old and new covenants, justice, holiness, the crucified life, the church, the ordinances, forgiveness, the second coming, and more are all topics God specifically and clearly addresses on the pages of Scripture. All of those subjects are clearly God's stuff, and we glean our understanding of them from applying good interpretive principles in our Bible study. By contrast, a therapist can observe enough people dealing with stress in the job place in order to glean certain helpful principles for relieving stress. A marriage counselor can observe enough people recovering from divorce to identify some helpful guidelines for navigating that crisis. Parenting experts can talk with enough moms and dads to be able to delineate some practical ways for raising strong-willed children. And while general Bible truths can be identified that relate to these and other life experiences, it would be difficult to conclude that God addressed any of them specifically and directly in His Word. That stuff is good stuff, but we can't categorize it as biblical truth.

Mark it down, fellow preacher. You haven't been given the responsibility of addressing all things good and helpful. You've been charged with the task of speaking only what God has spoken. Stott pointedly asks, "How dare we speak, if God has not spoken? By ourselves we have nothing to say. To address a congregation without any assurance that we are bearers of a divine message would be the height of arrogance and folly. . . . If we are not sure of this, it would be better to keep our mouth shut."[17] While all truth certainly is God's truth, He has sovereignly chosen to include in the Bible only the truth that's necessary to accomplish His eternal purpose. That means your authority to say "Thus saith the Lord" doesn't rest in good stuff, but God's stuff. So you're compelled to rightly exegete, interpret, and proclaim biblical truth in such a way that it's free to accomplish God's purpose. And that stewardship will issue forth in only one kind of sermon—an expository sermon. This practice is the only way for you to be true to the Bible's nature.

THE PURPOSE OF THE BIBLE

The nature of the Bible as God's stuff demands that we lean in a bit further and consider the specific reason for which the Bible was given, another reality that compels us to preach expository sermons. During the "battle for the Bible" that took place in my denomination during the last three decades of the twentieth century, issues like the Bible's inerrancy, infallibility, authority, and sufficiency were frequent topics of debate. But I don't recall a whole lot ever being said about the purpose of the Good Book. Yet this neglected issue has as much to do with how we preach as any of the others.

What you think about the purpose of the Bible largely will determine how you approach your preaching. If you think the Bible's purpose is just to get people converted, then most of your sermons will be evangelistic. If you think the Bible was intended to be an answer book for all of life's questions, then your sermons will generally pose and answer questions you think your listeners are asking. If you think the Bible was given to be a practical manual for daily living, then your sermons will take the nature of "how-to" messages on how to navigate life.[18] The simple fact, however, that the Bible says more to God's people than it does to unbelievers indicates its purpose couldn't be limited to conversion. All we have to do is come up with one question that the Bible fails to answer (e.g., What about dinosaurs?) or one life issue that it doesn't address (e.g., raising strong-willed children!) to prove the Bible wasn't given to us for those purposes. So why do we have the Bible? What purpose does it serve?

The answer is clear in just a brief survey of the biblical canon. The apostle Paul set the table for the answer when he told the Roman believers that the people whom God foreknew, "he also predestined to be conformed to the image of his Son, in order that he might be the firstborn among many brothers. And those whom he predestined he also called, and those whom he called he also justified, and those whom he justified he also glorified" (Rom. 8:29–30). Before time began, God determined to save a people from their sins and set them on a course to be shaped into the image of His Son, Jesus Christ. Consequently, every believer is moving toward perfect righteousness as part of God's plan for Christ to reign throughout all eternity over a holy race. That holy race will consist of people who are citizens of His divine kingdom and children in His divine family, all due to the redemption they received through the sacrifice of Jesus Christ.

This purpose is verified when we look at the big picture of the biblical canon. The Bible opens with the declaration that "in the beginning, God created the heavens and the earth" (Gen. 1:1). It closes with the creation of "a new heaven and a new earth, for the first heaven and the first earth had passed away" (Rev. 21:1). The Bible opens with God creating for Himself an even more precious possession than His physical world: "Let Us make man in Our image, according to Our likeness; . . . So God created man in His own image; in the image of God He created him; male and female He created them" (Gen. 1:26–27 NKJV). It closes with God re-creating mankind into His image (cf. 1 John 3:2; Rev. 21:3–4). Creation and re-creation of heaven, earth, and mankind essentially bookend the Bible with the resounding statement of God's purpose of redeeming and restoring His creation and His creatures to their intended state.

In between those bookends is the story of our tragic fall from God's design, His pursuit of us in Christ Jesus, and His redemptive plan to restore us to our intended purpose. Nowhere is this more evident than in the apostolic testimony of the new covenant. Paul told the Corinthians that "we all, with unveiled face, beholding the glory of the Lord, are being transformed into the same image from one degree of glory to another" (2 Cor. 3:18). He said to the Philippians that Christ Jesus "will transform our lowly body to be like his glorious body" (Phil. 3:21). The Colossians were reminded they had "put on the new self, which is being renewed in knowledge after the image of its creator" (Col. 3:10). Peter told his readers that Jesus' "divine power has granted to us all things that pertain to life and godliness, through the knowledge of him who called us to his glory and excellence, by which he has granted to us his precious and very great promises, so that through them you may become partakers of the divine nature" (2 Peter 1:3–4). This mission of God to recreate His creation is the clear purpose of the Bible.

That realization leads us down a path toward expository preaching in at least two ways. First, if the Bible's overarching purpose is to recount God's plan of re-creating mankind into His image through Christ, then the accurate declaration of that story becomes paramount. It just makes sense that if we want to use something effectively, then we use it for its intended purpose. We don't use a washing machine to fix a computer or a toaster to make ice cubes. What sense does it make, then, to use the Bible to try to answer questions it wasn't ever intended to answer, or to navigate aspects of daily life that it nowhere addresses? Discovering and proclaiming the Holy Spirit's intended meaning in every text of Scripture assures you of accurately reflecting God's voice so as to accomplish His agenda.

Second, the Bible's purpose of re-creation also compels the preacher to expose Christ in every text of Scripture. Every passage in the Bible either points to Christ futuristically, refers to Christ explicitly, or looks back to Christ reflectively. Consequently, the re-creation of individuals into Christ's image demands that you determine where your preaching text stands in relation to Christ, and then expose that relationship to your listeners. So in a very real sense expository preaching and Christ-centered preaching ought to be synonymous terms. Exposition gives you the confidence that God's agenda in Christ—the most relevant and urgent need in every person's life—will truly bring about life change in your listeners. In short, expository preaching simply allows the Bible to say what it was intended to say and do what it was intended to do.

THE POWER OF THE BIBLE

Serving as an accurate record of God's agenda of re-creation, however, is only part of the Bible's purpose. A careful reading of the New Testament reveals that God sovereignly has connected His Word with His agenda in a dynamic way. Specifically, God has ordained that the purpose of the Word isn't merely to recount the story of His redemptive activity, but also to be the means of bringing it about! In other words, the Scriptures are actually the supernatural agent that fosters this re-creative process in the lives of people. The truth of the Bible acts as the powerful sword (cf. Heb. 4:12) to accomplish God's purpose in our lives. So this cause-and-effect relationship demands that preachers unleash the Bible's innate power, allowing it both to say and do what it was intended. Expository sermons are the only way for that to happen.

God's Word makes incredible claims about its own spiritual ability to affect life change. Consider just a few examples of its own testimony. When Joshua was intimidated about trying to fill the shoes of Moses after the death of the great deliverer, God reminded him that meditating on and obeying His Word were the secrets to his success and prosperity (Josh. 1:8). The psalmists, meanwhile, emphasized how the Scriptures are able to impact human nature. In Psalm 19:7–11 God's Word is referenced by six different titles: *law, testimony, precepts, commandment, fear,* and *rules.* In those same verses, the psalmist mentions numerous characteristics of the Scriptures: *perfect, sure, right, pure, clean, eternal, true,* and *righteous.* It is more desirable than gold and "sweeter than honey." And we can't overlook all the blessings and benefits that God's Word brings: restoration of the soul, wisdom, joy, understanding, warning, reward, conviction, and cleansing. Verses 12–13 conclude that the Scriptures also bring protection from sin and blamelessness before God!

Clearly our Lord has given us every truth, principle, standard, and warning that we'll ever need for restoration into His image. Psalm 119 abounds with claims about the supernatural power of God's Word. In verses 1–5 it gives direction for navigating life's journey. In verses 9–11, heeding it results in spiritual cleansing and prevention of sin. In verse 18 it births awe-inspiring wonder.

The Old Testament prophets also knew the benefit of Scripture. God declares through Isaiah that His Word will give repentant sinners a heavenly drink that enables them to spiritually blossom upon their return to Him (55:10–11). Then they're able to receive the grace-gifts of His Word, sowing and eating instead of being paralyzed by sorrow. All of this describes the prosperity that God's Word brings! Jeremiah writes that God's Word is the source of joy (15:16). In 23:29, God declares through the weeping prophet that His Word is sufficient to confront hard hearts and difficult situations with consuming and forceful power!

The New Testament is also thick with claims by Jesus and His disciples about the awesome power of Scripture. It stirs the hearts of those who receive its explanation and application (Luke 24:32). Jesus Himself acknowledged that God's truth is the sanctifying agent in the disciple's life (John 17:17). The apostle Paul claimed the Word of grace would foster spiritual growth and advance the believer toward glorification (Acts 20:32). He also identified it as the producer of faith (Rom. 10:17) and the possessor of proactive and protective power for conviction (Eph. 6:17). He told Timothy the Scriptures provide everything that men and women of God needed for the entire salvation journey: wisdom for all godliness, instruction for knowing godliness, rebuke for straying from godliness, restoration to godliness, and training for pursuing godliness (2 Tim. 3:14–17).

The author of Hebrews noted the Word's ability to do soul-searching and spiritual examination (Heb. 4:12). James spoke of the Word's ability to foster the sanctifying wholeness of salvation (James 1:21). The apostle Peter said it purifies the soul, gives new birth to the dead heart, and fosters spiritual nourishment in infant Christians (1 Peter 1:22–2:2).

If these claims are true, then it follows that the preacher ought to do everything he can to make them available to people who desperately need the redeeming work of God in Christ in their lives. To do otherwise would be worse than possessing a cure for cancer and withholding it from the public. It begs the question, If this is where God has promised to invest His power, why would you want to give your people anything less than full exposure to this supernatural truth? If the Holy Spirit does all of this work and more through God's Word to affect life change, then the preacher has a high responsibility. He is charged with interpreting and preaching this truth in keeping with its full potency so that people aren't robbed of their only hope of being transformed into Christ's image through God's powerful, life-changing Word, empowered by the Holy Spirit within every believer.

CONCLUSION

These convictions are basic to right preaching and faithful sermon development. If the Bible is God's voice, it follows that as pastors, teachers, and evangelists, we're compelled to preach it. The prophet Amos rhetorically asks, "The lion has roared; who will not fear? The Lord GOD has spoken; who can but prophesy?" (Amos 3:8). The apostle Paul, citing Psalm 116:10, similarly confesses, "Since we have the same spirit of faith according to what has been written, 'I believed, and so I spoke,' we also believe, and so we also speak" (2 Cor. 4:13). Stott rightly concludes:

Here then is a fundamental conviction about the living, redeeming and self-revealing God. It is the foundation on which all Christian preaching rests. We should never presume to occupy a pulpit unless we believe in this God. . . . Once we are persuaded that God has spoken, however, then we too must speak. A compulsion rests upon us. Nothing and nobody will be able to silence us.[19]

Preaching, then, is rooted in basic assumptions that God has spoken, and He has orchestrated the record of His words to be compiled and preserved in our Bible. These assumptions drive us to interpret the Bible accurately, and they compel us to expose that interpretation accordingly in our sermons.

Gentlemen, this is a sermon!

READING FOR PROGRESS

Adam, Peter. *Speaking God's Words*. Vancouver: Regent College, 2004.

Johnson, Dennis E. *Him We Proclaim*. Phillipsburg, NJ: P&R, 2007.

Meyer, Jason. *Preaching: A Biblical Theology*. Wheaton: Crossway, 2013.

Stott, John. *Between Two Worlds*. Grand Rapids: Eerdmans, 1982.

2

A HOLY MAN OF GOD

LIVING AND PREACHING IN THE SPIRIT

Jerry Vines

H ere are some headlines from various newspapers:
"Pastor resigns after admitting to plagiarism." It gets worse.

"Nationwide celebrity pastor forced out of church for financial irregularities." It gets worse.

"Church fires pastor for alcohol, marriage issues." It gets much worse.

"Well-known pastor admits to multiple affairs." It gets much, much worse.

"Children's pastor caught in child sex sting."

Yes, all these are true headlines, adjusted somewhat. Such headlines seem to be monthly and unending. News reports about pastors guilty of financial dishonesty, sexual affairs, plagiarism, and even perversions are all too frequent. Of course, news of pastors who fail and fall is not all that new. Just read the Bible accounts of the spiritual leaders who failed in sundry ways. The warnings of the New Testament make it abundantly clear that the temptations and failures of pastors are not new news.

Nor is pastoral impropriety confined to one denominational group. Baptists, Methodists, charismatics, Catholics, and independents of all persuasions have to deal with such disastrous realities. Nor is any theological camp immune. Calvinists, Arminians, liberals, conservatives, etc. are caught in the pastoral sin web. Nor is any age group impervious. Recently there was the sad story of a seventy-one-year-old pastor who was caught in sexual immorality.

The church of Jesus Christ has had to deal with the follies, foibles, and failures of men of God since New Testament times. Yet a holy life is possible for every pastor and preacher. In the New Testament church it included Paul and Timothy. The apostle could write with integrity to the Corinthian church, "Be imitators of me, as I am of Christ" (1 Cor. 11:1). And to the young pastor Timothy, the apostle could write, "I am reminded of your sincere faith, a faith that dwelt first in your grandmother Lois and your mother Eunice and now, I am sure, dwells in you as well" (2 Tim. 1:5). And as we lead our local flocks, we are to imitate Christ, who is our good, great, and chief Shepherd (John 10:11; Heb. 13:20; 1 Peter 5:4), or pastor.

While none of us who preach, of course, will ever attain to the pristine holiness of our Savior, we should all aspire to have said of us what was said of Elisha: "I perceive that this is an holy man of God" (2 Kings 4:9 KJV). This is a basic essential to preaching. One may effectively teach algebra, instruct in art, and even train others in aeronautics, yet live a life of uncleanness. But we who preach the Word of God can do it effectively only from a heart and life that is seeking to live and preach by the power of the Holy Spirit. Isaiah says, "Purify yourselves, you who bear the vessels of the LORD" (Isa. 52:11). In the context of our passage that urges progress in the pulpit, Paul summarizes: "Keep a close watch on yourself and on the teaching" (1 Tim. 4:16). This imperative has special application to the preacher's life and preaching.

In this chapter we will revisit some of the issues presented in our first volume, *Power in the Pulpit*,[1] as well as extend several matters related to laying a solid foundation for the preaching ministry, particularly the anointing of God. In terms of personal holiness, we also will consider some important matters related to developing the preacher as a man of God and repave some of the lanes of the highway of holiness constructed in *Power*. Finally, we will add some new lanes that will facilitate your journey to being a holy man of God in your living and in your preaching.

Spurgeon said, "Holiness in a minister is at once his chief necessity and his goodliest ornament."[2] He added, "We have all heard the story of the man who preached so well and lived so badly that when he was in the pulpit everybody said he ought never to come out again, and when he was out of it they all declared he never ought to enter it again."[3] Hughes is even more emphatic: "In the law, the lips of the leper were to be covered; that minister who is by office an angel, but by his life a leper, ought to have his lips covered, he deserves silencing."[4] As we will see, the secret of being a holy man of God is found in living in the Spirit and preaching in the Spirit. In doing so, we will answer the question, What place does the Holy Spirit have in the preacher's life and preaching?

LIVING IN THE SPIRIT

Separation

Holiness. Sanctification. Separation. I've been a Baptist preacher all my ministry. These three words tend to cause us Baptists to break out in hives! But actually they are good Bible words. They explain a vital work of the Holy Spirit in the life of all believers. To summarize, the Holy Spirit is active in our salvation, the work God does *for* us; in our service, the work He does *through* us; and in our sanctification, the work He does *in* us. The Greek word for "sanctification," is in the same word family from which we get "holiness" and "saints." The basic idea is to "set apart." Though a full discussion is beyond the scope of this chapter, the Bible teaches, as to position, we *are* sanctified (Heb. 10:14). As to practice, we are *to be* sanctified (Heb. 12:14). Sanctification is a life bestowed and a lifestyle to be pursued. An often-used definition is that sanctification is a progressive growth in righteousness. All believers should seek to grow in their Christian life. The preacher is no exception.

Another Bible truth is closely related to sanctification, yet often neglected: the doctrine of separation. Now, that doctrine causes many preachers to head for the hills! There are several reasons preachers may run from the idea of separation. One is the danger of legalism. If not very careful, one's Christian faith may be defined by those things one does not do. This tendency is often seen in young preachers. I have said that many a young preacher gets perilously close to being a Pharisee at the beginning of his ministry. Another reason we hastily run from the idea of separation is the desire to reach others for Christ. Sound strange? Well, some adopt the position that the way to reach the world is to live like the world. Actually, the church has had the most influence on the world when it has been the least like the world. An understanding of what it means to be "separated" in the biblical sense is important here. I fear that there is a generation of young preachers that has never heard about this doctrine that is so crucial to a holy lifestyle.

Just what is separation? There is a negative side and a positive side to biblical separation. Negatively, believers should separate themselves from unholy things. Second Corinthians 6:17 puts it clearly: "Wherefore come out from among them, and be ye separate, saith the Lord" (KJV). The Greek word translated "separate" (*haphorizo*) is instructive. Our word *horizon* derives from it.

Life has a better horizon than just those things that pull us down. What are those things that drag us down? You fill in the blanks.

But Paul gives us the positive side. The apostle writes that he was "separated unto the gospel of God" (Rom. 1:1 KJV). The same Greek word is used here as in 2 Corinthians 6:17. When we live a lifestyle of separation, it is not so much what we are separated from; rather, it is what we are separated to! Life takes on a larger, more fulfilling, and more meaningful horizon! The Bible has many passages that teach this kind of separation. Romans 12:1–2 (KJV) comes to mind: "present," that's the positive; "be not conformed," that's the negative.

As preachers we must take seriously this call to pursue a holy lifestyle. Our preaching will have little to recommend itself if our living doesn't complement it. Stephen Olford tells of a letter found in Robert Murray McCheyne's desk after his death. It had never been shown to anyone. An anonymous writer told the preacher that he had been the human means of leading him to Christ. In conclusion he said, "It was nothing you said that made me wish to be a Christian; it was rather the beauty of holiness which I saw in your face!"[5]

Devotional Life

Just how is this separation or sanctification or holiness of lifestyle to be attained and maintained? Elisha, the holy man of God, had a prophet-mentor named Elijah. Two simple phrases from Elijah's life give us a clue. In 1 Kings 18:1 God said to him, "Go, show yourself . . . ." This had to do with his public proclamation to King Ahab. But previously in 1 Kings 17:3 God told him, "Hide yourself . . . ." Before public proclamation there was a time for private devotion. I believe this is the key to the preacher's preaching and his lifestyle. What goes on behind the scenes is often the secret of the preacher's success—or the reason for his failure.

During my freshman year in college I backslid. No, it's not a story littered with juicy morsels that you can put on the Internet. I didn't fall into deep sin. Outwardly, no one would have guessed it. I was taking Bible classes to prepare for ministry. I had to read large portions of Scripture. But I was reading my Bible for purposes of testing, not for spiritual growth. As a result I neglected my devotional reading of Scripture and my prayer life. My relationship with the Lord grew cold. Later, in response to the words of a lay preacher in a city-wide crusade, I faced up to my lack of a daily devotional life. I came to see I must "hide" myself before I am ready to "show" myself.

I have counseled many preachers through the years who have experienced moral failures. Without exception, they did not have, or had neglected, a daily devotional time when they read their Bibles and prayed. A preacher's devotional time is no guarantee, of course, that there will be no failure in his lifestyle. But neglect in that area certainly creates a greater possibility that a fall is ahead.

Let me suggest some ways the preacher may have a daily devotional time that will provide the impetus toward a spiritually consistent life. First, begin your days in the hidden place with God. Someone said, "Do not see the face of any man until you have first seen the face of God." Have a special place for your mornings with God. Scripture reveals rather unusual places used for devotion by its characters. Daniel had an open window. Jonah had the belly of a great fish! In earlier years I knew country preachers who had a rock altar in the woods. I have made my study my place of daily devotions for many years. In our retirement home I have a window with a kneeling rug before it. There is my daily meeting place with God.

Begin with Bible reading. Through the years I have used various approaches to my reading. You may go straight through from Genesis to Revelation. Or, you may read from several genres of Scripture each morning. Beginning in Genesis, Job, then the prophets and the New Testament is a helpful way to do it. Once you have finished in one translation, read your Bible in another one. Keep in mind when you read Scripture that God is talking to you. Don't be reading to find a sermon; read for your own spiritual nourishment and strength.

After your Bible reading, pray. When we pray we are talking to God. God talks to us through Scripture; we talk to God through prayer. There is communication and communion going on! There are no PhDs in the school of prayer. We are all in kindergarten in that school! Remember that our Lord's disciples didn't say to Jesus, "Teach us to preach," or "Teach us to administrate," or "Teach us to blog." They requested of Him, "Teach us to pray" (Luke 11:1).

Various methods of prayer may be utilized. Some preachers pray for different things on different days. One day may be given to praying for your congregation, if you are a pastor. Another day you may pray for missionaries. A prayer list may be helpful. Decide what method works best for you. There is no one way to pray. Whatever method you use, just pray! Spurgeon said, "The best and holiest men have ever made prayer the most important part of pulpit preparation."[6] Though devotional praying may not be specifically connected to your sermon preparation, it does prepare you for it.

In addition to Bible reading, reading devotional books also can be helpful. In the section on "The Worship of God" in *Power in the Pulpit* I list a number of these that have been helpful to me.[7] The ones I listed there might be considered devotional classics. There are newer ones that may be read with profit.

Also, reading books on the deeper life have been a blessing in my "hidden" place. I list several of these at the same place in *Power in the Pulpit*. In addition to these "deeper life" classics there are also newer ones that will help you better understand the things of the Holy Spirit.

I'm just emphasizing the importance of having that daily quiet time when you get your life in proper alignment with God. I repeat, it is no guarantee your lifestyle will be characterized by holiness. But, it surely provides all the spiritual high octane for such a journey on the highway of holiness. Get energized when you "hide" yourself; then you will be ready to "show" yourself.

Ministerial Ethics

Living in the Spirit should benefit ministerial ethics or morals. Yet when we polled several professors of preaching about ethical matters that confront young preachers, the one we heard about most often was plagiarism, which the Oxford Dictionary defines as "the practice of taking someone else's work or ideas and passing them off as one's own."[8] This is not a new problem. I do know of at least one pastor who was fired by his church for preaching one of my sermons! He was unwise to do it. He was even more unwise to steal mine! However, the problem seems to have exacerbated with the advent of the Internet, making it possible for preachers to access well-known preachers' messages.

The preacher who plagiarizes someone else's sermon is more easily caught in the act today. Detection software exists these days, you know. I don't think you have to give a prolonged citation for everything you get from others. W. A. Criswell said to me, "Lad, there has been nothing new since the early church fathers." Vance Havner said something like this: "When I started preaching I determined I would be original or nothing. I soon found out I was both!" Still, take what you glean in your reading, study it, reshape it, polish it and make it your own. I have tried to follow the counsel of Warren Wiersbe, who said, "I milk a lot of cows, but I make my own butter."

I do not think it is wrong to read commentaries, sermon books, or even sermons online. But, I do think it is unethical to preach someone else's sermon word for word, even telling "personal" illustrations of another as if they are your own. Paul said in 1 Corinthians 4:7, "What do you have that you did not receive?" If God has given me some insight into His Word that can be a blessing to others, I don't believe it is my property. Rather, it belongs to the church of the Lord Jesus Christ. So, I do not object to other preachers using my material. Adrian Rogers once said, "If my bullet fits your gun, shoot it!" I do think, however, proper attribution should be given along the way. I don't mean you should give author, chapter, and verse for everything. But significant material, not commonly known, should be acknowledged. In my later years of ministry I did a much better job of noting my sources.

The preacher who reads a great deal will run across much material that may be helpfully used in his messages. Though he may not intend to quote without attribution, it may occur. I would suggest that you carefully footnote portions you want to use. Through the years of my preaching I didn't always do this. Some quotes or statements have lodged in my mind, but I no longer can find the source. Advancing age can cause you to forget your sources for some things you might use. You can simply indicate you are using material you have read from others by saying, "Someone has said . . . ," or, "It has been said . . . ."

The preacher's ethics as they relate to the church where he is pastor will say much about holiness in his lifestyle. I always kept my distance from the finances in my churches. I never signed any checks. I always insisted on a church treasurer, finance committee, and the very highest ethical standards in the church's finances. The sad stories of preachers who got into trouble over mishandling of church funds are much too plentiful. Closely aligned to that is how the preacher handles his personal finances. More than one preacher has lost his testimony inside and outside the church by failure to pay bills promptly, shady business deals on the side, and extravagant spending.

Another area of ethics involves your words and attitudes toward any church where you once served. Often we preachers like to talk about how great things are going at the church, "since I came." And, if we aren't careful, we can talk about how bad things are now, "since I left." As a previous pastor, you really should keep your mouth shut, your knees bent, and your prayers going for the current pastor of your previous church. When I retired from First Baptist Church, Jacksonville, Florida, after almost twenty-four years there as pastor, Janet and I built a house in our native Georgia, and got out of Dodge!

I make it a policy to counsel those who might have a complaint with the current pastor to pray about it and go to see their pastor. I send the current pastor a text message every Sunday morning assuring him of my prayers as he preaches that day. More than one preacher has damaged his testimony and stained an otherwise successful ministry by his behavior after he is no longer the pastor.

Purity

Upon my returning from a preaching engagement, my wife surprised me with her announcement: "I will never listen to him preach again." Janet was referring to a visiting preacher she had heard that Sunday. He had used a great deal of crudity, coarseness and sexually suggestive references in his message. I said to her, "I hope I am wrong, but often when preachers talk like that publicly, worse behavior is going on privately." I regret to say it, but a month later the sad news came out about his sexual infidelity. There is a great deal of this kind of speech in the pulpit these days. Some use it with the rubric, "This is the way to relate to your listeners." Such questionable language can only lessen the people's respect for the preacher and cheapen his testimony. You don't have to descend into the gutter of suggestive language and innuendo to gain a hearing with a modern congregation.

I was brought up in simpler times. I must admit I catch myself singing Ronnie Milsap's "Lost in the Fifties Tonight" from time to time. Our list of things considered worldly was certainly different. The big debates in my teen years were about dancing and card playing, with the worldly habit of smoking rabbit tobacco thrown in! The list in our current culture is far more serious. Today's preachers are certainly not immune to the current vices. They face the relentless brainwashing from media all believers encounter. From all I can read pornography is an addiction that afflicts significant numbers of Christians, even preachers. Sexual temptations of various kinds have always been lurking, but they seem to be greater and more seductive with the availability of Internet pornography, immodesty in dress, and the close proximity of work environments. Difficulties with alcohol are increasingly common among preachers. Alcohol has many defenders, but no defense. As one who believes in total abstinence let me just say that moderation is the first step toward addiction. Here is my counsel to preachers and all Christians: don't get thrown into the miserable pit of addiction by the deceptive net of moderation. If you never take the first drink, there is no danger of becoming an alcoholic. My intent is not to discuss these sins, and others, in detail. I'm just trying to raise your awareness that there are "fleshly lusts, which war against the soul" (1 Peter 2:11 KJV).

In addition to "defilement of body" there are the sins that fall into the category of "defilement of . . . spirit . . ." (2 Cor. 7:1). In today's celebrity culture there is the danger of self-promotion. While I don't see a particular problem with having your own website (see mine at www.jerryvines.com), the preacher must not call more attention to himself than to his Savior. Preachers often receive a lot of attention and adulation. Don't let this rob you of holiness in your lifestyle. As someone pointed out, even the donkey carrying Jesus knew the applause was not for him! We may not be quite as great as some would have us think. The (perhaps fictitious) story is told of the preacher who was having his second cup of coffee with his wife on Monday morning. He was quite pleased with his "great" message the day before. He said to his wife, "You know, there are only a few great preachers left these days." To which his wise wife replied, "Yes. And there is one less than you think there is!"

Walk in the Spirit

The real secret of holiness in the life of the preacher is no different from the same in the life of any believer. The secret is a life lived by the Holy Spirit who is called "the Spirit of holiness" (Rom. 1:4). Galatians 5:16 and 25 point the way. Verse 16 indicates we get victory over the flesh by walking in the Spirit. This means we are to live our daily life by means of the power of the indwelling Holy Spirit. Daily we must ask the Holy Spirit to control our life. Verse 25 says we "live in the Spirit" (KJV). This means that we who are saved not only have the Holy Spirit dwelling in us; we also are living our life in the atmosphere of the Holy Spirit. Then it says, "Let us also walk in the Spirit." A different word for "walk" is used in verse 25. The idea is to be in line with or to step in order, to put one foot in front of the other. A progressive process is involved. As we walk day by day along the path the Holy Spirit lays down for us through the Word of God and prayer, we learn to walk in the right direction and avoid the wrong direction.

Books could be written about the importance of holiness in the preacher's lifestyle. My purpose here is to underscore that your holy life sets the stage for Spirit-anointed, Spirit-filled preaching. Let me leave this section by reminding you that the Bible says, "Be not conformed to this world: but be ye transformed by the renewing of your mind" (Rom. 12:2 KJV). Flee from anything that will rob you of a holy lifestyle. Follow after those things that will cause people to say, "I perceive that this is an holy man of God" (2 Kings 4:9 KJV).

PREACHING IN THE SPIRIT

"You're not a 'nointed man. I want to see Dr. Vines. He's a 'nointed man." So spoke the woman who came to our church to ask for a handout. My associate already knew she made regular calls on churches in the area. He was asking her some key questions. In her obviously irritated impatience she demanded to see me because I was a "'nointed" man.

I've often thought about her statement. Am I a preacher anointed by the Holy Spirit to preach? Have I always preached in the power of the Holy Spirit? I'm sure you will agree with me that this is always our desire. And will you not also agree with me that there were times when we preached and the anointing and power of the Holy Spirit seemed to be missing?

Preaching in the power of the Holy Spirit is closely related to the anointing of the Spirit.[9] Our understanding of this begins in the Old Testament. The picture there is the use of consecrated oil, smeared or spread to symbolize the presence and power of the Holy Spirit. Places could be anointed. Think tabernacle and temple. People were anointed. People in three special offices were to be anointed: prophets were anointed to speak to the people for God; priests were anointed to speak to God for the people; and kings were anointed to lead the people for God.

The beautiful picture of anointing is carried forward into the New Testament. Jesus Christ (the word *Christ* means "The Anointed One") was anointed, especially to preach the gospel (Luke 4:18). The New Testament also teaches that all believers have been anointed (see 2 Cor. 1:21; 1 John 2:20, 27). This anointing is an enablement all believers receive at the moment of salvation. All Christians have the power available for whatever service God intends of them.

There is a special application here for those of us who preach. The enablement to preach the gospel comes from God and is called the anointing. I believe the filling of the Spirit releases the power of the Spirit's anointing as we preach. As we yield to the Spirit's control (Eph. 5:18) He gives us fresh oil to preach the Word of God with power and effectiveness (1 Cor. 2:4; 1 Thess. 1:5). Olford ties the filling and the anointing of the Holy Spirit together in a helpful manner: "As the filling suggests an *inward* working of the Spirit, the anointing stresses the *outward* clothing with power."[10]

This kind of preaching must not be equated with merely human activities. Preaching in the Spirit doesn't mean loud preaching. The fanciful (perhaps!) story is told of the preacher who had a notation in the margin of one of his sermon notes, "Weak point; yell loudly!" Neither is anointed preaching to be confused with eloquence. Garretson writes, "Eloquence is one of the most dangerous gifts a minister may enjoy."[11] He also warns that eloquence can cause the preacher "to congratulate himself on his performance."[12] His definition of preaching anointing is helpful. Using the word *unction*, for the anointing, he says, "Unction is that facility of speech a man may experience in the act of preaching when the Holy Spirit empowers the message beyond the ordinary effect typically produced . . . ." It is "what happens when the glory and presence of God comes down upon a congregation during the preaching."[13]

Anyone who has preached for any length of time knows when his message has the blessing of the Spirit's anointing upon it. And he knows when there is no anointing. There have been times when I felt like a plane circling overhead in a fog, trying to land! On more than a few occasions I have felt like a pitcher throwing balls instead of strikes, looking at the dugout for relief! And the preacher knows those times when (much to his surprise!) the sermon preaches far better than he imagined and God comes down in power. As Childers and Schmit write in *Performance in Preaching*, "Any preacher who has ever 'preached above his . . . head' or taken a dog of a sermon into the pulpit only to have it fly, knows how irregular the preaching process can be."[14]

Something happens when the anointing of the Spirit is upon us when we preach. There is a power that is obviously not derived from any human source. We are given a fluency of speech and clarity of expression that don't come every time we preach. We are aware that our voice is just the method by which the voice of the Holy Spirit may be heard. We become a vessel conveying the life-giving water to our thirsty hearers. We are an instrument through which the Light shines upon our people who live in a world of darkness. Though we may not see the outward, visible results we desire, there is no doubt that the Spirit of God has brought home the truth of the Word of God in such a way that all who are present see the exalted Son of God. When the message is ended and the service is dismissed the word will be, "Surely the presence of the Lord is in this place."

How is the anointing in our preaching to be obtained? The words in *Power in the Pulpit* on "Obtaining the Anointing" have several suggestions.[15] In summary, I believe we can most expect the power of the Spirit's anointing upon our preaching when we are living a holy life and prayerfully yield to the control of the Holy Spirit before and in the moment of our preaching.

In *The Passion-Driven Sermon*, Jim Shaddix tells of reading a book on the subject of preaching to postmoderns. "I was blown away when I finished it without ever running across even one mention of the role of the Holy Spirit in the task." Then he says, "From beginning to end, preaching is the communication of the Holy Spirit. . . . The Holy Spirit inspired the Word of God that we preach. He illuminates our understanding to its meaning and anoints our communication of it. He enlightens the minds of listeners to the message, convicts their hearts, and prompts them to respond."[16]

READING FOR PROGRESS

Garretson, James M. *Princeton and Preaching*. Edinburgh: The Banner of Truth Trust, 2005.

Olford, Stephen F., and David L. *Anointed Expository Preaching*. Nashville: Broadman and Holman Publishers, 1998.

Shaddix, Jim. *The Passion-Driven Sermon: Changing the Way Pastors Preach and Congregations Listen*. Nashville: Broadman and Holman Publishers, 2003.

3

NEVER WITHOUT A WORD

PLANNING TO PREACH GOD'S REVELATION

Jim Shaddix

I don't have a word from God this morning." Those words have been seared into my mind ever since I heard them when I was serving on my first church staff over thirty-five years ago.

My pastor was going through a difficult time with our congregation. After a stressful week, he brought his frustrations into the worship service one Sunday morning. When it came time for him to preach, he placed his Bible on the pulpit, looked at the congregation, and said those words: "I don't have a word from God." Our people sat stunned and silent. To this day I'll never forget what I was thinking as I sat on the front pew staring down at my Bible and gripping it tightly with both hands. *There are sixty-six books of the Word of God in here, and you don't have a word from God?*[1]

In Psalm 19:1–6 we're told that God reveals His glory through the natural revelation of creation. But then in verses 7–14 the psalmist contrasts that revelation with a better way to see God's glory, and that's through His written revelation in Holy Scripture. It's as if the psalmist is pointing out that the physical creation is susceptible to greater misinterpretation. And because

God doesn't want any of us to miss His glory, He wrote about it in what has become our Bible. And while I believe that He sometimes leads preachers to specific passages for particular sermons, I think His general plan is to say, "I've spoken and I've written it down for you to give it to My people; now, knock yourself out!"

We should never be without a word from God—even if we don't have a tingly feeling running up and down our spine, an audible voice in a Damascus Road experience, or a dream with a man from Macedonia in it. And my pastoral experience tells me that the weeks in our ministries that we have some mystical leading toward a particular text or subject will be the exceptions, not the rule. Most weeks it's just us and our Bibles. But I have so much confidence in the Bible as God's Word that I'm convinced I can open my Bible, point to a place on a page with my eyes closed, interpret that text with integrity in its context, and still be able to stand before people and declare, "Thus saith the Lord!"

That's why I believe planning our preaching is not only allowable, but essential if we're going to preach the whole counsel of God faithfully, diligently, and purposefully. So let's consider some things to keep in mind when it comes to planning our preaching.

PLAN WITH PURPOSE

When I arrived at the second church I pastored, I immediately began doing the only thing I knew how to do as a young pastor—preaching systematically through a Bible book. After I'd been there a couple of months, one Monday morning an adult Sunday school teacher walked into my office and asked me a question that I'll never forget: "Why don't you get your messages from God?" He said there was no way I could be hearing from God simply by moving consecutively from one passage to the next each week. What he said next clarified for me how he had arrived at such a conclusion. He said he was accustomed to preachers who usually got their messages from God while they were on the way from their office to the sanctuary on Sunday mornings![2]

If we listen carefully, our people will tell us a lot about what they think about preaching and how they listen to sermons. Obviously this Sunday school teacher and I differed greatly on some theological issues, including the implications of the closing of the canon and the subsequent source of preaching content. But I also learned something very practical from him that day. I learned why he and the other folks in the church didn't think their pastor needed to study during the week, much less plan a preaching calendar. I understood better why they expected me to spend all my time visiting the hospitals, drinking coffee with church members on their front porches, planning the annual church reunion, and running errands for the flower and cemetery committees. In their minds I didn't have to do things like study or plan to preach, so obviously I could devote all my time to those other pastoral duties!

My experience at that church was not at all uncommon. Many congregations have a theology and philosophy of pastoral ministry that's directly tied to their view of the preaching event. They believe sermons come directly and instantaneously from God, and consequently the pastor can dedicate all of his time to tasks that characterize more of a "family chaplain" role. This scenario causes many pastors to yield to such expectations and, therefore, neglect their preaching. Most pastors need to grow in their own understanding of the importance of planning. But they also will need to shepherd their congregations to an appreciation for it as well. Consider just a few of the reasons why planning a preaching calendar can be important and beneficial.

First, planning underscores the importance of our preaching. Planning says something about the weight we put on our most important pastoral responsibility. This makes pulpit planning advantageous for our overall leadership as pastors. Not only is our preaching where we are helping to shape people into Christ's image, but it's also our strongest leadership venue. It's where we cast vision and provide direction. The preaching moment is when we help our congregation see where we're going as we follow God's leadership for the future. Annual planning helps us to clarify the vision and direction that we'll be taking our congregation in the coming year.[3]

Second, planning helps us preach the whole counsel of God. Preaching the whole counsel of God doesn't necessarily mean we must preach on every verse of the Bible before our ministries are over. But it does mean that we should intentionally preach the whole gospel from the breadth of Scripture. Planning helps me to preach from a wider segment of God's Word, teaching my congregation systematically and intentionally. It helps me be intentional about preaching from both Testaments, every major literary genre, foundational areas of systematic theology, and the purposes of the church. I want to be purposeful about proclaiming the gospel to unbelievers, grounding new believers, and taking seasoned believers deeper into the beauty of the gospel.[4] Planning compels me to think more broadly than just my favorite Bible books or approaches to sermon development, as well as to think about the best ways to communicate all facets of God's redemptive plan.

Third, planning maximizes our time, energy, and emotion. Determining what to preach can create a lot of stress for most pastors. Instead of spending your time each week frantically searching for a topic or a text, advanced planning enables you to spend your time actually preparing your message. Not knowing where you're going often leads to defaulting to the latest hot topic on Christian blogs, or to downloading a well-known preacher's sermon off the Internet. Advanced planning helps you know where you're going so you can begin your preparation immediately. It enables you to funnel your time, energy, and emotion to actually studying God's Word and preparing to preach it.

Fourth, planning extends our ministry of God's Word. When you provide your ministry leaders with some advance insight into your preaching direction, they have more time to creatively reinforce the teaching of God's Word. Musical worship leaders can work in advance to develop meaningful worship services where song selection and other worship elements connect to what's being preached. In some churches, Bible teaching staff and volunteers are able to write small-group curriculum, study guides, discussion questions, family worship guides, Bible reading plans, and other resources that coincide with the sermon texts and topics. Advanced planning can also enable media personnel to supplement the preaching event with additional elements such as videos, visual aids, stage décor, and more. All of these elements reinforce God's Word and extend it beyond the actual preaching event.

Fifth, planning prepares people for outreach. A carefully planned and packaged sermon series can supplement the preaching event by giving church members another "talking point" with their friends. When a sermon series is publicized in advance, churchgoers have one more resource to use in inviting friends to the gathering of God's people. After church leaders announce from the platform, "Come join us for this new teaching series," church members later can extend the same invitation to their neighbors. The kickoff of a new series also provides fresh opportunities to launch new small groups with new curriculum, distribute new publicity pieces, and develop creative graphics and environmental elements that may foster interest among people who are not yet a part of the fellowship.[5]

PLAN TO PASTOR THE PEOPLE

Similar to Paul saying that some have the gift of tongues and some have the gift of interpreting tongues, my wife has the gift of "kitchen" and I have the spiritual gift of "eating kitchen." I love to eat. And I love to watch her plan her cooking almost as much as I like eating it. She approaches it with the same intensity that I approach sermon preparation. Once each week she pulls out her notebook, iPad, and cookbooks and sits down at the table to make out her grocery list and plan her menus for the week. She's truly an artist! And she's been that way throughout our marriage. Why does she put so much into planning and preparing meals? Because, like most wives and mothers, she wants her family to be properly nourished with a balanced diet.

Similarly, planning to preach helps pastors to take a holistic approach to preaching so they can shepherd the people well and feed them a healthy diet of spiritual food. Pastors want their congregations to grow up in maturity so they might look more and more like Christ. So it's important for pastors to consider a balanced diet by planning to preach purposefully. To help me do that as a pastor, I've found it beneficial to plan to feed my people intentionally from three particular spiritual food groups: systematic exposition, doctrinal instruction, and prophetic interpretation. These three areas capsulize my own philosophy of pastoral preaching.

Systematic Exposition

The bread-and-butter of a pastor's preaching ministry ought to be systematic exposition. Such exposition consists of the consecutive and exhaustive treatment of a Bible book, or at least an extended portion of one. The book or section is divided into paragraphs and the preacher expounds on them consecutively each week. That's the best way for a pastor to hold himself accountable to accurate interpretation of each passage in its context.[6] F. B. Meyer describes this kind of preaching as "the consecutive treatment of some book or extended portion of Scripture on which the preacher has concentrated head and heart, brain and brawn, over which he has thought and wept and prayed, until it has yielded up its inner secret, and the spirit of it has passed into his spirit."[7] What better way for me to shepherd my people than to get the spirit of God's voice into my spirit and then share it with those for whose souls I'm responsible!

Planning a systematic exposition series reaps numerous benefits, none more important than meeting the basic spiritual needs of your congregation that are necessary for re-creating them into Christ's image. That's God's primary agenda in giving us the Bible. In *Power in the Pulpit*, Jerry and I discuss a few other fruitful benefits as well.[8] First, systematic exposition helps the preacher fight against the culture's rampant biblical illiteracy by enhancing knowledge of the Bible. Second, it holds you accountable for saying what God says and not what you want to say. Third, it makes you work hard by studying and interpreting the Bible in its context. Fourth, systematic exposition forces you to deal with passages that you might otherwise overlook or even intentionally avoid, and it reigns you in from always gravitating toward your favorite subjects. Fifth, it guards you against using the Bible as a club and using your preaching to rebuke an erring parishioner in the public arena. Sixth, it helps to remove anxiety about what to preach by enabling you to know exactly where you're going the next time you preach. Seventh, it fosters an appetite for God's Word in your people and encourages them to go home and search the Scriptures for themselves. So plan to do a systematic expositional series as part of your regular preaching fare.

Doctrinal Instruction

In addition to a steady diet of systematic exposition, pastors need to feed their people regularly with the doctrine of the Christian faith. In his final sermon series at Bethlehem Baptist Church in Minneapolis, Pastor John Piper described the foundational doctrines that he expounded. Such doctrines, he said, "are wildly untamable, and explosively uncontainable, and electrically future-creating. They don't just sustain the present and explain the past. They are living and active and supernaturally supercharged to take this church where it has not yet dreamed, in ways we have not yet dreamed."[9] That's what doctrine is—the supernatural, dynamic truth of God that sanctifies believers and empowers the church to fulfill its mission. And that makes it absolutely essential in pastoral preaching.

Certainly, the church is going to learn doctrine through systematic exposition of Bible books. Biblical theology will surface in every message as texts are expounded paragraph-by-paragraph and Scripture is allowed to interpret Scripture. Similarly, one of my favorite ways to teach doctrine is simply to expound one key passage that addresses a particular doctrine and then support it with other texts that help to flesh out that doctrine. For example, I once presented a series entitled "Jesus on Church Discipline" from Matthew 18. While the whole series was an exposition of that one passage, I also treated 1 Corinthians 5 and other key texts within the exposition. But most of the time our people will only get doctrine in sample sizes if we limit it to an exposition of one text. We need to make sure they get the whole package if they're going to grow to full spiritual health. So at the risk of sounding heretical, let me suggest that expositors need to do some periodic "topical" messages on the foundational doctrines of the faith in which they expound them systematically for the people. Plan periodically to treat particular doctrines in pure topical fashion, supporting each point from multiple places in God's Word.

Prophetic Interpretation

Systematic exposition and periodic doctrinal instruction are vital, but they periodically need to yield to strategic opportunities to shepherd people with a word from God about what's currently happening in their world. Such prophetic interpretation can occur when observing events in the community and nation. I was pastoring Riverside Church in Denver, Colorado, on April 16, 2007, the day of the shooting on the campus of Virginia Tech University in Blacksburg, Virginia. Thirty-two people were killed and seventeen others wounded in what came to be known as "The Virginia Tech Massacre." At the time I was in one of my usual Bible book series with our congregation. But I had multiple adults in my congregation who had been students at nearby Columbine High School when a similar attack on students had happened almost eight years to the day prior to the Blacksburg shootings. They had been there when twelve of their fellow students and one of their teachers had been murdered. The events on the Virginia Tech campus opened up all kinds of deep wounds for them and the rest of our faith family, and they needed to hear from God about what they were experiencing. So I shelved my systematic exposition series for the following few weeks and preached a doctrinal series entitled "Answering Blacksburg and Columbine: A Biblical Perspective on Unrestrained Evil." As their pastor, I needed to help them see what the Bible says about the problem of evil in our world.

As we shepherd our congregations to health through a regular diet of systematic exposition and doctrinal instruction, we're also responsible as pastors to nourish them with God's perspective on significant contemporary events and trends. Such Bible teaching is a form of prophetic interpretation. As I write these words in the late summer of 2016, our country is facing a confusing presidential election, a rise in racial tension, and an increasing frequency of domestic terrorist attacks. Our people need to know what God thinks about issues like these, as well as how they're to respond to them. Contemporary issues give pastors great opportunity to bring right theology to bear on them so our people develop healthy worldviews that will serve them well for a lifetime. Pastor, don't fail to prophetically interpret contemporary events through the lens of God's Word. Your people need to hear His perspective on what's going on in our world.

PLAN IN COMMUNITY

It's generally understood that people are better together than they are alone. And the Bible isn't at all silent on the subject—"Two are better than one" (Eccl. 4:9) and "a threefold cord is not quickly broken" (v. 12). Even Jesus sent His followers out on mission in pairs (cf. Luke 10:1). And in 1 Corinthians 12:18–21, the apostle Paul compared the mutual dependency of believers to the awesome design of the human body:

> But as it is, God arranged the members in the body, each one of them, as he chose. If all were a single member, where would the body be? As it is, there are many parts, yet one body. The eye cannot say to the hand, "I have no need of you," nor again the head to the feet, "I have no need of you."

So why not apply this truth to sermon planning? Here are some ways to plan better by involving others.

Consulting Spiritual Leaders

During my first three years on the faculty of Southeastern Baptist Seminary, I also had the privilege of serving bi-vocationally as a teaching pastor at The Church at Brook Hills in Birmingham, Alabama. The senior pastor at that time was David Platt, now president of the International Mission Board of the Southern Baptist Convention. For many years David shepherded that congregation with great skill and wisdom. One of the things we did every year was to ask our elders to help us determine what to preach the following year. Before we went on our annual retreat, we would ask these men—who shepherded our people through small groups week in and week out—to prayerfully determine the spiritual needs of our congregation and what we needed to hear from God. Then we would gather at our retreat, put everyone's thoughts on the table, and try to discern where God was leading us to go. After the retreat, the teaching pastors would then prepare next year's preaching plan based on that input.

Including other spiritual leaders in developing a preaching plan is a wise thing for pastors to do. The emphasis in the New Testament on the plurality of leadership in Christ's church implies our need for help in shepherding God's people. Let me challenge you to involve other spiritual leaders in your congregation in determining what you should preach. Of course, the operative word here is *spiritual*. If you have a body of elders or deacons who meet biblical qualifications, or a staff that's biblically grounded and spiritually discerning, consider using them to give you input on your congregation's spiritual condition and needs. And then work with them in determining where in the Bible God addresses those needs. Do your people need to grow in their awe of God's greatness and glory? Consider teaching through the Psalms. Do they need to be challenged to pursue God's presence? Consider Haggai. Do they need to be established in their understanding of the gospel? Consider Luke. Do they need to be exhorted from Hebrews not to shrink back from God's mission in the face of persecution? Even if you don't have a trustworthy group of official leaders, try to identify some godly men in your church who you can enlist to give you wise input about what your people need to hear from God.

Working with a Team

I've often said (halfway jokingly!) that the key to pronouncing Bible names is to say them fast and confidently. Then people just assume you know what you're talking about! So whether it's a list of David's mighty men or one of the genealogies in the Gospels, the best thing to do is move through them rapidly and boldly. But because these lists of names are included in inspired Scripture, they're always important and have a reason for being there. Two of my favorite lists are those found in Nehemiah 8:4, 7. These groups of scribes and Levites assisted Ezra in teaching the people and helping them to understand God's law. And there's no doubt that they served an offline purpose as well—helping Ezra to interpret God's Word correctly before they ever got to the public arena. I like to refer to these guys as "Men Whose Names We Can't Pronounce," and I use them to illustrate the host of commentaries that pastors use to help them interpret the Scriptures. Every week we invite these godly "Men Whose Names We Can't Pronounce" to sit around our study desk and help us gain insight into God's Word.

Receiving input on what to preach from a group of spiritual leaders in your church is not the only way to use others in your process. If Ezra used a group of men to help him interpret and teach God's Word (Nehemiah 8), and the apostles consulted the elders to interpret the implications of the gospel for the Gentiles (cf. Acts 5), then surely you and I can use some trusted people in our church to help us actually put together a preaching calendar. Matt Carter, pastor of preaching and vision at Austin Stone Community Church in Austin, Texas, uses a team of leaders not only to determine the congregation's spiritual needs, but also to develop the specific plan for preaching the various Bible texts. After the team members do some individual spade work, the group has an annual retreat to hammer out the organization of specific Bible books and various preaching series for the year. In other words, they develop the preaching plan together.

Again, even if you don't have an established body of leaders at your disposal, you can still accomplish the same thing by enlisting some trusted individuals in your congregation. You don't have to plan in isolation.

PLAN FOR INTERRUPTIONS

Let's be honest—planned preaching can sometimes come across to our people as being canned, academic, and less than spiritual. Recall the earlier story about my Sunday school teacher who didn't think I got my messages from God because I was preaching through a Bible book systematically. I can understand how some people might think that working too far in advance might be getting a little bit ahead of the Holy Spirit. While I certainly believe the Holy Spirit can and should lead our advance planning, I also believe there's a mystery to the preaching event that demands a sensitivity to Him throughout the process.

That's one of the reasons our planning should be done with an open hand. We need to keep it in check by always surrendering it to the sometimes spontaneous leadership of God's Spirit and the larger nature of our callings as shepherds of God's people. A planned preaching calendar should never control the preaching ministry. It should serve the preaching ministry, not be the master of it. I've already implied as much above in the discussion of the pastor's responsibility to prophetically interpret contemporary events. So it's wise to actually *plan* for some interruptions to what you've already planned. Consider some occasions when you will want to press Pause on your preaching calendar, as well as some ways to actually plan for that very thing.

Anticipated Breaks

It's always best to build some intentional interruptions into your preaching plan. I guess in one sense it's really not an interruption if you plan for it, but it still helps to incorporate some rhythms into your schedule that enable you and your people to take a breath before moving on. One way I've found it helpful to do that is to take one or more breaks for a few weeks in the midst of lengthy systematic exposition series. Preaching journeys through books like Genesis, Isaiah, Psalms, Acts, and Revelation can get somewhat heavy if we don't provide some "rest areas" for people to get off the road and refresh. Taking a few weeks to preach a miniseries on some aspect of the Christian life, or even just a handful of unrelated messages, can infuse new life into a congregation and help them be ready to jump back into the series. I often will label these planned "time-outs" as messages "From the Pastor's Heart," providing the opportunity for me to address certain congregational needs while taking a needed break from the larger series.

Another way I've planned interruptions in my preaching series is to disguise breaks as actual component parts of Bible book series. I refer to these as *series-within-series*. In other words, instead of just preaching through the whole book of Matthew under one big heading like "The King Has Come: A Study of Matthew," I might break the book up into multiple miniseries. So I could launch the study after Thanksgiving with a Christmas series on Matthew 1–2 with its own series title. Then in January I might start a new doctrinal series on baptism that encompasses chapter 3 under a brand new title that reflects that subject. Then chapter 4 might be another message on gospel ministry with its own title, and chapters 5–7 could be another one on kingdom citizenship from the Sermon on the Mount, again with a new title. And so on, where each miniseries has its own series title and is organized according to the natural divisions of Matthew's gospel. Such an approach gives the feel of movement and accomplishment in shorter segments while I'm actually just doing a long series through the whole Bible book.

Unexpected Crises

Like most Americans, I remember exactly where I was on September 11, 2001, when those two airplanes hit New York's Twin Towers. I remember sitting in my living room on the campus of New Orleans Seminary watching the horrific events unfold on national television. At the time, I was serving as dean of the campus chapel and responsible for coordinating our three chapel services each week, one of which involved me preaching a systematic exposition series every semester to our students, faculty, and staff. But in the days immediately following 9/11 I watched with interest the frequency with which the words "God Bless America" showed up on school marquees, storefront windows, and even on the lips of senators and representatives as they sang that song by the same title on the steps of the capitol building in Washington, D.C. As those events unfolded, my Bible book series for that semester seemed to be of secondary importance to the need for a timely prophetic response.

So I interrupted that series on my next assigned date and, instead, preached a message from Matthew 5:1–12 entitled "God Bless America: What's It Going to Take?" I think our seminary family was better served in hearing what God says His blessing really looks like as opposed to subtly buying in to the perception that it meant His revenge on terrorists on behalf of our country.

The 9/11 terrorist attack on the World Trade Center was an unexpected crisis in the life of our country that affected all of us. Nobody was planning for it. Nobody had it on their calendar. And no preacher had previously scheduled himself to preach the following Sunday on "What to Do When Terrorism Comes to America." But crises like that are going to happen. They're just part of the stuff of life in a depraved world. It may be a national tragedy like 9/11, a global scare like Ebola or the Zika virus, or a congregational heartbreak like a group of students being killed in a car accident. Whatever form they take, unexpected crises will periodically raise their ugly heads and demand pastoral attention. And whether the need is for prophetic interpretation or compassionate pastoral care, the wise and discerning shepherd sometimes will need to interrupt his preaching plan in order to minister God's grace to his hurting and confused flock. Don't allow your preaching schedule to cause you to miss potent opportunities to apply the healing balm of God's Word to open wounds.

Unpredictable Pastoral Work

Pastoral work can be messy business. People don't have crises on schedule, and the pressing needs of people never go away. An infinite number of variables are at play in the lives of people that make up any given congregation. All of this and more come together to make pastoral ministry an unpredictable enterprise. We frequently are required to deal with emergencies, interruptions, and unforeseen circumstances. All of these things and more can mess up your preaching schedule. Sometimes I find that it takes me two weeks to expound a text I had planned to complete in one week. At other times—although it be the exception—God does lead me to abandon my scheduled sermon and go in a completely different direction.

These are just a few of the unpredictable circumstances of pastoral ministry that can interrupt a preaching plan. Every week pastors approach the pulpit to preach with a feeling of inadequacy because something unforeseen disturbed their sermon preparation time. The way to rise above and win over this tyranny of the urgent is to plan for these interruptions in your preaching schedule. Stephen Rummage suggests two ways to do this. One, schedule one "flex" day every twelve weeks on your preaching calendar where you don't put anything on the schedule. That practice will help you be able to adjust along the way without disrupting your plan. Two, only share a portion of your yearly preaching plan with your people at a time. Then you don't have to agonize over changing the plan in light of unanticipated circumstances. You can modify it as God leads and circumstances require.[10] In these ways, you can be ready at all times—a preacher never without a word.

READING FOR PROGRESS

Gibson, Scott M. *Preaching with a Plan*. Grand Rapids: Baker, 2012.

Rummage, Stephen Nelson. *Planning Your Preaching*. Grand Rapids: Kregel, 2002.

4

PULPIT DISCIPLESHIP

SHEPHERDING PEOPLE TO CHRISTLIKENESS THROUGH PREACHING

Jim Shaddix

A few years ago I was attending a conference on discipleship. During one of the breaks I visited the conference bookstore to see if I could take advantage of some of the discounts. When I didn't find a particular work I wanted, I asked one of the salespersons about it. He emphatically replied, "That's a preaching book. This conference is on discipleship."

I walked away from the display tables pondering that dichotomy. The book I was after actually addresses the relationship between preaching and helping people to grow in spiritual maturity. So I couldn't help but wonder, *Why are these two ministries considered to be so different?*

We live in a day of specializations. Everyone wants to focus their time and energy in a particular area. From college majors and business fields, all the way to seminary degrees, spiritual giftedness, and ministry callings within the church, everybody wants to be a specialist. Nobody wants to be a generalist. While there's nothing wrong with specializing in and of itself, sometimes I wonder if our affinity for finding just the right niche has caused us to over-analyze certain ministry disciplines. In the process we may actually convolute the meaning of some ministries, erroneously redefine others, and even create new ones that seem to be dangerously exclusive. Similar to the false dichotomy between preaching and worship, it appears that for many believers preaching and disciplemaking have become mutually exclusive. I believe that we need to fix this unhealthy separation.

While preaching and disciplemaking are not synonymous terms or ministries, they are closely related. The process of disciplemaking is most often initiated by preaching and is always carried along by it. And preaching bears its ultimate fruit in disciplemaking as individuals grow to look more and more like Jesus. In my own pastoral ministry, I've found it helpful to look at the relationship between preaching and disciplemaking as a set of concentric circles, and then to follow certain rules for fleshing it out in a pastor's ministry.

CONCENTRIC CIRCLES OF DISCIPLEMAKING

I remember the first time I heard someone suggest that preaching was a species of rhetoric. I balked at the assertion, wanting to defend my calling and discipline from being a component part of anything else. Could anything be bigger than preaching God's Word? But the more I processed it, the more I realized the truth of the claim.

The field of rhetoric is the field of persuasive public speaking. Preaching is a very specialized form of that field. It's public, and it's persuasive. But it has a very narrow and specific content—the gospel of Jesus Christ as revealed in the written Word of God. That makes preaching a species of rhetoric, in the same way that political speeches and infomercials are species of rhetoric. Although I think preaching is the most important kind of rhetoric, it really is just one of many disciplines in the rhetoric family.

Maybe that's one of the reasons some pastors create such an unhealthy division between the disciplines of preaching and disciplemaking. In reality, preaching is a species of disciplemaking. The process of making disciples takes place on many levels, not all of which involve the public proclamation of God's Word. Spiritual formation takes place in personal devotions, one-on-one interactions, small group conversations, life-on-life engagements, and numerous other venues and expressions. People are helped to look more like Jesus through various encounters with God's truth. But while it's important for preachers to remember that disciplemaking is more than preaching, it's equally important to remember that preaching is not less than disciplemaking.

Aiming at the Target

Understanding the relationship between preaching and disciplemaking begins with having the right goal—or target—in mind. Have you ever thought about the probability that when Jesus gave the Great Commission there were only eleven individuals present?[1] When He gave the marching orders for all believers for the remainder of our days on earth, the eleven remaining apostles likely were the only ones who heard it! That seems a bit strange. It just seems that something of that magnitude would have merited Him gathering together every one of His followers, at least those in reasonable proximity to Galilee. So why did He limit His audience to the eleven?

Part of the reason is that those eleven were the only ones really prepared to receive the Great Commission and to embrace it with the gravity it deserved. Jesus had spent three years pouring into them—so that when the time came for Him to check out and go back to heaven, there would be a group of men with whom He could entrust the gospel. And His plan worked. That's why we're writing and reading books like this one two thousand years later. Jesus' plan worked. He *discipled* twelve guys with whom He could entrust this precious gospel. And one of them didn't make it! But eleven of them did, and the gospel is still advancing today because of it.

FIGURE 1

CONCENTRIC CIRCLES OF DISCIPLEMAKING

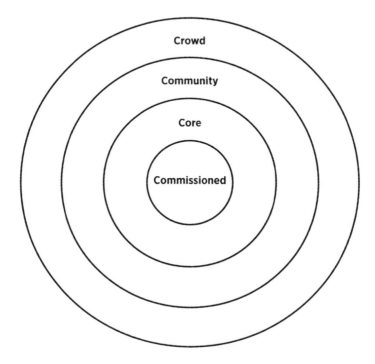

Realizing this truth has led me to find it helpful to think about the relationship between preaching and disciplemaking in terms of concentric circles. We challenge our congregations today with this Great Commission because we know it's the primary reason Jesus left us on the planet. Yet few Christians in proportion respond by embracing that commission and carrying it out. Let's be honest; the Great Commission is for every believer, but not every believer is spiritually ready to allow their lives to be driven by it. And that's why spiritual disciplemaking is necessary. Christians are not just going to move from conversion to Great Commission living. They need to be discipled to the point that they are ready to be trusted with the Great Commission. I like to refer to these disciples as the *commissioned* (see Figure 1, center circle). They are among the Christians in our congregations who take the Great Commission seriously, allow their lives to be defined by it, and are committed to fulfilling it and passing the gospel on to others who will do the same. That's our target—to develop more Great Commission Christians.

Understanding the Journey

But notice in Figure 1 that the *commissioned* don't exist in isolation, nor do they automatically arrive at that position upon conversion. They get there by process, by traveling on a discipleship journey. And that's the way it happened with Jesus' original twelve disciples. I think Jesus discipled people at different levels. He preached often to the *crowd* and proclaimed the gospel to them. But He also ministered to various expressions of *community*, which were smaller groups than the crowds. One example might be the group that heard the Sermon on the Mount referenced in Matthew 5:1. Matthew's account seems to suggest that this group—while smaller than the crowds from which they were summoned—likely included more than just the twelve apostles. Another might be the seventy-two He sent out on mission in Luke 10. These groups were engaged with Jesus and His work to a greater degree than the crowds. But there were also people who were closer to Jesus than the community. I refer to them as the *core* of His ministry. These would include the Marys and Marthas and Lazaruses of the world. These people experienced life with Jesus on an even more intimate basis than the crowd or the community.

Obviously the largest number of people make up the *crowd*. This is where commitment is at a minimum and it's easy to just blend in as a spectator. There are fewer people in the *community* than in the crowd. It takes a little more skin in the game to live there. In the *core* there are even fewer people, but even greater commitment. Their lives are more intimately tied together

64

by the things of the gospel. Among the *commissioned*, however, is where we find the greatest level of surrender and the highest degree of involvement in our Lord's mandate to make disciples of all nations. And how do people get there? People get to the *commissioned* group the same way the eleven apostles got there—by someone pouring his or her life into them, helping them mature in Christlikeness, and entrusting them to own and advance the gospel. In other words, someone guides them on the journey. And that's what we do when we disciple people in our churches.

Beginning the Process

That's why and how we as pastors disciple people in our churches. Taking people on a successful discipleship journey doesn't happen automatically. We intentionally move them from the *crowd* (worship gatherings?) to the *community* (midweek gatherings? special events?); then we move them to the *core,* (small groups? ministry teams?), and ultimately to the *commissioned*, where they will live out the gospel and pass it on to others. So that raises an important question: how does this process usually begin?

Most often the disciplemaking process begins when the Word of God is preached to the crowd. Something mysterious takes place there. As the Scriptures are expounded, people are convicted about sin and complacency (see Neh. 8:1–12). Their hearts burn within them as did the hearts of the two disciples on the Emmaus road (see Luke 24:27, 32). As the Word is read, explained, and applied, people are compelled to greater holiness (see 1 Tim. 4:13–16). They are convinced that something otherworldly is taking place, and they are constrained to yield their lives a bit more to the things of God. While some discipleship journeys begin on more intimate levels, most of the time people are moved to greater commitment by hearing the public proclamation of God's supernatural Word among the crowds. And therein lies an important aspect of the relationship between preaching and disciplemaking.

Pastor, don't ever underestimate the role that your week-by-week preaching plays in the fulfillment of the Great Commission. The people you're preaching to every week make up a host of individuals who are candidates for being entrusted with the gospel and living out their lives for its advancement. Every worship gathering in which you preach provides a ripe opportunity to foster reproductive disciplemaking in your church.

FIVE PRINCIPLES
OF PULPIT DISCIPLESHIP

Once one has the right lens, it's easier to see the landscape more clearly. While I'm sure there are more, I've identified five principles that I believe govern the territory of the relationship between preaching and disciplemaking. They can help you to intentionally move people from your weekend crowds to the point of owning their commission to make disciples among all people. For each principle I'll offer a couple of selected applications for pastors who desire to shepherd their people to Christlikeness through their preaching.

Principle 1: Discipleship is driven by personal discipleship.

There's a symbiotic relationship between what we do in our sermons and what we do in personal spiritual conversations. As an example, consider the public appeals we make in our sermons for people to respond. Every sermon ought to include a call for listeners to respond to the preached words. Whether we ask people to express their response immediately and physically in some form of "altar call" is negotiable. But we must appeal to them to say "yes" to whatever has been preached. Doing so will be determined in part by what we do in spiritual conversations as part of the normal course of our own lives. If I'm calling on people to confess Christ and to walk with Him in holiness in my daily encounters, then I'm more likely to genuinely call on people to respond to God's truth when I preach. If my heart breaks for people so much that I regularly appeal to them to follow Christ in daily conversations, then I'm more likely to appeal to people in my sermon with a broken heart. And the opposite is equally true. If I'm not sharing Christ with people one-on-one, my public calls for response during my sermons are going to be less than heartfelt and passionate, if existent at all.

The same is true in the relationship between a pastor's pulpit discipleship and his personal discipleship. If you and I aren't making disciples offline (that is, outside the pulpit) as part of our weekly routine, it's highly unlikely that we'll make any intentional effort to seek disciples during our preaching. But if personal disciplemaking is part of our life and ministry, then that passion and commitment naturally will carry over into our preaching. Every time we prepare a sermon and every time we get up to preach, we will be conscious of the role our preaching plays in the disciplemaking process. Consequently, we'll be looking for ways to purposefully engage in disciplemaking through our preaching.

Challenge 1: Keep growing in personal spiritual maturity.

So let me offer a couple of challenges to foster this relationship.

First, keep growing in your own spiritual maturity. Don't ever forget that you're not just a disciplemaker, but you're also a disciple. And your personal growth as a disciple will influence your work as a disciplemaker, both offline in personal journeys as well as online in your preaching. While this may seem both routine and repetitive, let's never grow weary of reminding one another of the indispensable place our personal spiritual growth has in our ministries. And I'm not just talking about having your quiet time. I'm talking about actually progressing in your walk with Jesus, taking strides in your relationship with Him. Ask yourself often, "Do I look more like Jesus today than I did this time last year?"

Challenge 2: Disciple other believers "offline."

Second, always be discipling a few other believers offline. This is huge. You can't expect to be an effective disciplemaker through your preaching if you're not doing it as a lifestyle. Remember, Jesus discipled people at multiple levels (look back at Figure 1). Yes, He engaged them to some degree when He preached to the crowds. But He obviously called some out of the crowds into more intimate relationship with Himself so He could prepare them to be trusted with the gospel. And there's no doubt that His interaction with the twelve apostles fueled His preaching ministry with the crowds. It's not different for us. There will always be somewhat of a circular dynamic going on between our pulpit discipleship and our personal discipleship—our "offline" discipleship. The more you disciple people one-on-one or in small groups, the more effective you will be in making disciples through your preaching. And the more you engage in disciplemaking in your preaching, the more passionate you will be about pouring into others in personal relationships.

I'm convinced that my legacy in the churches I've pastored (if I have one!) won't be my preaching. It won't be some sermon series I preached or some program I initiated. In fact, it won't be anything that was even ever announced or featured on the platform during worship gatherings. I think—at least I hope—my greatest legacy will be the lives of some men in those churches that I met with weekly and with whom I attempted to share life in various other offline contexts. I pray that my legacy will be an army of reproducing disciplemakers that was birthed out of groups of two or three men who went on a journey with me to learn how to steward the gospel. And I trust that those journeys have made a difference in how I preach and how I make disciples through my preaching.

By the way, even though my preference for offline disciplemaking is groups of two to three plus myself, you may prefer one-on-one relationships. Regardless of how you do it, make sure you're feeding your pulpit disciplemaking with your personal disciplemaking.

Principle 2: Preaching is the seedbed for disciplemaking.

Disciplemaking doesn't happen organically or passively. We have to be intentional about it. Jesus was. He prayed all night before He chose the twelve apostles, and He selected them from among a larger group of His followers (see Luke 6:12–13). In choosing those twelve, He must have had some criteria. If He was going to invest three years in twelve men in order to move them toward Christlikeness and prepare them to be trusted with the gospel, He had to have the right guys. There's no doubt that His preaching ministry to the larger group of His disciples played an important role in preparing the twelve for their selection to this task. Jesus' preaching was a seedbed for the selection and development of the twelve apostles.

Finding Candidates with Heart

We need to be intentional about selecting discipleship candidates as well. The stakes are too high and the time is too short for us to be random or haphazard when it comes to the gospel. And we need to rightly understand how preaching provides fertile soil for the development of discipleship candidates.

Let me explain. When I choose guys to disciple I always look for men who have *HEART*. I developed this acrostic years ago to serve as a lens through which I look at potential candidates for a discipleship journey. In my estimation a man who has the HEART of a disciple is a man who is:

*H*ungry.   *He desires to pursue Christ's kingdom and likeness.*
*E*ngaged.   *He's already involved in church life to some degree.*
*A*vailable. *He's willing to give time needed for discipleship.*
*R*eliable.   *He can be trusted to handle important matters.*
*T*eachable. *He's humble and open to counsel and instruction.*

None of these qualities is dictated by how long a man has been a Christian or how much Bible knowledge he has. A potential discipleship candidate may be a new believer, or he may have walked with Christ for decades. But he needs to possess some qualities that indicate he's ready to take a journey that leads to greater Christlikeness and responsible gospel stewardship.

In my disciplemaking experience the HEART rubric doesn't come into play practically until the *core* and *commissioned* stages of disciplemaking (see Figure 1). This is the lens through which I look at men who are part of the core of my church when I'm determining who I want to invite on a discipleship journey that will lead to ownership of the Great Commission. But I've found that having these criteria in mind is very helpful when I'm preaching to the crowds. And while you may use a different and even better rubric than mine, your set of criteria will serve you well as you use your preaching to prepare people for potential discipleship journeys down the road.

Preaching that Prepares People for Discipling

Here are a couple of ways for you to be intentional in your preaching about fertilizing the soil of your congregation to grow potential disciples.

First, connect biblical truths to qualities of potential disciples. Whatever criteria you plan to use when you and other leaders in your church choose discipleship candidates, have those criteria in mind as you prepare and deliver your messages. And then be intentional about connecting spiritual truths from your text to those qualities. So for me, I'm asking questions like:

- How can this truth foster a deeper hunger for Christ? (Hunger)
- Can I use this truth to challenge people to greater involvement in church life? (Engaged)
- Does this truth say anything about yielding more time to spiritual growth? (Available)
- What does this truth say about being trustworthy with weighty matters? (Reliable)
- Are there applications of this truth to being a lifelong learner? (Teachable)

Obviously, you won't be able to legitimately connect all the qualities on your list to every text you preach. But keeping those qualities in mind will enable you to identify potent opportunities to apply your preaching truths to the preparation of future discipleship candidates.

Second, provide sermon discussion guides for small groups. If our goal is to move people from just being a part of the *crowd* to ultimately being a part of the *commissioned*, it makes sense to look for ways to connect the sermon to those smaller concentric circles (Figure 1) of disciplemaking. One way to do that is by providing your people with discussion and application questions based on your preaching text. Some churches actually use sermon discussion guides as their curriculum for small-group Bible studies. This is a wonderful way to encourage the crowd in the preaching event to be involved in more intimate circles of discipleship. But even if your small group ministry uses a separate curriculum, you can still make discussion questions based on the sermon available to families, discipleship groups, and informal gatherings. And if the questions you develop take particular aim at your list of qualities for potential disciples, then you double your effort at making your preaching a seedbed for future disciplemaking.

Principle 3: Preaching combines the power of the Word and prayer.

There's an interesting relationship suggested in the Bible between prayer and the ministry of the Word. When Jethro counseled Moses to reduce his ministry job description down to essential priorities, he said: "You shall represent the people before God and bring their cases to God, and you shall warn them about the statutes and the laws, and make them know the way in which they must walk and what they must do" (Ex. 18:19–20). Basically, Jethro told Moses to pray and teach God's Word! And the New Testament parallel to that ministry crisis is similar. When the apostles began to spread the wealth of ministry involvement so the church's growth wouldn't be hindered, they said, "We will devote ourselves to prayer and to the ministry of the word" (Acts 6:4). And when you consider that they had used the word *preaching* to describe their primary work earlier in the narrative (see Acts 6:2), one can build a case that the apostles actually considered preaching to be comprised of the component parts of "prayer and . . . the ministry of the word." In other words, true biblical preaching includes prayer as an essential component.

Praying that Engages the Holy Spirit in Preaching and Gospel Advancement

In addition to the evident relationship between prayer and the ministry of the Word, there's no doubt that God ordained prayer to be the primary trigger for engaging the Holy Spirit in our lives and ministries, including our preaching. Jesus was clear on the subject. When the apostles asked Him to teach them to pray, He responded by suggesting that the end of prayer actually was to get more of God through the Holy Spirit (Luke 11:1–13, esp. v. 13).

He later taught them that prayer would be the key to having the Holy Spirit attend their efforts at doing the greater works of redemption after His departure (John 14:12, 14; 15:7, 16; 16:23–24).

Apparently it was just an assumption in the Acts narrative that prayer was absolutely essential for effectual gospel proclamation. The book opens with the small band of believers praying as they wait for the power of the Holy Spirit (1:14). Then the newly birthed church prioritizes it as one of its four major devotions (2:42). The apostles are shown to be about this business as they begin their marketplace preaching ministry (3:1). And the church defaults to it as the source of otherworldly boldness amid persecution (4:23–31). Later, the church would launch its missionary enterprise out of the activity of prayer (13:1–3). The biblical record is clear that prayer is an essential partner to the ministry of God's Word and the effective proclamation of the gospel.

Yet even with this resounding clarity of the absolute necessity of prayer in gospel advancement, most pastors and preachers woefully neglect its practice, at least in comparison to the time they spend on the ministry of the Word. I've frequently—and painfully—compared the number of seminary courses I've taken related to the ministry of the Word. I took Old and New Testament, theology, biblical backgrounds, Greek, Hebrew, hermeneutics, homiletics, numerous preaching electives, and a host of other courses that have informed the work of preaching and teaching God's Word. But when I compare those courses to the number of courses I've taken on prayer, there's a massive difference. The emphasis on prayer in my own theological education journey is probably limited to one spiritual formations course in which prayer was simply one of many topics addressed. Since finishing my seminary education I've diligently practiced the ministry of the Word, written several books on the subject, and spent much of my ministry teaching it in the classroom. Yet my own emphasis on and involvement in prayer pales in comparison to the amount of emphasis I put on handling the text correctly and developing expository sermons. I'm guessing that such is the case with most pastors. It's no wonder that we have so many powerless pulpits and churches!

Praying and Preaching for Your People's Growth

Because the work of prayer and preaching are interrelated, we must understand the mutual relationship between prayer and pulpit discipleship. We can't expect people to be matured into Christlikeness through our preaching if our preaching is not saturated in the waters of sacrificial prayer. And we can't expect our homiletical prowess to be sufficient. E. M Bounds said, "The preacher who has never learned in the school of Christ the high and divine art of intercession for his people will never learn the art of preaching, though homiletics be poured into him by the ton, and though he be the most gifted genius in sermon-making and sermon-delivery."[2] Pastor—for the sake of your people's growth in Christlikeness—give yourself to prayer for them as much as you do preaching to them. Below are a couple of suggestions on how to make both part of your disciplemaking efforts through preaching.

First, pray intentionally for your people's spiritual growth. I'm humbled when I compare the substance of my prayers with those of the apostle Paul. I'm so temporal in my praying—physical needs, temporary circumstances, personal aspirations, and the like. Paul was so spiritual and eternal in his praying, always focused on the spiritual well-being and development of the people. Consider his prayers for the believers in the churches at Ephesus, Philippi, and Colossae:

> For this reason, because I have heard of your faith in the Lord Jesus and your love toward all the saints, I do not cease to give thanks for you, remembering you in my prayers, that the God of our Lord Jesus Christ, the Father of glory, may give you the Spirit of wisdom and of revelation in the knowledge of him, having the eyes of your hearts enlightened, that you may know what is the hope to which he has called you, what are the riches of his glorious inheritance in the saints, and what is the immeasurable greatness of his power toward us who believe, according to the working of his great might. (Eph. 1:15–19)

> I bow my knees before the Father, from whom every family in heaven and on earth is named, that according to the riches of his glory he may grant you to be strengthened with power through his Spirit in your inner being, so that Christ may dwell in your hearts through faith—that you, being rooted and grounded in love, may have strength to comprehend with all the saints what is the breadth and length and height and depth, and to know the love of Christ that surpasses knowledge, that you may be filled with all the fullness of God. (Eph. 3:14–19)

> It is my prayer that your love may abound more and more, with knowledge and all discernment, so that you may approve what is excellent, and so be pure and blameless for the day of Christ, filled with the fruit of righteousness that comes through Jesus Christ, to the glory and praise of God. (Phil. 1:9–11)

And so, from the day we heard, we have not ceased to pray for you, asking that you may be filled with the knowledge of his will in all spiritual wisdom and understanding, so as to walk in a manner worthy of the Lord, fully pleasing to him: bearing fruit in every good work and increasing in the knowledge of God; being strengthened with all power, according to his glorious might, for all endurance and patience with joy. (Col. 1:9–11)

If you want to grow your people into Christlikeness, learn to pray like Paul. Pray intentionally for their spiritual maturity. Plan designated times in your week—and especially in your sermon preparation process—to pray for your people's spiritual development, especially as it relates to your preaching text each week. Undergird your preaching by crying out to God on behalf of those that He so desperately desires to grow up into the fullness of His Son.

Second, preach expositionally for your people's spiritual growth. At the risk of sounding like a looping song on iTunes, I'm convinced that expository preaching is our only hope of seeing people grow spiritually. Paul claimed to have become

> a minister according to the stewardship from God that was given to me for you, to make the word of God fully known, the mystery hidden for ages and generations but now revealed to his saints. To them God chose to make known how great among the Gentiles are the riches of the glory of this mystery, which is Christ in you, the hope of glory. Him we proclaim, warning everyone and teaching everyone with all wisdom, that we may present everyone mature in Christ. (Col. 1:25–28)

Paul told Timothy to devote himself to reading, explaining, and applying the Scriptures because that was the only way to save (sanctify) both himself and his people (cf. 1 Tim. 4:13–16). Later he encouraged him to continue in the Scriptures because they were able to mature him in his salvation and make him complete, prepared for every good work (cf. 2 Tim. 3:15–17). Peter encouraged his readers to desire the pure spiritual milk of God's Word so they might grow up into salvation (1 Peter 2:2).

The most effective and direct way to foster spiritual growth in your people is to lay open this supernatural text, called the Scriptures, in such a way that the Holy Spirit's intended meaning and attending power are brought to bear on their lives. Expository preaching unleashes the full transforming and re-creative power of God's truth. It enhances biblical literacy by explaining truth in context and allowing Scripture to interpret Scripture. It develops people's appetite for God's Word and encourages them to go home and search the Scriptures for themselves. And expository preaching models for your people how they should study the Bible and interpret it with integrity. If you want to see your flock grow spiritually, expose them to God's truth on a regular basis.

Principle 4: The preaching of the gospel encourages the stewardship of the gospel.

I love the relay races that are part of track-and-field competitions. Four runners participate in the event, with each one running a leg of the race, and then handing a baton to the next runner. Relay races are unique because the team that wins the race isn't necessarily the team whose last runner crosses the finish line first. The team who wins the relay race is the team whose last runner crosses the finish line first *carrying the baton*. You have to get the baton around the track to win!

Finishing the Race

The apostle Paul described what I would liken to a relay race when writing his second letter to young Timothy. Paul had received a gospel baton from his ancestors (2 Tim. 1:3), which he passed on to Lois and Eunice, who then passed it on to Timothy (cf. v. 5). It was now Timothy's responsibility to carry it faithfully, proudly, and confidently (cf. vv. 8, 12, 16), and then to pass it on to others who would be able to do the same (cf. 2:1–2). And it's clear what Paul was expecting Timothy to transfer from one party to the next—the gospel of Jesus Christ (1:8–10, 13–14; 2:2) What an incredible description— and prescription—of a pastor's responsibility to spend himself on the work of reproductive disciplemaking!

But the great apostle wasn't through. Before closing his letter he gave the young pastor one additional command regarding his stewardship of the gospel: "I charge you in the presence of God and of Christ Jesus, who is to judge the living and the dead, and by his appearing and his kingdom: preach the word; be ready in season and out of season; reprove, rebuke, and exhort, with complete patience and teaching" (2 Tim. 4:1–2). Paul instructed Timothy not only to perpetuate the gospel offline, but to extend it online as well through his public proclamation. The aged apostle apparently believed that gospel advancement required both personal disciplemaking and pulpit disciplemaking.

The foundational goal of disciplemaking is to mature people into Christ-likeness. Such character is ultimately expressed in this life in our ability to steward the gospel well during our own legs of the race, and then entrust it to others who will run their legs behind us. From a practical standpoint, that has to be the goal of our disciplemaking efforts. The gospel must keep going, and God has no plan B to make that happen. His only plan is life on life, men to men, women to women. And the preaching event serves as a wonderful help to make that happen. While we ultimately want to move people from the crowds into more intimate venues for disciplemaking, the public proclamation of the gospel naturally helps prepare people for that stewardship. About his preaching Paul said to the Corinthians, "I decided to know nothing among you except Jesus Christ and him crucified" (1 Cor. 2:2).

How to Encourage Gospel Stewardship

If Paul believed that all of preaching is characterized by the gospel, and the desired end of disciplemaking is gospel stewardship, then it follows that the preaching of the gospel will help prepare people to steward it well. Here are a couple of ways for you to encourage gospel stewardship in your preaching.

First, teach the gospel—or at least some component of it—in every sermon. One of the welcomed discussions in contemporary Christian preaching is the renewed emphasis on Christ-centered and gospel-driven preaching, a subject we will address in more detail in chapter 7. Jesus taught that all of Scripture was about Him (e.g., Luke 24:44–45; John 5:39, 46), and so must we. If we preach it like that, then there ought to be some legitimate pathway to the gospel in every message. You may actually preach on the subject of the gospel because it's the intended subject of your text. At other times your passage may address just one particular aspect of the gospel that you can highlight. In almost every text there's some place to give either a capsule of the gospel or a full presentation of it. Without compromising exegetical integrity or engaging in hermeneutical gymnastics, you can be intentional about teaching the gospel or some facet of it in every sermon.

Second, highlight the Great Commission at every opportunity. Effective missional, disciplemaking congregations never grow weary of talking about the Great Commission. When I served as a teaching pastor at the Church at Brook Hills in Birmingham, Alabama, I experienced firsthand why that church has the reputation of having a huge heart for the nations. The pastoral staff talked about it all the time! We were intentional about finding ways to connect the church's mission to every worship experience, including the sermon. Sometimes it came by way of a quick word of application. Sometimes we used a video testimony by a mission partner to illustrate something in the text. At other times we would stop and pray for a missions endeavor that was an expression of something in the text. And if we ever did miss an opportunity in the sermon, we always concluded every worship gathering by asking the congregation to stand and quote the Great Commission together as our benediction.

Pastor, look for creative ways to feature the Great Commission in your preaching. Doing so will go a long way in establishing a Great Commission worldview in the lives of your people.

Principle 5: Preaching matures communities as well as individuals.

The final principle that governs the relationship between preaching and disciplemaking is probably the most overlooked because it's the most difficult for us to measure: preaching helps in forming the community of faith—not just individual believers—into Christlikeness. Most of the time when we're talking about the journey of transformation into Christlikeness, we're thinking about individual believers. Paul, however, often addressed the corporate community in his writings when referring to their spiritual growth. He intentionally wanted to build a mature community, not just mature individuals.[3] When you stop and think about it, there are lots of things in the Christian life that can only be realized and manifested in community. Love, unity, spiritual giftedness, peace, and patience are just a few of the qualities of the Christian life that imply the experience of body life. They take more than one person to happen! And preaching helps to foster those things.

At the beginning of this chapter we used a set of concentric circles to show groups included in disciplemaking. Now let's conclude with a different set to show the elements of incarnational preaching. Several years ago I developed a diagram (Figure 2) of how I believe preaching God's Word fosters spiritual growth in the community of faith. It's an incarnational process as Jesus takes on an increasingly more influential role in our lives.[4] In other words, spiritual growth of an individual works from the inside out. As the Spirit of Christ gets bigger and bigger within a person, He begins to affect the conscience—the way one thinks, feels, and desires. When Christ's lordship is a reality in our conscience, He begins to influence our conduct, or the way we act. And when Christians begin to think, feel, and act like Christ in community—in the context of being the church—then they start looking like the body of Christ.

FIGURE 2

INCARNATIONAL PREACHING

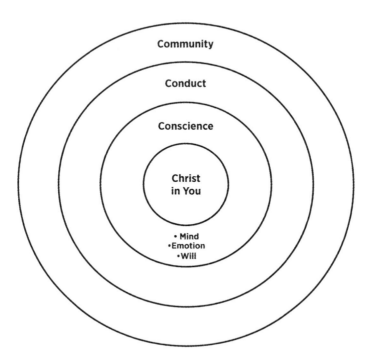

Changing Behavior from the Inside Out

We take great pains sometimes to convince unbelievers who visit our worship gatherings that we're no different than they are, that we're just regular folks like them. But the truth is that we are different because Christ in us is different. Figure 2 shows the influence that preaching has on each of the aspects of our existence, including our identity as a covenant community that is the very house of God and the true bride of Christ. We don't change behavior from the outside in, but from the inside out. Preaching shapes Christ's image in us; it can make Him more influential so He affects our thinking and acting. And our acting ultimately affects how we relate to one another in the community of faith.

Creating a Corporate Body with Common Values

Preaching creates in us a corporate consciousness and a sense of common bond. It shapes us into a corporate body that has corporate values or goals.[5]

Consider a few ways to make this happen in your preaching.

First, address the identity and mission of God's people frequently. The question "Who are we and what are we to do?" was at the forefront of Israel's consciousness in the Old Testament. And Paul made great effort to maintain that awareness in the church.[6] When he wasn't addressing some particular crisis in one of the congregations, he was usually writing about such topics as who they were in Christ and the mission they were on together. These issues remain huge for Christian communities today, arguably even more so than much of the practical application we attempt to offer individuals in our sermons. And the most logical way for believers to remain aware of their identity and mission is for preachers to address them in corporate worship gatherings. Seize every opportunity to address these corporate identity elements with your people.

Second, use—and explain—the language of Zion. One of the most significant characteristics that defines community is language. People are bound together by their ability to communicate with one another. Their "ownership" of terminology ties them together. And that's what's so ironic about many contemporary calls for preachers not to use terminology that's unfamiliar to the unchurched. We're frequently warned about using "the language of Zion." But we need to think critically about this counsel. If the church loses its language, it will lose an important aspect of its community. When we lose some of our terms that define us as a people, as well as their distinctive meanings, we lose some of that which sets us apart from our culture.

Paul's extensive education didn't keep him from educating first-century believers in their own lingo because he knew that owning their own terminology was necessary for building community.[7] So, pastor, be intentional about using and explaining theological terms like "election" (1 Thess. 1:4; Rom. 9–11), "sanctification" (1 Thess. 3:13; 4:3, 7; 5:23; 1 Cor. 5:1–11:1), "propitiation" (Rom. 3:25; Heb. 2:17; 1 John 2:2), and "redemption" (Rom. 3:24; Eph. 1:7; Col. 1:14). When you use them and explain them, you get the best of all worlds. You do good exposition by explaining unfamiliar terms to people, and you reinforce the community's ownership of its language. And ultimately, you make disciples by shaping your congregation into Christ's image and challenging them to steward the gospel well.

READING FOR PROGRESS

Shaddix, Jim. *The Passion-Driven Sermon*. Nashville: Broadman & Holman, 2003.

Thompson, James W. *Preaching Like Paul*. Louisville: Westminster John Knox, 2001.

PART 2

DEVELOPING THE SERMON

5

KING JAMES,
PRINCE,
AND MERLE

PREACHING LITERATURE

Jerry Vines

As a pastor, I recall West Rome Baptist Church in Rome, Georgia, as a fun church. The church included a good cross section of people from the city of thirty-five thousand people. We had day laborers and medical workers, widows and young couples. I also had quite a few educators.

One of my members, Sandra, was a high school English teacher. She asked me to visit her eleventh grade English literature class and speak on the Bible as literature. I was happy to do so.

In my presentation, I talked about the various kinds of literature found in the Bible. I pointed out that the Bible has hundreds of stories in it, beginning with the historical stories of the human race and the Hebrew race recorded in Genesis. Also, I showed them that there were beautiful poems in it, which we call the Psalms. I talked about prophetic literature in the Old Testament, where prophets proclaimed a message for their day and sometimes foretold a message for a future day. I carried them to the New Testament, showed them the historical accounts of the life of Christ, beginning with Matthew and the history of the early church in Acts. From there I went to the letters written by several of the apostles. I concluded with a reference to the book of Revelation, which is apocalyptic literature, presenting the account of final things.

When I finished my presentation Denise, one of the brightest students in the class, asked this question: "If the Bible is literature, just what makes it different?" Ah, that was my opening! "Well, Denise, the Bible is different from other literature in that it is sacred literature. In particular, it is literature that conveys the very words of God to us. When we study the Bible we are in a literature that is unique."

One of my mentors, evangelist Jesse M. Hendley said, "When I study my Bible, my finite mind is in touch with the infinite mind of God." Northrop Frye says, "A literary approach to the Bible is not in itself illegitimate . . . but the Bible is just as obviously 'more' than a work of literature. . . ."[1] With this in mind, we will consider preaching the Bible as literature—but literature that is sacred, divinely inspired, and without error.

TRANSLATIONS

Because the original documents contained in the Bible came from the East, their original manuscripts were written in non-English languages, primarily Hebrew and Greek (and also some Aramaic). In the twenty-first century we have more than fifty English translations and paraphrases. (See a listing at www.Biblegateway.com.) When I began preaching, the only version of the Bible with which I was familiar was the King James Version. Not until I went to college did I know there were others. At the university I was exposed to the Revised Standard Version. In my conservative circles, this was not a popular version. Critics charged that the liberal bias of the translators affected their renderings. I also became aware of the New American Standard Bible. Most conservatives seemed to be quite happy with it. When I was ordained to the gospel ministry the State Executive Secretary of the Georgia Baptist Convention sent me a free copy of the NASB.

Translation Choices

Others were equally interesting. Charles Williams's translation of the New Testament, published in 1958, was thrilling to read. This proved very helpful and opened my eyes to new ways of reading the words of Scripture. Early on I became familiar with J. B. Phillips's New Testament translation (1960) as well. Norman Geisler explains, "A translation is simply the rendering of a given composition from one language to another."[2] Frye reminds us, "Christianity as a religion has been from the beginning dependent on translation."[3]

I have grown in my understanding of the words of Scripture by reading the New American Standard Bible, the English Standard Version, the New International Version, the Holman Christian Standard Bible, the New King James Version, and others. David Allen, dean of the school of preaching at Southwestern Baptist Theological Seminary, encourages using many translations in the preparation of a sermon. He suggests such an exercise will "validate one's own exegesis and translation of the passage from the Greek" (and Hebrew), and it "provides ideas on how to say the same thing in different ways, which is vital to creative preaching."[4]

Choosing a Bible for Scripture Memorization

We can be grateful for all textually accurate new translations. However, the large number of newer translations can be confusing at times. Though the positives of newer translations are major, there can be some negatives. One issue most churches face is what translation to read from the pulpit, since many members may have different translations and may have difficulty following the Bible reader or the pastor quoting a particular set of verses. One solution is to project the passage on an overhead screen; a second is to equip the church with pew Bibles of the same translation.

Another issue is the difficulty of memorization with the rash of new translations. Although a pastor may recommend one, the new (or older) believer may have already purchased or received one and is familiar with it. Should he or she use it to memorize Scripture? The answer is yes, as long as it is an accurate translation. Those would include the King James Version, the New American Standard Bible, and more recent translations, such as the English Standard Version and the Christian Standard Bible (formerly HCSB).

Considering the King James Version

I continue to use the King James Version in my memorization and preaching. (Some things old preachers just don't "progress" in!) There is a beauty and flow to the language that lends itself to memorization. Do not misunderstand. I am far from a King James Only preacher. However, there are some advantages to the KJV in that regard.

Wheaton literary scholar Leland Ryken has quite a bit to say about the positives of the KJV. He says, "To make the Bible readable in the modern sense means to flatten out, tone down and convert into tepid expository prose what in the KJV is wild, full of awe, poetic, and passionate. It means stepping down the voltage of KJV so it won't blow any fuses."[5] Gustavus Paine also says, "They knew how to make the Bible scare the wits out of you and then calm you, all in English as superb as the Hebrew and the Greek."[6]

Ryken grants the point, however, that "the real case against the KJV for regular use today is the archaism of the language."[7] By all means, we want the Bible to be understandable to modern readers. But, he continues, "Even if we use a modern translation most of the time, there are good reasons to read the King James Bible some of the time."[8] Paine says of the King James: "But at the time of translation, a Bible 'appointed to be read in churches' was made to be listened to and remembered. Its rhythms were important as a prompting for memory."[9] We must take care that, in our progress, we do not lose in our translations something of the beauty and force of the words of Scripture.

PARAPHRASES

When I began my preaching ministry I knew very little about paraphrases. Again, at my university I was introduced to them. The first one I encountered was by J. B. Phillips, *The New Testament in Modern English*. A better-known one was Kenneth Taylor's *The Living Bible* published by Tyndale House in 1971. There was quite a bit of controversy surrounding *The Living Bible*. I never understood the uproar. A paraphrase is merely a free rendering that seeks to give the original sense of Scripture in a simpler manner. This is not dissimilar to what we do when we attempt to preach the Word of God in our words. We seek to convey the meaning of Holy Scripture clearer and with more understanding to those before whom we speak. I have found them to be helpful. In recent years Eugene H. Peterson's *The Message* (2002) has given me different ways of looking at the text, especially in the narrative sections of Scripture. Just keep in mind that a paraphrase is not an attempt to give a word by word, literal rendering of Scripture. Paraphrases can be helpful in getting people started reading their Bibles. But, the need to move to a good translation is imperative.

GENRES IN THE BIBLE

I remember well my first acquaintance with the word *genre*. Many years ago someone asked me, "What is your favorite genre of music?" I thought it was a musical instrument or something! They were actually referring to different types of music, whether country, pop, rock, rap, classical, gospel, etc. Some people prefer country; others like pop; still others prefer classical; and some are eclectic. If you like Prince, your genre of choice is rock. If you listen to

Merle Haggard, yours is country. The word can also be applied to the different kinds of literature found in the Bible.

Actually, the word is rather simple and quite helpful. Etymologically, *genre* is a French word meaning "a kind." We discuss the concept of genre in *Power in the Pulpit*, revised edition.[10]

Kinds of Genre

As applied to the Bible, *genre* means a category of literary composition. Several kinds of genres are found in the Bible. In his excellent volume *Recapturing the Voice of God*, Steven W. Smith says there are at least nine discernible literary genres: Old Testament narrative, Law, Psalms (or poetry, which also includes Job and Proverbs), wisdom literature (which can include Job, Proverbs, Ecclesiastes, and Song of Solomon[11]), prophecy, Gospels/Acts, parables, epistles, and Revelation (apocalyptic).[12] Jeffrey Arthurs writes, "(The) Amazon rainforest hosts 20 million species of insects! That's species, not individual bugs. This world bursts with an inventive, wise, sometimes wry display of God's power and glory, and variety is part of that glory."[13] As we approach Scripture we see that the Holy Spirit has used a variety of genres to display God's revelation and glory to us.

In the course of my preaching ministry, I came to see that understanding the genre of the Bible book from which I was preaching was vital to my overall comprehension of the passage at hand. I could not preach the narratives of the Old Testament as I did Paul's letters in the New Testament. Each had its own style, feel, and flow. Smith has helpfully arranged the various Scripture genres under three simple, easy to understand headings: story, poem, letter. *Story* primarily encompasses the narrative portions of the Old Testament, the Gospels, the Acts of the Apostles, and the parables in the New Testament. *Poem* is the category that contains the Psalms, prophecy, and the wisdom literature. *Letters* include the epistles of the New Testament and the Revelation to John. Smith says we are to understand the scene structure in story, the strophe structure (verse division) in poem, and the paragraph structure in letter.[14] McCarty succinctly says the keys to genre are: *letter*—verbs; *poetry*—strophe; *story*—scenes.[15] Both are right when they indicate that we need to master these three templates if we are to preach effectively all sections of Scripture.

During my twenty-four years as pastor of First Baptist Church, Jacksonville, Florida, I preached a series of messages from each book of the Bible. This took me to every genre of literature found in God's Word. I became keenly aware that each genre had to be approached with its particular style in mind. Narrative sections are telling a story. The stories have a plot. Each author has a purpose that is intended to carry the movement of the story from scene to scene. I am to carefully look for those various scenes. The narratives have characters. I need to identify both the main and minor ones. There is normally a problem presented in the narrative that creates tension. And, most of the time, there is some resolution to the problem. Arthurs points out that Hebrew narrative communicates on three levels. The top level is the "macro-narrative" that points to the overall narrative of Scripture: creation, fall, redemption. The middle level shows in particular how God dealt with His chosen people, Israel, to accomplish redemption from sin through a coming Savior. The bottom level focuses attention on the individual characters in the narrative and God's dealings with them.[16]

I learned a great deal about how to approach biblical narrative on a trip to DreamWorks studios in Hollywood, California, in 1997. Stephen Spielberg was producing an animated movie on the life of Moses entitled *The Prince of Egypt*.[17] He invited a number of religious leaders to see what he was doing and to offer input. I found the way Hollywood approaches narrative to be fascinating. And very helpful for my preaching. I was especially captivated by the studio's use of storyboards. On a wall, the storyboards served as a visual blueprint of the story line, action, characters, and dialogue of the movie. The directors could see how they moved the story line along. I saw how they zoomed in closer at key points in the action to highlight different characters and actions.

Understanding Various Genres

This has significant application for the preacher as he approaches the narrative portions of Scripture. Arthurs writes, "Like the movie director using close-up and panorama, storytellers [I might add, preachers] also zoom in and out."[18]

The poetical books are styled according to the Hebrew approach to poetry. Unlike our poetry that has a parallelism utilizing rhyme, the poetry in Hebrew uses a parallelism of thought. This is especially prevalent in the Psalms. Like the stanzas of a song, the reader is to look for the main divisions of the psalm. Also, he must find the kind of parallelism used. I find it helpful to arrange the parallelism of the poetic books into three main categories. First, some parallelism is *completive*. We see this in Psalm 46:1, "God is our refuge and strength." This is the first line of the stanza. The second line reads, "A very present help in trouble." Do you see the completion? The second line states the same thought, but in a different way, with perhaps some added information.

Second, some parallelism is *contrastive*. Proverbs 3:5 is an example. Line one says, "Trust in the LORD with all your heart." Line two gives the contrast: "and do not lean on your own understanding." Thus the message: We are to put our trust in the Lord and not trust in own understanding. The third kind of parallelism is *constructive*. Constructive parallelism contains a succession of parallels. Proverbs 30:17 is an example. Notice how the verse builds: "The eye that mocks a father and scorns to obey a mother will be picked out by the ravens of the valley and eaten by the vultures." Each statement builds on the previous one. Finally, it expresses the basic idea—the importance of obedience to one's father and mother. Understanding the characteristics of poetic genre in Scripture is vital in preaching from that section of the Bible.

The epistles are more didactic in style. I found that the letters of the New Testament have a structure that is normally easy to discern. In particular, Paul's style is to give the doctrinal section first, then move to the practical section. Very often there is a word that gives us a clue that a shift is taking place. Romans 12:1 is a case in point. After presenting the doctrinal section (chapters 1–11) as a foundation, Paul begins 12:1 by saying, "I appeal to you therefore, brothers. . . ." The word *therefore* makes the transition from the doctrinal to the practical sections of Romans. Also, in most of the letters, there is an introduction, body of the letter, and a conclusion.

As is the case in such literature, we find there are many commands, couched in biblical imperatives. These commands are built upon indicative statements. For instance, 1 Corinthians 6:20 says, "You were bought with a price [indicative]. So glorify God in your body [imperative]."

OUTLINING

Understanding the particular genre of the Bible book is very helpful in entering and developing the preaching passage. It also allows us to correctly identify the structure of the passage and thus the structure of our message. As we shall see in the chapter on preaching the language of Scripture, we are to draw out the meaning of the passage itself. This brings us to the matter of outlining.

To Outline or Not?

Much has been written about *points* or *divisions* in a sermon. Whatever position one takes, many would agree that one's points or divisions should be taken from the Bible passage itself. Some suggest we should do away with the idea of outlining altogether. David Buttrick called for sermon structure to be more of a series of "moves" rather than be composed of a number of "points."[19] Buttrick's viewpoint has been influential in the field of homiletics. One current homiletician says about sermon outlines, "Such propositions and points, as seminary students are taught to create, are inherently stagnant, resulting in 'static and turgid' sermons."[20]

As an advocate of using points or divisions in sermons, let me state my case. I do believe much can be learned from the questioning of the validity of points. Without a doubt, the same sermon template cannot be used for every genre of Scripture. Three points and a poem isn't a one-size-fits-all for sermonic passages. And I do agree with the text-driven approach to sermon preparation that one's divisions should be derived from the Scripture passage itself. David Allen writes, "A good text-driven sermon that explains the meaning of the text can be couched in a variety of forms. . . . Good text-driven preaching will reflect this variety as well. There is a broad umbrella of sermon styles and structures that can rightfully be called 'expository' or 'text-driven.'"[21]

Using "Tags" in Narrative Scenes

Having said that, there does seem to be a valid place for the use of an outline in every genre of Scripture. The passage itself should determine the number of divisions of the sermon. If the passage has three clear divisions, then let that be reflected in the sermon. If it has only two or one, let the sermon outline be shaped by that. This can be done, even in the narrative (story) sections of Scripture. Zack Eswine writes, "Instead of using traditional sermon points, the preacher will want to think of the sermon as a series of scenes that are identified from the biblical narrative itself."[22] Granted. But, can't these scenes be given helpful tags or words to give the listeners some idea about what is the subject matter of the scene? We see this in the case of plays where audiences are provided a helpful program to guide them through the various acts and scenes of the play.

For example, in one sermon I prepared about Joseph from Genesis 39, I identified the plot by reference to the fourfold repetition of the storyline: "God was with him." The phrase is repeated twice at the beginning and twice toward the conclusion of the story. Building around that, I pointed out that this truth is illustrated in the three scenes. God was with Joseph in his *vocation* (Gen. 39:1–6), in his *temptation* (Gen. 39:7–18), and in his *incarceration* (Gen. 39:19–23). The problem or tension in the chapter is actually three in one. First, Joseph is working in a different vocation in a distant land. Second, he is faced with the advances of Potiphar's wife and her subsequent false accusations. Finally, he finds himself in prison. Each problem is resolved by the truth that *God was with him* in all three times of difficulty.

Using "Tags" in Poetry

The same may be done in the poetic genre of Scripture. In my message from Psalm 126, I identified three main stanzas (strophes) in the poem (some prefer only two stanzas). I gave each of these stanzas a point or division; they are as follows:

Praise for Spiritual Returning: verses 1–3
Prayer for Spiritual Reviving: verse 4
Promise for Spiritual Reaping: verses 5–6

There are difficulties in outlining certain books, however. The book of Proverbs is a case in point. Actually, I'm not sure preaching through Proverbs consecutively, verse by verse, is desirable. I know of only one preacher who did so. I wondered how his people survived! In passing, I'm not sure you even want to preach through the Psalms consecutively. Again, I know of one pastor who attempted that. It about killed his church! As an aside, you might do better to preach certain of the psalms around the particular kinds of psalms. There are lament psalms, thanksgiving psalms, etc. Perhaps it would be best to select psalms from these subgenres. And, you could do a few, move to other books, then return from time to time.

Back to Proverbs: how best to preach this book? When I did a series from Proverbs I picked certain passages and topics. I preached twelve messages from Proverbs in this manner. I built the messages around the overall theme, Proverbs for Parents. Let me give a few examples. I preached a message from Proverbs 1:20–22 entitled "How Not to Raise a Rebel." I pointed out in my introduction that Solomon in Proverbs is giving instructions to a son. He uses "my son" twenty-three times. Thus we find in Proverbs a manual for child-rearing. Then from 1:20, I drew three words that track the stages that cause a child to become a rebel. I categorized "the simple" (v. 22 KJV) as "The Delightful Simple." From verse 22 (NKJV), I tagged "the scorners" as "The Difficult Scornful." Finally, in verse 22 I labeled the term "fools" as "The Dangerous Rebel."

As I moved through Proverbs I preached messages on certain topics. Do I mean you can do exposition in topical sermons? Yes. Exposition has to do with how a passage is handled. I preached a message on "The Strange Woman" from Proverbs 5:3–23 and 7:6–27. Still, I continued the overall theme that these are words from parents to children. I said parents have a responsibility to "Expose Sexual Immorality" (5:1–14, 20–23) and "Encourage Sexual Purity" (5:15–19). So my message had two points or divisions. Follow the themes of Proverbs, treat them in an expository fashion, then give pegs to enable your people to retain what you are preaching.

There is another way to utilize Proverbs. As you preach in other parts of the Bible, you will often find that you can draw on verses or sections of the Proverbs to provide helpful illustrations or pithy statements. If you review some of your messages, you might be surprised how many times you made reference to Proverbs. If you don't find many references, you are missing a treasure house of preaching material!

Through the years of my pastoral preaching, I found a clear, discernible outline was very helpful in teaching my people the Word of God. There is growing scientific evidence that the human mind tends to organize the material it hears (information processing). Human mental processing functions much like a computer, receiving and organizing information.[23] Is it not helpful, then, to enhance that tendency to organize by giving a clear, easy-to-follow outline of a Scripture passage? Be careful to let your divisions arise from the passage you are expounding.

There is evidence that the human mind has some difficulty in processing more than seven pieces of information at a time.[24] Interestingly, the old *three points and a poem* concept seems to still have some validity. Gallo says, "The rule of three pervades every aspect of our business and social lives."[25] In citing the effectiveness of a Steve Jobs presentation, he says that Jobs understood that "the 'rule of three' is one of the most powerful concepts in communication theory."[26] However, this should not cause us to impose three predetermined points or divisions upon our preaching passage.

I do recognize the danger of making the outline so prominent that the skeleton overshadows the body. But there is the opposite danger that a body with no skeleton (outline) can often look like a big, cumbersome blob of material! Steven Smith, author of *Recapturing the Voice of God: Shaping Sermons Like Scripture* is helpful at this point:

> Every sermon has to have a structure, even when it is not obvious.
> The metaphor I like best is that some sermons have an exoskeleton
> and some have an endoskeleton. Both are appropriate. Of course,
> some time showing the shape of the text explicitly clarifies the point
> of the sermon.[27]

The metaphor makes good sense. In the latter years of my ministry, I have had subpoints in my message. But I didn't always use them in the delivery of the message. However, I did find them useful as an *endoskeleton* to assist my recall of the message.

PASSAGE PATHOS

Much has been written about Aristotle's three elements of rhetorical persuasion: ethos (the character of the speaker), logos (the reasoning involved), and pathos (the appeal of the speaker to the emotions). In *Power in the Pulpit,* Jim Shaddix and I make reference to these in terms of the speaking moment.[28] In a development that was new to me, Adam Dooley takes the idea of pathos to the emotion found in a particular passage of Scripture.[29] He quotes Bryan Chapell who says, "Accurate exposition requires us to reflect a text's tone as well as define its terms."[30] I think I instinctively grasped this in my preaching of the Bible. But, Dooley is helpful in elucidating this pertinent observation.

Every passage of Scripture has an emotional element. One cannot preach the prophets without being aware of the emotions that swirled in their hearts as they brought God's message to His people and to all the peoples of the world. In preaching the narrative passages the preacher needs to carefully consider the emotions that are present. One cannot adequately preach about the prophet Nathan confronting the sin of his friend and Israel's king, David, unless he digs deeply into the sorrow, anger, outrage, and compassion that Nathan must have been feeling (see 2 Sam. 12:1–14). Nor can one preach without sensing the pathos of David's anger, shock, fear, guilt, remorse, and repentance as his sin is exposed. The emotional states of characters in a narrative must be elicited from the passage. The preacher's task is to reflect those emotional states in his message.

The poetic genre is rich in pathos. Each of the psalms, for instance, has a distinct kind of pathos. A confession psalm like Psalm 51 has a different emotional *feel* than a praise psalm like Psalm 8. Emotional dissonance would surely result if we preach the sad passages with a smile and happy-go-lucky delivery. Conversely, the same would occur if we preach the glad passages with a frown on our face or a sad-sack countenance.

The letters in the New Testament also have their own pathos. One can easily sense Paul's amazement and even anger as he comes down hard on the Galatian believers who so quickly had deserted their Lord (Gal. 1:6). Not much room for grinning there! Conversely, Paul's great joy over his relationship with the Philippian believers is not hard to discern (Phil. 1:3–8). It wouldn't do to preach that passage with a scowl on your face!

The thrust here is that understanding and reflecting the passage pathos in whatever Bible genre one is preaching is vital to biblically faithful exposition. I realize there is some overlapping here between the reading of a passage and the delivery of that passage. In chapter 10, I will more specifically address how we are to reflect passage pathos in the varied emotions of our delivery. Dooley says, "Ideally, a preacher's personal pathos will correspond to the emotive intention of the biblical passage he preaches."[31] Now, what's that about genre and country music?

READING FOR PROGRESS

Akin, Daniel L., David L. Allen, and Ned Mathews. *Text-Driven Preaching*. Nashville: Broadman and Holman, 2010.

Eswine, Zack. *Preaching to a Post-Everything World: Crafting Biblical Sermons That Connect with Our Culture*. Grand Rapids: Baker, 2008.

Kuruvilla, Abraham. *A Vision for Preaching: Understanding the Heart of Pastoral Ministry*. Grand Rapids: Baker, 2015.

Smith, Steven W. *Recapturing the Voice of God*. Nashville: B&H Publishing Group, 2015.

6

WE DEAL IN WORDS, MY FRIEND

PREACHING LANGUAGE

Jerry Vines

As I was working on this chapter, Supreme Court Justice Antonin Scalia died. Date: February 13, 2016. Place: a hunting lodge in Texas. Immediately there was widespread discussion about how to choose his successor. Should the outgoing president Barack Obama choose his successor, or should the winner of the fall presidential election submit a name?

The result would be far-reaching for the court and for the nation. President William Howard Taft and later chief justice of the Supreme Court said, "Presidents come and go, but the Supreme Court goes on forever."[1] Justice Scalia was one of the most conservative justices on the court. His opinions and dissents were brilliant. The jurist believed the Constitution of the United States should be read from an originalist perspective. He preferred to refer to his position as textualism. That is, the Constitution should be read as the words were intended by its original authors.

Justice Scalia could be colorful in the way he emphasized his commitment to the original meaning of words. When the majority of the Supreme Court issued its rulings legalizing universal medical coverage, known as Obamacare, and later same-sex marriage, Scalia minced no words. He talked about "pure applesauce" and "jiggery-pokery." He warned that the result of such rulings meant "words have no meaning."[2]

This is no minor issue. The whole thrust of postmodernism is about the meaning of words. Do they mean what those who originally wrote (spoke) them meant? Or do they mean whatever those who read (hear) them want them to mean? The assumption of postmodernism is that once words are used in a text those who read them give their own interpretation of them. The meaning they assign to the words becomes "their truth." So, whatever the words mean to you are what they mean in your experience. Justice Scalia begged to differ.

THE IMPORTANCE OF THE WORDS OF SCRIPTURE

Scalia's insistence on textualism as it refers to the Constitution is like the insistence of conservative Christians that the words of Scripture are not only inerrant, but they also mean what the original authors (human and divine) intended for them to mean. Walter Kaiser broaches this subject when he indicates where meaning in the Bible is to be found. His words are pertinent and helpful. "On the question of where meaning is to be lodged (i.e., in the text, in the community, or in the individual reader), we answer it is in the text as it is found in the context of the writer's assertion."[3]

Because of my commitment to biblical inerrancy, the words of Scripture have been important to me throughout my ministry. Whether it has been reading them, studying them, or preaching them, my ministry has been much involved with words. Paul clearly teaches in 1 Corinthians 2:13 that the words of Holy Scripture are the words of God. In a sermon before the 1987 Southern Baptist Convention sermon, "A Baptist and His Bible," I explored the apostle Paul's statement that "all Scripture is given by inspiration of God" (2 Tim. 3:16 NKJV). I said, "The word for Scripture is *graphe*, which means 'to write.' The obvious reference is to the words. The words of the Bible are God-breathed." I further stated, "No one has ever explained to me how it is possible to have thoughts without words. . . . Remove the words from the page and the thoughts disappear. There can be no music without notes; no math without numbers; no geology without rocks; no thoughts without words."[4]

Then I referenced the words of Jesus when He said, "Man shall not live by bread alone, but by every word that proceedeth out of the mouth of God" (Matt. 4:4 KJV). And, "For verily I say unto you, Till heaven and earth pass, one jot [the smallest letter in the Hebrew alphabet; a breath mark, the stroke of a pen] or one tittle [a little horn on a Hebrew letter; only about 1/32nd of an inch] shall in no wise pass from the law, till all be fulfilled" (Matt. 5:18 KJV).

The words of Scripture are important. I have spent my entire ministry trying to understand for myself and explain to others the meaning of those words. Think about the words of Scripture: *salvation, justification, sanctification, faith, love,* and *hope.* No wonder the hymn writer Philip Bliss composed these words: "Sing them over again to me, wonderful words of life. Let me more of their beauty see, wonderful words of life."[5]

My love for the Bible led me to minor in Greek at the university I attended. At seminary I took all the Greek and Hebrew courses available. Through the years of my ministry I have sought to progress in my understanding of the words of Scripture in the original languages. I would encourage every preacher and teacher to do everything possible to engage with those words. Fortunately, there are tools available today that were not available when I began ministry. Since that time there has been a large volume of writing in the fields of literature, language, and textual study. The preacher who wants to grow in his preaching needs to avail himself of these new studies.

TEXT-DRIVEN PREACHING

In recent years helpful new terminology has appeared to describe sermon preparation. Through the years I have used the term *expository preaching.* This is the term to denote that an expository sermon expounds a passage of Scripture, organizes it around a central theme and main divisions, then decisively applies its message to the listeners.[6] Today the newer term often used is *text-driven preaching.* The use of this newer terminology seems to be an effort to more clearly define the need to let the sermon come out of the text.

It also stems from the fact that some preachers classify their sermons as expository when in actuality they are not. Marvin R. Vincent tells of the preacher who said he liked expository preaching because "when he was persecuted in one verse he could flee to another!"[7] Too often preachers go way beyond the meaning of the text in their comments.

In *Text-Driven Preaching,* editor David Allen defines a text-driven sermon as one that "develops a text by explaining, illustrating, and applying its meaning." He continues, "Text-driven preaching stays true to the substance of the text, the structure of the text, and the spirit of the text."[8] The terms "expository" and "text-driven" use similar wording to describe the same endeavor.

When preachers are "expository" or "text-driven," they are taking the message of Scripture from the text and delivering it to the people. Hughes says, "Expository preaching is a verbal conveyor belt that digs gold from the Scriptures and transports the nuggets of God's word to the hearts and minds of people."[9]

This kind of preaching is built upon the conviction that the words of Scripture are inspired by the Holy Spirit. And it assumes that the meaning of a passage intended by its human author and the inspiration of the Holy Spirit is the meaning we are to expound. Walter Kaiser says, "Let us say it clearly: The text has but one meaning, the meaning intended by its author; and there is but one method for discovering that meaning, the grammatical-historical method."[10]

Text-driven or expository preaching is also built upon the assumption that it is vital that the preacher conveys to his listeners what God has said, rather than his own ideas and words, regardless of how creatively the preacher may deliver them. Again, Allen writes, "It is the height of arrogance to substitute the words of men for the words of God."[11] Today's preacher must decide if he will serve people a diet of sugar-filled junk food or a nourishing meal of the milk, the meat, and the manna of the Word. For the preacher who believes God has spoken in the words of Scripture, there can be no doubt about his decision. Expository or text-driven preaching is solidly built upon the foundation that when we thus preach the Bible we are giving and applying to the people the meaning of the very words of God.

THE ROLE OF LINGUISTICS

Tom Shelton (not his real name) was one of my members at Second Baptist Church in Cedartown, Georgia. He lived across the street from me in the mill village just behind the church. Tom likely never finished high school. He spent his entire working life at the Goodyear Fabric Mill. Never owning a car, he walked to and from the mill every day. Tom worked on the second shift and returned home at midnight. In the summers he'd be drenched with sweat; he would bathe and then eat the sumptuous meal his wife had prepared for him. Then he studied his Bible.

His insightful understanding of Scripture was remarkable. Often after Sunday services Tom and I would walk together to our homes. "Preacher, that was a marvelous message today. I was studying that passage recently and I had never seen that—" Then he would explain what God had taught him from the Bible. I was often astonished. Looking back, I wonder why I didn't talk with Brother Shelton about my sermon before I preached it!

Tom Shelton probably never heard the word *linguistics*. He could read neither Hebrew nor Greek. He read only from a well-worn King James Version of the Bible. So what could linguistics do for him? What can it do for you?

Linguistics is the study of the structure of language, including phonology, morphology, syntax, semantics, and pragmatics.[12] In particular, we are interested in the field of linguistics as it applies to our study of the Hebrew Old Testament and the Greek New Testament.

The role of linguistics in biblical expository preaching grew during the 1980s. David Alan Black wrote, "The 1980s . . . have seen a genuine awakening to the substantive contribution that linguistics can make to biblical exegesis."[13]

The Benefits of Linguistic Study

The field of linguistics is too large and involved to deal with it extensively in this section. I do want to suggest some advantages to the preacher however, to be found in several areas of linguistic study. Noam Chomsky, called by some "the Einstein of linguistics," claims that there are linguistic universals in syntax.[14] Recognizing these universals will assist us in our biblical analysis and exegesis.

Analyzing Structure and Types of Words

Analyzing the structure of a Bible passage can be of great benefit to the preacher. Such study can be applied to an entire Bible book. I recently did a study of the book of Jude. Applying principles from linguistics, the overall structure of Jude became clear. Most of the elements of the rhetorical style of writing in the first century are found. There is *exordium*: the case to be argued (vv. 1–3), *narratio*: concerns raising the argument (v. 4), *probatio*: illustrations and supporting arguments (vv. 5–16), and *peroration*: summary and appeal (vv. 17–24). Placed in terms more familiar to us, and with some slight tweaking, Jude is organized as follows: greeting (vv. 1–2), theme (vv. 3–4), evidence (vv. 5–16), summation (vv. 17–23), and doxology (vv. 24–25).

Because words are the material we use to form sentences, it's important to discern the various kinds of words used in a Bible passage. Linguistics helps us understand that two basic kinds of words are used: function words and content words. Function words are those that hold the passage together. These are the articles, prepositions, and conjunctions found in the passage. Primarily, they are very important in pointing to relationships within the Bible passage. They can also be helpful in placing the passage at hand in its context. D. A. Carson says that in textual preaching we must not overlook the old adage that "a text without a context becomes a pretext for a proof text."[15] Hershael York, pastor and professor of Christian preaching at Southern Baptist Theological Seminary, once told me he often reminds his college students as well as his church congregation, "Context is everything." I agree with the often used statement, "Text is king; context is queen." Structure words help keep context before us.

Some of the structure words are referred to as "discourse markers." That is, they are words that bracket off units of the biblical text that hang together. This is true of conjunctions. The Greek conjunction *kai* serves the purpose of connection. Constantine Campbell says it is "a coordinating conjunction used to connect words, phrases, clauses, or paragraphs, linking items of equal status."[16] *De* is another coordinating conjunction. When the biblical author uses this particular conjunction, it's a "heads up," alerting readers to a new development in the flow of the text. As Campbell points out, the use of the Greek *gar* "adds 'background' information that strengthens or supports preceding material."[17]

The Key Roles of Function and Content Words

Function words often have rich meaning. Again in Jude, look at how function words are helpful to our understanding of the passage of Scripture. The use of the definite article in "the faith" (v. 3) gives emphasis to the fact that Jude is referring to a body of belief known in Scripture as "the faith," that is, that body of truth that constitutes the essentials of Christianity (cf. Romans 6:17). As another example, look at the words "just as" in verse 7. The subordinate conjunction seems to tie the sin of Sodom and Gomorrah to the sin of the angels in verse 6. This is certainly pertinent to a careful exegesis of the passage.

The content words of a Bible passage are even more important. Content words are nouns, verbs, adjectives, and adverbs. Content words in Jude deliver loads of information and inspiration. For example, the verb "kept" (Gk. *tereo*), is used five times in Jude (vv. 1, 6, 13, 21 [translated "reserved"], 24). The verb gives the idea of being kept safe from harm. And its uses in verses 24 and 21 indicate there is a keeping God does and a keeping we must do.

Think with me further about the importance of verbs in a Scripture passage. Verbs are the load-bearing words in a text. The tense, voice, or mood of a verb sequence can be very helpful in interpretation. This can even be seen in an overall view of a book. As an example, consider the opening chapters of the book of Romans. Chart carefully the verbs as you move through Romans. You might be surprised to find where the first imperative verb occurs. You don't find it in the introductory verses (1:1–17). The section that could be labeled "Sin" (1:18–3:20) has no imperative verbs. Nor does the section on "Salvation" (3:21–5:21) have imperative verbs either. Indicative statements of fact are made. When we come to the section on "Sanctification" (6:1–8:39) we find our first imperative verb in 6:11: "reckon [or consider] . . . yourselves to be dead indeed unto sin" (KJV). (Note that the imperative in 3:4 is extraneous to this point.)

Is this significant? Indeed, it is. When it comes to man's sin problem, there is nothing we can do about that. The Bible makes statements of fact: we are sinners, period. When it comes to God's great plan of salvation, there is nothing we can do to merit or earn that. God has done everything necessary to make that possible, period. But sanctification is our progressive growth in righteousness. Thus, we are given commands (imperatives), for we do have an involvement in that! There are things we can and must do if we are to grow in our Christian lives.

Understanding this distinction between function and content words can be very helpful in properly exegeting a preaching paragraph. David Alan Black says, "Structure words are the mortar of language, content words are the bricks that provide the substance of a sentence."[18]

The Future Role of Linguistic Study

There is much, much more in play in this new and exciting area of textual study. Matters such as verbal aspect and grammatical analysis promise to aid the preacher in understanding what the text is saying. Campbell points out that "genuine advances in Greek linguistics can lead to new insights into the text."[19] In actuality, when all is said and done, the new insights may just be the natural extensions of what earlier biblical language scholars suggested. A. T. Robertson is considered by many to be the greatest New Testament Greek scholar of all time. His exhaustive grammar is the sine qua non in the field. Scholars today acknowledge his scholarship and their indebtedness to him. Campbell says, "The most distinct feature of Robertson's grammar is that even today, a century later, it seems remarkably modern."[20] He adds, "Robertson handles Greek in a way that is not (on the whole) overturned by modern linguistic principles and methodology."[21]

Do I have you sufficiently confused? If so, let me seek to alleviate some of your confusion. We must keep in mind that linguistic study of the Scripture is relatively new. Though there is a great deal of agreement among Greek scholars in accepting these new insights, the field is far from settled. Black is helpful here: "Linguists themselves seem uncertain about their conclusions, and the entire discipline is in a state of flux."[22]

Cautions in Linguistic Studies

I do believe there are some dangers we must avoid as we enter the world of biblical linguistics. First, we must be aware of the possibility that there are influences from a more liberal approach to hermeneutics. D. A. Carson warns, "With complex roots in linguistics and structuralism, radical hermeneutics has fostered an array of interpretive approaches (the best known of which is deconstruction) that are grounded in postmodern epistemology."[23]

And, there is another concern we must consider. There is the danger that scholars in the field might suggest that only expertise in linguistics will enable one to understand the text of Scripture. Whether intended or not, some of those I have read in this field seem to give that impression.

So, I am back to Tom Shelton. None of the information I have shared in this section was available to him. I rather doubt he could have understood it if it had been. Does this mean that a simple Bible-studying Christian cannot understand the Scriptures and find truth to feed his/her soul and guide his/her life? The answer is obvious. The same Holy Spirit who inspired men to write the Scriptures can illuminate those who read them to understand what they are reading (1 Cor. 2:9–16 and Eph. 1:17–18 are helpful here). Insights are available through our relationship with God the Father and Son and the presence of the Holy Spirit. It's not unlike the old man who sat by the roadside during his lunch hour, reading a worn New Testament. A traveler who noticed him asked, "How can an old fool like you understand that book?" "It would not be possible sir, in the ordinary way," replied the old man, "but you see, I happen to know the Author."

Is there any reason, then, to spend our time with such a complicated discipline as linguistics? Emphatically, yes. God gives the Tom Sheltons of the faith pastors to teach them. Those pastors should be able to expand and enrich the understanding of the people who listen to them. The pastors should be trained by faithful teachers who give them further insight into the meaning of the texts of Scripture. Those teachers should derive the tools for in-depth study from Bible scholars in the disciplines.

The authors of *Going Deeper with New Testament Greek* conclude that new linguistic insights "are beginning to trickle down to the average New Testament scholar, with promise for future students and pastors." They continue,

"While we have little confidence that pastors will ever use terms like 'sequential head,' 'conjoining head,' and 'alternating head,' we do look forward to helpful insights from discourse analysis finding their way into the preaching of the church."[24] Here is my appeal to our scholars and teachers: take the profound information you have discovered and simplify it for those who can benefit from it. If this is not done, very little of this scholarship will ever make its way to those who sit in the pews.

WORD STUDIES

Perhaps you're thinking, *Whew, glad that's over!* Well, not quite. Effective expository or text-driven preaching also means giving attention to the *words* of our preaching passage. Word study has been a fruitful and rich source of material throughout my preaching ministry, helping the people understand what the passage was saying.

Word Etymology and Usage by Writers

Looking at the etymology of the words of Scripture can be very helpful in expounding meaning. A great deal of our preaching is derived from ascertaining the meaning of the words of our preaching passage. "Every word has a range of meaning . . . and also a specific meaning that can only be determined with the context in which the word is used," note Köstenberger, Merkle, and Plummer.[25] They illustrate by pointing out that the Greek word for "world" (*kosmon*) in 1 John 2:15 means "things in this world that entice and gratify the longings of humanity's sinful nature" and "humans in their desperate lost state" in John 3:16–17.[26]

Also, we must keep in mind that the different Bible writers assign different meanings to different words in different contexts. For example, the writer of Hebrews uses "faith" (*pistis*) in one way (Heb. 11:1ff) and Paul uses it in a different way (cf. Eph. 2:8). Be aware also that the same Bible writer may use the same word in a different sense. Does he mean something else in another passage where the word is used? With the technology available to us, this is rather easy to determine today. So, it's rather simple to just find out what the word meant in the context of a particular Bible author. Or is it?

Enter D. A. Carson again. His book *Exegetical Fallacies* really got my attention, as it did many, many expositors. He was building on other volumes. He points out that "there now exist several excellent volumes to introduce the student to the general field of lexical semantics and to warn against particular abuses."[27] One of those volumes is *Biblical Words and their Meaning*, by Moisés Silva. Silva gives a helpful definition: "Lexical semantics is that branch of modern linguistics that focuses on the meaning of individual words."[28]

In Carson's chapter "Word-Study Fallacies," he cautions readers not to make some common mistakes in word study. Here's one that many tend to make. I remember when I first saw the Greek word for power: *dynamis*. Of course, that's where we get our English word for dynamite! So, in Romans 1:16, we see that the gospel is the dynamite of God to everyone who believes. Well, not hardly. Carson points out that there was no such thing as dynamite when Paul penned the word.[29] There is the danger that we may read back into the text of Scripture something that isn't there. But, does this mean there is nothing instructive to be learned from *dynamis*? No. As I understand it, the word carries the meaning of inherent power. There is inherent power in the gospel to change a life. Clearly there is value in doing word studies.

Though I am very limited in my understanding, I do take issue with some of their conclusions. For instance Silva writes, "We must accept the obvious fact that the speakers of a language simply know next to nothing about its development; and this certainly was the case with the writers and immediate readers of Scripture two millennia ago."[30] Two questions come to mind. First, did the human Bible authors know anything of the etymology of the words they were using? Surely they knew something; and probably more than we do. In some instances the human authors of Scripture pointed to the etymology of certain words they used. The etymology of Jesus' Hebrew name is clearly alluded to when Matthew uses it in his statement, "You shall call his name Jesus, for he will save his people from their sins" (Matt. 1:21). Second, did the divine Author, the Holy Spirit, know the etymology of the words He inspired the human authors to use? The answer is definitely yes. I guess that sounds very unscholarly. But, I believe there is value to be derived in studying the etymology of the words and the way the words are constructed.

In no way do I intend to minimize the value of the new information we are receiving from the scholarly study of lexical semantics. Yet we should not completely give away all the richness and fullness available to us as we exegete Scripture. Even Carson says, "It is possible to go too far with this sort of criticism."[31] Do all the word studies, structural linguistics, etc. you can, gleaning insights that will help you have a good meal for those who hear you preach. Then, "deliver to them the finished product—grain threshed, ground, and baked into bread."[32]

Suggestions for Doing Word Studies

Here are several suggestions to assist you in doing word studies as you expound your preaching paragraph. Seek to determine what the human author intended when he used a certain word. Take into consideration the etymology of the word and its use in the particular context where it is used. Check with several lexical sources to help you determine the most accurate meaning of the word.

Be aware that words often change their meaning over time. "Gay clothing" as used in James 2:3 (KJV) may mean something entirely different than in the current use of the word. Avoid reading back into a word some meaning in current usage that would not have been understood or intended by the Bible writer. Check several English versions of the passage to determine whether your interpretation of the word's meaning is accurate. Draw deeply from the rich nectar of the words the Holy Spirit inspired men to write.

My personal conviction is that expository preaching is the only way to produce spiritual growth in the people of God. Only by preaching what God says may believers be kept from the entangling wilderness of worldliness. This kind of preaching will not be well received by all. The current trend toward self-help, felt-need sermons will probably resist such preaching. Many of the sermons one hears today are more in the category of motivational talks. Such talks may begin with a verse or two of Scripture at the beginning to provide a diving board to what the speaker wants to say. Or, a verse may be hitched to the back of the talk to lend some biblical credibility to what has just been said. The preacher who wants to give his people the words of God will perhaps notice that some churches where pastors speak pious platitudes to crowds with "itching ears" (cf. 2 Tim. 4:3) rapidly increase in attendance. He may be tempted to ditch expository preaching. He must resist the temptation.

Speaking before a large audience, David Allen once recounted perhaps the most dramatic scene in the classic western movie *The Magnificent Seven,* the story of how Chris Adams (Yul Brynner) led a band of seven hired guns to protect a Mexican village from marauders, headed by Calvera (Eli Wallach). They train the villagers how to defend themselves. When Calvera and his forty bandits ride into the village, they are met in the town square by Chris, who firmly tells Calvera: "Ride on."

Calvera protests. "I'm going into the hills for the winter. Where am I going to get food for my men? Somehow, I don't think you have solved my problem."

"Solving your problem is not our line," Chris replies.

The camera cuts to a lean, cool character standing a few feet to the right of Adams, Vin Tanner (Steve McQueen). With a you-know-I-mean-business look and voice, he utters my favorite line in the movie: "We deal in lead, friend."

To which David Allen added about preachers and preaching, "We deal in words, friend!"[33]

And so we do. Let us make progress, seeking to share the words of Scripture as we preach.

READING FOR PROGRESS

Akin, Daniel L., David L. Allen, and Ned L. Mathews, *Text-Driven Preaching*. Nashville: B&H Academic, 2010.

Black, David Alan. *Linguistics for Students of New Testament Greek: A Survey of Basic Concepts and Applications*, 2nd edition. Grand Rapids: Baker, 1995.

Carson, D. A. *Exegetical Fallacies*. Grand Rapids: Baker, 1996.

7

IS A BEELINE THE BEST LINE?

GETTING TO THE CROSS IN EVERY SERMON

Jim Shaddix

I take my text and make a beeline to the cross." While it's certainly not the only great quote attributed to him, this declaration has been hailed as the sum of Charles Haddon Spurgeon's preaching method.

Although some question whether "the prince of preachers" actually said these words,[1] most agree that the statement accurately reflects his commitment to get to Jesus in every sermon. He didn't care who or what stood in his way. Spurgeon was going to find a path to Calvary every time he preached. And every self-respecting expositor should do the same. But is a beeline the best line for getting to the cross every time we preach?

THE WEATHER ON
OUR WAY TO THE CROSS

My wife and I love road trips. Although I fly a lot, if all things are equal and we've got the time, the two of us would prefer to load up the car and make our journey by land. When we do, we use a lot of apps on our smartphones

107

and tablets to help us enjoy the trip. Whether it's finding restaurants, rest areas, points of interests, or the closest Starbucks, we rely heavily on our technology. But starting out, two particular apps are especially important to me: the weather app and the GPS app. I want to know the forecast along my route, and I want to hear the lady on my GPS app say, "You're on the fastest route and your route is clear."

In determining how to make the best line to the cross, it's probably wise for us to know a little bit about the current climate of the conversation.

What We Agree On

I don't know many expositors who wouldn't agree that evangelical pastors need to preach Christ in every sermon. After all, that's the primary distinguishing factor between Christian preaching and the moralistic, God-themed sermons that characterize most theistic world religions. As has often been suggested, a truly Christian sermon should never be welcome in a Jewish synagogue or a Muslim mosque, at least sermons spoken by preachers who have any convictions about what they believe. And it's Christ and His cross that should create the fundamental rub. The apostle Paul said the cross was a stumbling block to Jews and foolishness to everybody else (cf. 1 Cor. 1:18, 23).

The Bible's Theme: God's Redemptive Work in Christ

More importantly, it's hard to read the New Testament and not come away with the clear understanding that all Scripture is about God's redemptive work in Christ. The New Testament obviously is comprised of a clear retelling of the gospel (Gospels), the story of its expansion (Acts), and an exposition of gospel truths (Epistles). But Jesus, the apostles, and other early church leaders evidently believed that Christ was the theme of the Old Testament as well. In the most famous sermon ever preached, Jesus claimed to be the intended meaning of the Old Testament: "Do not think that I have come to abolish the Law or the Prophets; I have not come to abolish them but to fulfill them" (Matt. 5:17). He told his critics, "You search the Scriptures because you think that in them you have eternal life; and it is they that bear witness about me. . . . For if you believed Moses, you would believe me; for he wrote of me" (John 5:39, 46). And after the resurrection, Luke records a couple of telling conversations that Jesus had with His disciples:

> And beginning with Moses and all the Prophets, he interpreted to
> them in all the Scriptures the things concerning himself. . . . Then he

said to them, "These are my words that I spoke to you while I was still with you, that everything written about me in the Law of Moses and the Prophets and the Psalms must be fulfilled." (Luke 24:27, 44)

Jesus clearly saw Himself as the intended meaning of the Old Testament Scriptures.[2]

Jesus' followers embraced the same conviction after He rose from the dead and ascended back to heaven. At Pentecost and in the days following it, Peter preached about Jesus fulfilling God's promises that were foretold by the prophets about the Messiah (cf. Acts 2:14–34; 3:18–25). Philip told the Ethiopian eunuch the good news about Jesus by expounding from Isaiah 53 (cf. Acts 8:27–35). In Paul's first recorded sermon he preached Christ from Psalm 2:7, 16:10, Isaiah 5:3, 49:6, and Habakkuk 1:5 (cf. Acts 13:13–43), a practice he would continue throughout his missionary journeys (e.g., Acts 17: 1–3; 26:22–23; 28:23). And his epistles are filled with clear connections he made between the Old Testament and the person of Christ (e.g., Rom. 1:1–3; 16:25–27; 1 Cor. 15:3–4). Maybe the most pervasive example of Christ being interpreted as the theme of Old Testament Scripture is found in the book of Hebrews. Guthrie counts "roughly thirty-seven quotations, forty allusions, nineteen cases where OT material is summarized, and thirteen where an OT name or topic is referred to without reference to a specific context."[3] The author of Hebrews—in sermonic fashion throughout the letter—clearly exposes Christ from all of these places.

The Spirit's Theme: To Glorify Christ

In addition to Jesus and His followers considering all of Scripture to be about Him, the Holy Spirit shares the same conviction! Jesus told His disciples that the Spirit would "bear witness about me" (John 15:26) and "glorify me" (John 16:14). The Spirit of God is to make much of the Son of God. So it just makes sense that if the Spirit of God's job is to draw attention to the Son of God, and the Spirit of God inspired all of Scripture (cf. 2 Peter 1:20–21; 2 Tim. 3:16), then all of Scripture must be about the Son of God. Ware writes, "For although the Spirit is primarily responsible for producing the Bible as the inspired Word of God, the Bible is not primarily about the Spirit but rather it is about the Son."[4] From Genesis to Revelation, the Holy Spirit wrote about the Lord Jesus Christ.

It's clear that the New Testament church believed the focus of the Old Testament was Jesus Christ. The vast majority of contemporary expositors share this same conviction that both Old and New Testaments are about Him. Azurdia says the Bible is "a record of the redemption of the people of God by His Son, Jesus Christ."[5] Wright concurs: "The Old Testament tells the story which Jesus completes."[6] Even the statement of faith in my own Southern Baptist denomination acknowledges this truth: "All Scripture is a testimony to Christ, who is Himself the focus of divine revelation."[7] Because we believe the whole Bible is about Jesus, it makes sense we agree that every sermon should reveal that relationship in some way—so we show people the gospel. I don't hear much argument over these two contentions. So what's all the fuss about?

What We Don't Agree On

To Beeline

While expositors tend to agree that Christ is the theme of all Scripture, and that the gospel subsequently should show up in every sermon, we don't always agree about how we get there and what exactly that Christ-always theme ought to look like. In fact, the approach that Spurgeon supposedly professed to preaching Christ in every message has been met with mixed reviews among some today who champion expository preaching. Mohler, a clear proponent of Spurgeon's beeline approach, hails the great British pulpiteer for his alleged beeline homiletic, saying that he

> preached a full-bodied gospel with substantive content and unashamed conviction. In this he was regarded as something of an exception, but he held fast to his biblical faith, Calvinist convictions, and evangelistic appeal. . . . But whatever the text—Old Testament or New Testament—Spurgeon would find his way to the gospel of the Savior on the cross. And that gospel was put forth with the full force of substitutionary atonement and with warnings of eternal punishment but for the grace of God in Jesus Christ.[8]

According to Mohler—and myriads of other contemporary expositors—Spurgeon serves as a healthy model of Christ-centered, gospel-driven preaching.

Or Not to Beeline

Other expositors, however, have balked at the wisdom of the approach Spurgeon is believed to have embraced. Thabiti Anyabwile, for example, minces no words when suggesting that

Spurgeon was wrong. We're not to take a text and make a bee-line to the cross. In fact, if you've read a number of Spurgeon's sermons you've no doubt noticed that often he seems to take the long way around. He was no expositor and he seemed to make a bee-line away from the text, which is not the same as making a bee-line to the cross.[9]

By contrast to the beeline approach, Anyabwile contends, preachers have the responsibility to reveal the meaning of every text for its original author and hearers, according to its immediate context (a contention with which I'm quite confident Mohler would agree!). Then and only then can they make their way to the cross in a responsible manner. He says,

> A bee-line to the cross might just be bad exegesis and a neglect of the Bible. The gospel preacher's task is to explain what God said and meant in a given text in context, answer what it meant for the original hearers—whether Israel or the early church, then show how it relates to the Person and work of Christ, before applying it to our contemporary hearers.[10]

For Anyabwile and many others, this approach fosters a better understanding of the whole Bible, exposes Christ in richer ways, avoids canned presentations of the gospel that get tacked on to the end of the sermon, and makes the gospel integral to every text with integrity.[11]

Now I'm not suggesting that Al Mohler condones every approach Spurgeon took. Nor am I suggesting that Thabiti Anyabwile disagrees with everything Spurgeon did. But I am suggesting that these two expositors represent the fact that there are differences of opinions regarding how we get to the cross, or at least regarding the validity of the approach credited to Spurgeon. So what's an expositor to do? Do we find our way to Jesus in every sermon regardless of the historical context and meaning of our passage? Or does our preaching text establish some guidance—and boundaries—for making our way to the cross? What exactly does it look like for us to be Christ-centered and gospel-driven in every sermon we preach? And how do we get there?

What We Should Agree On

I don't claim to be smart enough to settle a debate that now has spanned almost two decades. Nor am I naïve enough to think there's a place where we'll all agree on every facet of Christ-centered, gospel-driven preaching. But I do suspect that Mohler and Anyabwile—and the various camps they represent—actually wouldn't disagree much with one another if they sat down in the same room and talked through this issue. Furthermore, I'm not convinced that Spurgeon himself would disagree too much if he could sit in on the conversation! So how are these differing perspectives reconciled?

A Unifying Purpose: The Bible's Story Line of Redemption and Re-creation

I'm convinced that the best way to bring these positions together is to keep in mind not just the *theme* of all of Scripture but the *purpose* of all of Scripture. In chapter 1, I proposed that the primary purpose of the Bible was to unfold God's redemptive plan of re-creating mankind into His image through Jesus Christ. The apostle Paul said of the people whom God "foreknew he also predestined to be conformed to the image of his Son, in order that he might be the firstborn among many brothers. And those whom he predestined he also called, and those whom he called he also justified, and those whom he justified he also glorified" (Rom. 8:29–30). And that truth frames the Bible and serves as its primary theme (cf. Gen. 1:26–27; 2 Cor. 3:18; Phil. 3:21; Col. 3:10; 2 Peter 1:3–4; 1 John 3:2; Rev. 21:3–4).

Basically what I'm talking about is using sound biblical theology. That's what we're doing when we interpret all of Scripture in view of the Bible's overall story line of redemption and re-creation. We're operating with the conviction that the Old Testament sets the stage for our need to be restored to God's image and points us to Christ as the agent of that process; the Gospels reveal Jesus as the Christ, unfolding the redemptive work He did to restore us to God's image; and the rest of the New Testament explains the implications of Jesus' death and resurrection for our re-creation, culminating with the full accomplishment of God's mission of restoring us to His image in Christ that we might enjoy and worship Him forever. Surely we have to agree on these things.

If we agree that all Scripture is about Jesus, and that the Bible is one big story about what God has done in Christ to restore us to His image, then it follows that every text stands somewhere in relation to Christ. My friend and colleague Tony Merida contends, "Every text will point to Christ futuristically, refer to Christ explicitly, or look back to Christ implicitly."[12] So the most important question for me to answer is, "Where does my text stand in relation to Christ?"

Answering this question about New Testament texts should be relatively simple. The Gospels are the historical account of Jesus' life and work; Acts is about the advancement of His mission in and through the early church; the Epistles are reflections on His life, work, and character as they are to be lived out by His followers; and Revelation is the foretelling of His triumphant return and future glory. Just about every text in the New Testament is speaking directly about Jesus' person and work, the advancement of His message and mission, and His return in glory. So if we interpret these texts with integrity, their historical meaning is going to lead us naturally to Christ and His gospel.

The Old Testament, however, is a bit trickier. Why? Because no Old Testament text mentions "Jesus of Nazareth" specifically, and most don't even explicitly reference the concept of the Messiah. So moving forward, I want us to dedicate most of our attention to the biblical revelation before Jesus ever showed up. While the principles we discuss in the rest of this chapter apply to both Old and New Testaments, we'll concentrate on how we get to the cross in every sermon from passages in the Old Testament.

So keep in mind that the need to answer the question *Where does my text stand in relation to Christ?* doesn't in any way imply that Jesus, any titles referring to Him (i.e., Christ, Messiah, Savior, Deliverer, etc.), or even the idea of His person are referenced in every biblical text. Block says, "On the surface it may appear spiritually edifying, but it is exegetically fraudulent to try to extract from every biblical text some truth about Christ. The Scriptures consist of many different genres and address many different concerns. Not all speak of Christ."[13] Merida agrees:

> I am not advocating *allegory* or clever "Jesus-jukes" (also called *spiritualizing*). Some well-intended but misguided people, in their zeal to preach Christ, sometimes play fast and loose with the Bible, making cavalier and fanciful correspondences that are not in the text. Every time you read about *wood* in the Old Testament, it does not stand for the cross. Every time you see the color *red*, it does not signify blood. These are examples of silly, unfounded allegorical readings.[14]

To force connections to Jesus on any text is nothing short of exegetical gymnastics and hermeneutical treason. We are responsible for discovering the Holy Spirit's intended meaning in the text, beginning with what the human author intended the original audience to get. And the human authors in the Old Testament certainly weren't thinking about Jesus of Nazareth and a bloody cross every time they wrote.

Finding Connections that Lead to Jesus

Instead of allegorizing, spiritualizing, or fabricating unintended allegory, we need to be looking for the inner-biblical connections within Scripture that lead to Jesus. The Bible is a unified book in which all the plot lines and embedded gospel themes converge on Christ.[15] Geisler says, "Christ is presented as the tie between the Testaments, the content of the whole canon, and the unifying theme within each book of the Bible."[16] As an interpreter, my job is to find the connections in my particular preaching text to that unifying theme.

Finding those connections means that we must study, prepare, and preach every sermon with our biblical theology in mind: the overarching narrative and redemptive purpose of the Bible—re-creation into God's image through Christ. I love Jeramie Rinne's analogy that likens this approach to Bible interpretation and preaching to having good "court sense" in a basketball game:

> Good basketball players don't just focus on dribbling the ball to the hoop. They are aware of the location of their teammates and defenders on the court as well as the flow of play. Similarly, good exposition doesn't merely provide a running commentary on the verses at hand. It also has a court sense of what else is going on before and after the text, and how it all relates to overall progression of God's big story.[17]

Our basketball court is the whole Bible that tells a single story of God's mission to re-create a people into His image through Christ and establish a kingdom for His glory. If we can determine how every passage fits into that story, then we will have found a clear path to the glorious gospel of the cross. I think all expositors must agree on that. So let's explore some ways to help us do it.

SEEING OUR WAY TO THE CROSS

The older I get the more I struggle with seeing well. I'm not at the point yet where I need to wear glasses all the time, but the doctor tells me I do need them when I drive at night and when I look at a computer screen for long periods of time. The lenses he prescribed make words on road signs and electronic documents actually readable for me. That's what corrective lenses do—they help us see things in the right way instead of the convoluted way our unaided degenerating eyes see our world. Eyeglasses help us see the right route as we walk or drive. In the same way, we have to choose the right lenses in order to find our way to the cross in every sermon. Our fallible nature as interpreters can cause us to see texts in convoluted ways they weren't intended to be seen. So our choice of lens is critical if we're going to see Christ in the right way in every text.

Three Ways to View Scripture Connections to Christ

In recent years preachers and scholars have proposed several hermeneutical lenses to help us see appropriate Christ-connections. The three primary lenses that seem to get the most airtime are *christocentric*, *christotelic*, and *christiconic*. Each of these three approaches is considered to be an overarching hermeneutical rubric to be applied to the whole of Scripture. The christocentric approach sees all of Scripture as having Christ as its central theme. The christotelic approach sees all of Scripture as having Christ as its end, or fulfillment. The christiconic approach sees all of Scripture as having Christ—or His character—as its goal in the lives of the readers.

Because each one of these perspectives is considered to be a lens through which all of Scripture should be viewed, they most often are considered in juxtaposition to one another. In other words, it's implied that we have to pick only one of them as our path to getting to the cross. And I'm convinced that's one of the biggest reasons we end up with opposing positions among like-minded expositors who share similar theological views.

My question is, Why can't we use all three? Just like some people have a pair of prescription glasses for everyday use and then a pair of reading glasses for the small print, it makes sense that we might need to look at different texts through different lenses. So isn't it possible that different literary genres and even different passages might require a different hermeneutical key? Instead of embracing one particular method as the only way, isn't it more likely that one approach may work for a given passage but may not work for others? Murray thinks so: "I increasingly saw the vital necessity of flexibility in interpreting each Old Testament genre and passage, the need to have a variety of interpretive keys at my disposal if I was to accurately unlock the Christ-centered message that God had packed into that book or passage."[18] With the wide variety of biblical literary genres, it seems best to adopt a paradigm that enables us to choose the appropriate interpretive key to unlock the gospel connection in each genre and text.

I'm convinced that the christocentric, christotelic, and christiconic lenses can combine to make a strong process for getting to the cross from every text in every sermon. So I don't feel like I have to choose one of them as an exclusive approach. Instead, I keep all three at my disposal so I can determine which is the best approach to discovering the Christ connection in my particular preaching text. So think about these three lenses as they relate to helping us see where our text stands in relationship to Christ.

The Christocentric Approach

The term *christocentric* has a broad history that encompasses a variety of styles, approaches, and methods. It's been popularized in recent years by men like Sidney Greidanus and Graeme Goldsworthy. Greidanus says, "*God's* story of bringing his kingdom on earth is centered in *Christ*: Christ the center of redemptive history, Christ the center of the Scriptures."[19] Again, Greidanus is speaking about the whole of Scripture. But if we think of the term *christocentric* as meaning Christ is the center, then it can be a very helpful tool in interpreting and preaching many individual texts in the Bible. Why? Because many texts do have Christ at their center—they are speaking directly and specifically about Jesus. The author's intent was to tell people something about the Messiah to come.

So the first thing we want to do is look to see if Christ is the center—or central theme—of the preaching text. In the Old Testament, the most direct route to the cross is what we call promise/fulfillment. That's when the preaching text contains a prophecy or promise that specifically addresses Christ and His work, and is clearly fulfilled in some aspect of the gospel. These texts are christocentric in that they're speaking directly about the Messiah.

Think about the many passages in the Old Testament that specifically and directly address the subject of the Messiah. For example, consider the host of Messianic Psalms (e.g., Pss. 2, 22, 110) as well as passages like Isaiah 9 and 53. These are texts that have Christ as their theme. If I'm preaching from the prophets, I want to note when they're specifically speaking about the messianic event. Micah's prophecy about a ruler coming out of Bethlehem (Mic. 5:2), for example, provides a direct path to Matthew 2:6 where the prophecy is fulfilled in the birth of Jesus. When I'm preaching on Abraham, I want to be sure to take my people over into the New Testament to see how Jesus fulfills God's promises to bless Abraham's offspring or "seed" (Gal. 3:16; cf. Gen. 12:7; 13:15; 17:8; 24:7). Many passages address the Christ event explicitly and directly. These texts usually provide the easiest pathways to the cross.

The Christotelic Approach

The term *christotelic* is relatively new in the field of Bible interpretation. It likely was coined by Peter Enns in an effort to describe the apostolic method of interpreting the Old Testament.[20] Enns explains that the Greek word *telos* means "end" or "completion." So, to read the Old Testament christotelically means to read it already knowing that Christ is somehow the *end* to which the Old Testament is heading.[21] Again, Enns is speaking of a lens through which to look at the Old Testament as a whole. But if we apply the idea to individual texts, it serves to help us identify the gospel connection in passages that don't speak of Christ specifically (christocentric), but instead find their ultimate realization in Him (christotelic).

The christotelic approach enables the Bible expositor to determine how a particular text points toward Christ so one doesn't have to force Him into every text. Additionally, it holds the expositor accountable to being true to the historical meaning of the text for the original audience. Championing for a christotelic approach, Block writes:

> While it is hermeneutically irresponsible to say that all Old Testament texts have a Christocentric meaning or point to Christ, it is true that all play a significant role in God's great redemptive plan that leads to and climaxes in Christ. This means that as a Christian interpreter my wrestling with an Old Testament text must begin with trying to grasp the sense the original readers/hearers should have got, and authoritative preaching of that text depends upon having grasped that intended sense first.[22]

It's vital that we let the original meaning direct us to God's redemptive plan in Christ. The christotelic approach to certain texts helps us arrive at the cross without straining to make Christ fit into every passage.

Some of the most fertile soil for making christotelic connections is in the area of typology. A type is a correspondence between some aspect of the gospel in the New Testament with people, offices, events, and institutions in the Old Testament. Specifically, the Old Testament type foreshadows Jesus and His work. New Testament writers frequently refer to things in the Old Testament as types of Christ, which makes it different from allegory. Allegory makes unsubstantiated leaps to the gospel. True typology, on the other hand, is comprised of Old Testament patterns, language, and themes that are clearly given a new—often escalated—meaning in the New Testament. For example, in the New Testament Jesus is the last Adam, a priest greater than Melchizedek, a prophet better than Moses, the true Israel, David's ultimate Son, the true Passover lamb, our final sacrifice, and more.

One of the things I've found helpful in identifying these types is to ask the question, What does this look like on this side of the cross? Asking this question forces me to consider whether there is a clear New Testament correspondent to the person, office, event, theme, or institution that I'm dealing with in my Old Testament preaching passage. This allows me to interpret and expound the text according to its historical context and meaning, and then move my audience to see what that truth looks like in light of the New Testament and its gospel message.

For example, some time ago I was preaching through Haggai and dealing with God's command for the returning Jewish exiles to rebuild the temple. The temple in Jerusalem played a crucial role in the Old Testament as the place of God's saving and ruling presence among His people. The original temple was a literal physical structure located in a specific geographic place. And through Haggai God was telling the Israelites to rebuild it with real brick and stone and mortar and wood. But surely the book of Haggai wasn't telling my congregation to launch a church building program! So I had to ask, "What does the concept of the temple look like on this side of the cross?"

The answer to that question is that the Old Testament temple merely foreshadowed God's presence among His people through Jesus Christ. In the New Testament, Jesus Himself claimed to be the temple (John 2:21). He—like the temple—is the physical presence of God among His people to save and reign. Later Paul said—as a result of Christ's work—individual believers are the temple (1 Cor. 3:16; 6:19–20). When Jesus takes up residence in someone's life, God dwells there! Paul also said the church is the temple (Eph. 2:19–22). When Jesus gets in the lives of believers, and believers unite to form the church, God is resident in their midst. Ultimately the New Testament says the eternal presence of God in Christ is the temple (Rev. 21:22). So once I explained the meaning of Haggai's words to its original hearers, I took my people to the New Testament passages above to show them the priority we must place on pursuing and experiencing the presence of God, even above our own comfort and convenience. That's what the Holy Spirit—through Haggai—is saying to people on this side of the cross. This kind of christotelic connection allows me to preach Christ without compromising original authorial intent.

Certain biblical themes are similar to types, except they don't point as directly to Christ. These are recurring motifs and images that often help us see where our text fits in the larger biblical story. These themes often are best seen christotelically. Some of the more common biblical themes include creation, covenants, the exodus from Egypt, the day of the Lord, and the kingdom of God. Tracing these themes as they are woven throughout biblical history provides a framework for organically moving from many texts to the key turning point of their fulfillment in the gospel. For example, when I'm expounding Numbers 13–14 in the Old Testament, the letter to the Hebrews in the New Testament helps me challenge believers not to resist participating in God's missionary enterprise. Conversely, understanding the timeline of Israel's exodus from Egypt helps me to understand and preach the message of Hebrews as a missionary appeal to God's people to fulfill their purpose of getting the gospel to unbelievers.

The Christiconic Approach

Of the three terms, *christiconic* represents the newest approach to be proposed for interpreting and preaching Old Testament texts. It's the brainchild of Abraham Kuruvilla, who suggests that the Bible as a whole projects an image of Christ, with each text portraying a facet of what it looks like to be Christlike.[23] These facets—or icons—of the image of Christ are presented through the theological sense of the given passage, providing listeners the opportunity to align themselves with God's divine demand for holiness and thereby be conformed to the image of Christ. I don't necessarily agree with all of Kuruvilla's assertions (nor would he probably agree with all of my application of his assertions!). But I do think his paradigm can be useful in my approach to individual texts. While some texts have Christ as their center (christocentric), and others have Christ as their intended realization (christotelic), some texts simply reflect the character and image of Christ into which God is re-creating us (christiconic).

The christiconic connection is particularly helpful in practically applying the dos and don'ts of mature Christian living to our listeners. Kuruvilla contends:

> Application involves discovering the world projected in front of the text and aligning oneself to that world. Such an alignment restores the relationship between God and his community. A periscope, by way of its theology, thus contributes to the corporate mission of covenant renewal. I submit that what God would have is that his people be captivated by the world projected in front of the text, and that they seek to be its inhabitants, aligning themselves to its precepts, priorities, and practices. This is God's gracious divine demand.[24]

When the natural outgrowth of a text is the identification of Christlike qualities or practices that God intends for our lives, there's a direct application for listeners to embrace, adopt, or align themselves with those qualities. Doing so fosters restoration into His image.

The christiconic approach helps me to answer the question, "What does my text say about our need for Jesus?" I think this is Bryan Chapell's intent when he tells us to look for the *fallen condition focus* (FCF) in every passage. He defines FCF as "the mutual human condition that contemporary believers share with those to or about whom the text was written that requires the grace of the passage for God's people to glorify and enjoy him."[25] When I'm able to identify "the mutual human condition" between the original audience and my audience, I then can find a redemptive solution in the Christ life that faithfully reflects the meaning of the text, and at the same time gets me to the cross in my sermon. I like to think of that solution as the *crucified condition needed* for us to look like Jesus. It's the aspect of sanctification that's required by the gospel.

Specific moral commandments—reflected in such laws as the Ten Commandments, aspects of the Levitical law, the Proverbs, and implied in the lives of many Bible characters—fill the biblical story with pathways to the cross. Rinne identifies three particular ways we get to Jesus from Scripture's moral and ethical commands. First, those commands lead us to Jesus by showing us our sin and need of a savior. They're like a mirror to confront us with our moral deformity and inability to be justified by keeping God's law (cf. Rom. 3:20). Second, biblical commands point us to Jesus as the one who perfectly kept them and brought them to their intended goal (cf. Matt. 5:17). The prodigal nature of Adam and Israel, as well as Israel's judges and kings, all demonstrate man's inability to earn God's approval. Third, through reliance on God's Spirit through the resurrected Christ, we can now keep God's laws as obedient sons and daughters. Jesus rescued us from the power of sin "in order that the law's requirement would be accomplished in us who do not walk according to the flesh but according to the Spirit" (Rom. 8:4).[26]

One example is Proverbs, a book filled with wisdom-sayings that I think are best interpreted and preached with a christiconic approach. The apostle Paul wrote that "because of him [God] you are in Christ Jesus, who became to us wisdom from God, righteousness and sanctification and redemption" (1 Cor. 1:30). That means whatever manifestations of wisdom and righteousness and sanctification we find in the Proverbs are found in Jesus! So let's say I'm preaching on Proverbs 30:7–9:

Two things I ask of you; deny them not to me before I die: Remove far from me falsehood and lying; give me neither poverty nor riches; feed me with the food that is needful for me, lest I be full and deny you and say, "Who is the LORD?" or lest I be poor and steal and profane the name of my God.

If I stop after expounding the human author's intended meaning for the original audience, I'll have nothing more than a moralistic sermon on telling the truth and being content. But if I look at the divine Author's intent by peering through a christiconic lens, I can point my listeners to Jesus' embodiment of truth and contentment, not to mention His willingness to deny Himself of the things of this world in order to give His life for us. And I can easily connect this text to the truth and contentment we can have through the power of Christ's Spirit.

Another way to look for christiconic gospel connections in the Old Testament is by looking for the attributes of God in the text. References to God's mercy, grace, justice, and power will always point us to Christ as the one who fleshed out these qualities. Specifically, look to see how your preaching text reveals the nature of the God who provides redemption.[27] Again, these connections are immediately applicable in helping people worship the Lord Jesus as well as embrace His character as their own.

ONCE WE GET TO THE CROSS

Finding the best line to the cross is only half the battle. Getting to the cross with a christocentric, christotelic, or christiconic connection can all be undone if the connection you make isn't communicated in the most effective way. Be sure to include the following when you preach Jesus from every text of Scripture.

Show Your People How You Got There

Earlier I mentioned my use of the GPS app on my smartphone when I travel. I've discovered that the way I use it often gravitates to an unhealthy place. I've found myself getting into a "plug-n-play" routine of just entering my destination and listening to the directions, but not paying attention to the actual route. In other words, I don't learn the directions to new destinations. So every time I get ready to go back to someplace I've been before, I still depend on my GPS to get me there. Preaching can do that to listeners if we're not careful.

One of the responsibilities we have as expositors is to teach our listeners how to read and study the Bible rightly. Our people learn more about how to do those things by listening to us preach than any other way. So we live in a constant tension between overloading them with needless exegetical details, and simply giving them conclusions that we've drawn from our study. Neither extreme is helpful to them in learning how to handle God's Word with integrity and hear His voice when they read and study their Bibles. So we have to make it our practice to show them enough of our exegetical journey to validate our conclusions and strengthen their confidence in God's Word.

This responsibility includes our efforts at connecting every text to the Christ event. If we just say "This is talking about Jesus" or "That's a reference to the gospel" without showing people how we arrived at that conclusion, we do one of two things. We create doubt in their minds, cause them to cynically wonder *Where did that come from?* and thereby undermine their trust in us as messengers of God. Or—like me with my GPS app—we foster in their lives an unhealthy dependence on us to tell them what the Bible means instead of them learning to read and study it with integrity themselves.

Neither is a desirable outcome. Therefore, be sure to show your people enough about the journey for them to see how you got there. Clearly explain how certain aspects are referring to Christ. Take them to New Testament references that show Christ's fulfillment of Old Testament prophecies. Show them descriptions of the person of Christ that indicate qualities that need to be in their lives. Don't offer just the bottom-line truth in your preaching text for your people. Help them learn the routes so they can get there on their own. In doing so, you will help to strengthen listeners in their faith and their confidence in the Bible. Let them see the wonder of the riches of God's Holy Word!

Talk about Jesus like He's Important

Rick Warren and I would disagree on a lot when it comes to preaching philosophy. But one thing I totally resonate with is his conviction that preachers ought to be interesting when they talk about the Bible. He says:

> **It never ceases to amaze to me how some Bible teachers are able to take the most exciting book in the world and bore people to tears with it.** I believe it is a sin to bore people with the Bible. The problem is this: **When I teach God's Word in an uninteresting**

way, people don't just think I'm boring, they think God is boring! We slander God's character if we preach with an uninspiring style or tone. The message is too important to share it with a "take-it-or-leave it" attitude.[28] [Boldface emphasis in original.]

There's no excuse for preachers talking about the lofty things of God and His eternal truth in a mundane way.

This is especially true when it comes to how we talk about Christ and the gospel. When you land on the best line to the cross, make sure you take people on the journey in such a way that convinces them that it's important. D. A. Carson reflects on his own experience:

> If I have learned anything in 35 or 40 years of teaching, it is that students don't learn everything I teach them. What they learn is what I am excited about, the kinds of things I emphasize again and again and again and again. That had better be the gospel.[29]

The same is true for preaching. People have a better chance of embracing what we're excited about, not what we present to them in a way that gives the impression that it doesn't seem to matter much.

David Hume, a well-known Scottish philosopher and historian in the eighteenth century, was also a deist. Hume didn't believe in the inspiration of the Bible or that Jesus was the Son of God. But reportedly he thought it was worthwhile to travel twenty miles to hear the evangelist George Whitefield preach. Early one morning he was headed down a street in London. He came around a corner and encountered a man who recognized him and asked, "Aren't you David Hume?"

"Yes," he replied.

"Where are you going at this early hour?" the man asked.

"I'm going to hear George Whitefield preach," Hume said.

Perplexed, the man said, "You don't believe a word Whitefield preaches."

"No," Hume answered, "but he does!"[30]

Even a deist who didn't believe in Jesus knew when a man was not just "talking theology." And your people know it as well.

When you prepare to preach Christ in every text, be sure to ask yourself, "Does this truth light me up?" If it doesn't, take some time to get on your face before God and beg Him to grip your heart with His truth. And stay there until He does! Whatever you do, don't enter the pulpit until you can talk about the gospel in a way that portrays it as nothing less than the most incredible news in the universe. When you discover the best line to the cross, share it as the best news in the world—because it is! The gospel is great news, so sound like you are declaring such news when you talk about the gospel!

Present the Gospel Every Time

Whether the best line to the cross is a beeline, or whether you and I need to take a few side roads in order to preserve hermeneutical integrity, we must make sure we reach the cross in every message. And when we do, we must make sure to unpack the good news enough that people have the whole story. I have a firm conviction that the gospel should be presented clearly and wholly in every sermon, enough that an unbeliever is able to get it. Even if my preaching text is primarily aimed at believers, at some point in the message I want to directly address unbelievers and share the gospel with them.

Very few of our preaching texts are going to include a whole presentation of the gospel as part of the biblical record. And most texts in the Bible actually are primarily addressed to the people of God. But regardless of whether my text is christocentric, christotelic, or christiconic, it's still in some way connected to Christ. And that connection opens the door for me to flesh out the gospel, make sure the listeners understand it, and appeal to them to embrace it.

So let me encourage you to master at least one synopsis—or capsule—of the gospel that you can use in every message. The apostle Paul seemed to have several at his fingertips (e.g., 1 Cor. 15:3–4; 2 Tim. 1:8–10). Very rarely do I preach a sermon that at some point I don't say some version of the following:

> Jesus came to earth and lived a life that you can't live, meeting God's standard of perfection for getting into heaven. Then He took that perfect life to the cross and died a death you should've died, incurring God's wrath against your sin on your behalf. Then He defeated death and the grave by rising again, buying the right to give you back the life God created you to have. And He'll give it to you right now if you'll change your mind about your sin and trust Him alone to save you.

My gospel capsule isn't perfect, but it's at least an effort to include some summary of the whole gospel in every sermon.

A gospel capsule can be inserted at different places in different sermons. It doesn't always have to look the same. Sometimes I will include it in the middle of a message when I make a Christ connection in my preaching text.

I might say something like, "This truth is only part of the whole story of the Bible that tells us. . . ." And then I will launch into a brief gospel capsule like the one above. At other times—having made a Christ connection somewhere in the course of the sermon—I'll save the gospel capsule for the end of the sermon as part of the conclusion. I might say something like, "Before we finish I want to make sure that we understand that this truth is part of the larger Bible story about how. . . ." And again, that's where I'd give the gospel synopsis. But I try to always make sure that before the sermon is over, I summarize the whole gospel clearly at least once and make some appeal for unbelievers to embrace it.

Make sure you don't find the best line to the cross but then fail to give people the best news in the world! Present the gospel at some point in every sermon.

READING FOR PROGRESS

Chapell, Bryan. *Christ-Centered Preaching*. Second Edition. Grand Rapids: Baker, 2005.

Greidanus, Sidney. *Preaching Christ from the Old Testament*. Grand Rapids: Eerdmans, 1999.

Kuruvilla, Abraham. *Privilege the Text!* Chicago: Moody, 2013.

Merida, Tony. *The Christ-Centered Expositor*. Nashville: B&H, 2016.

8

"TURPENTINE" THE IMAGINATION

IMAGINING THE SERMON

Jerry Vines

M ama, Mama," Johnny shouted as he ran into the kitchen, "There's a big bear in the backyard!" Terrified, Johnny's mother rushed to the window. In the backyard was a scrawny little dog.

"Johnny, that's not a bear; it's a tiny dog. Go upstairs to your room and don't come down for supper until you tell God what you did." Johnny went upstairs. Much too soon, he came bounding down the stairs into the kitchen. "Did you tell God about it?" his mother asked.

"Yes, Mama."

"Well, what did God say?" she replied.

"Oh, God just said, 'That's all right. First time I saw the dog I thought it was a bear, too!'"

That imaginary story illustrates the real truth that children are born with lively imaginations. Then somewhere on the journey from childhood to adulthood the imagination tends to get extracted from our minds. There is such an emphasis on the scientific and technical aspects of learning that the artistic and creative melodies of education get lost in formulas and mathematical constructions. D. Martyn Lloyd-Jones said, "We have all become so scientific that there is but little room left for imagination."[1]

What does this have to do with preaching? Much indeed. Consider the rest of Lloyd-Jones' quotation: "This . . . is most regrettable, because imagination in preaching is most important and most helpful."[2] John Phillips said to me, "The difference between an average preacher and a great one is imagination." Without imagination our preaching can become boring and dull. And unreal. When I was a seminary student, actor Gregory Walcott spoke to us. He said, "Too often preachers speak of truth as if it were fiction, and actors speak of fiction as if it were truth."

We who preach the eternal Word of God need to know how best to transition from the ancient text to our current audiences. One of the best ways to do that is by the use of what has been called a "sanctified imagination." The imagination can be used in devious, lustful, destructive ways—or it may be sanctified to wholesome and holy uses. What is imagination and how do we "sanctify" it to the task of preaching?

Pastor and author Warren Wiersbe to the rescue! The man who got me started on the path of expository preaching now helps me make progress in understanding the importance of imagination in preaching. In his classic book *Preaching and Teaching with Imagination*, he writes that imagination is "the image-making faculty in your mind, the picture gallery in which you are constantly painting, sculpting, designing and sometimes erasing."[3] W. Macneile Dixon put it a slightly different way: "The human mind is not, as philosophers would have you think, a debating hall, but a picture gallery."[4] This does not mean that we are to deal with the unreal or make-believe. There must be a clear distinction between creating something that isn't the real thing and turning the real into images that can be visualized and understood more clearly.

Imagination is not so much creating something that doesn't exist. Instead, imagination is the mind's ability to reproduce reality in new and creative ways. Preaching doesn't seek to illustrate something that does not exist, like a Harry Potter world. Preaching takes the eternal truths of God and penetrates the real world in which people live today. Imagination is vital in bringing that to pass. As many have suggested, imagination enables us to turn our listeners' ears into eyes.

BRAINY PREACHING

How does imagination do this? It does so by creating word pictures that connect with people's means of receiving information, through verbal and visual communication.

Verbal communication becomes verbal learning as it is processed through the brain's left hemisphere. Such communication is the primary means by which people comprehend information. This is why the preacher's major means of communicating God's eternal Word is through his spoken words. In visual communication, the brain's right hemisphere processes visual information. Because of the advent of television—now in high definition—and additional technology, such as images and video via Internet shown on large (personal computers) and small (electronic notepads and smartphones) displays, our culture is much more inclined to receiving information visually. "Don't just tell me about it. Show me!" is the slogan of our day.

Some tend to say that we have right-brain and left-brain people in our congregations. Though certain tendencies are there, actually both sides of the brain are used by everyone to receive information.

Think with me now about how the brain learns. Our brain receives information through the senses. Humans have five senses: the sense of hearing (the ears), seeing (the eyes), tasting (the taste buds), smelling (the nose), and touching (the nerve endings in the skin). Isn't it reasonable to think that the preacher should engage as many of these senses as possible as he seeks to communicate God's Word? Though the spoken Word is primary, the other senses may be targeted as well.

The apostle John had something interesting to write about our senses and the witness of Jesus' disciples: "That which was from the beginning, which we have heard [hearing], which we have seen with our eyes [seeing], which we have looked upon and have touched with our hands [touching] concerning the word of life . . . we proclaim also to you" (1 John 1:1, 3). A. T. Robertson writes of verse 1: "Three senses are here appealed to (hearing, sight, touch)."[5] By the use of imagination the preacher can utilize word pictures to trigger his congregation's brains' reception to these sensory vehicles to more readily receive the message. (We will say more about how the human brain receives information in chapter 9.)

There does need to be a note of caution here. Arthur Hunt points out that God's revelation to us in Scripture is primarily verbal, not visual. He references God's warnings about worshiping idols, visible expressions of a god. Yet Hunt also recognizes the use of visual imagery in the Bible and correctly points out that God often uses visuals to convey propositional truth. For example in the Old Testament the imagery of the tabernacle and the temple teach salvation truths very graphically. But he also cautions that we are not to abandon or diminish the verbal for the visual.[6]

As we shall see, the Bible abounds in word pictures. Jack Hughes gives a helpful definition of a word picture: "Any word, phrase, story, analogy, illustration, metaphor, figure of speech, trope, allegory, graphic quotation, historical reference, cross-reference, or comparison used to help the listener see, imagine, experience, sense, understand, remember and/or relate to abstract facts."[7]

WORD PICTURES

The Bible is a marvelous treasure chest of word pictures. There is no better place to go than the Holy Scriptures to find scores and scores of word pictures. I often tell congregations that one of the best ways to study the Bible is to look for the word pictures. Though some genres of Scripture have more than others, they all have ample pictures to make the Bible come alive. Let me illustrate in my own early study of the Bible.

Pictures in the Old Testament

I remember well my first fledgling attempts to read through the Bible. Things went quite well until I reached Leviticus. Oh, my! I found myself immersed in repetition, unfamiliar terminology, and ancient Jewish worship instructions. I stopped. This happened several times. Then, I came to understand that many of the unfamiliar, somewhat tedious sections of Leviticus point to various aspects of the person and work of the Lord Jesus Christ. This transformed the book for me. I came to see the many word pictures to be found there. Even this morning in my daily devotions, before I began writing this chapter, I was reading Leviticus 23. The chapter is about the various festival days God provided for His people. Immediately the word pictures began to leap off the page. I saw the vast host of pilgrims headed up to Jerusalem (v. 2). I smelled the unleavened bread (v. 6). I touched the sheaves of first-fruit grain (v. 10). I tasted the meal and wine (v. 13). I heard the blowing of the silver trumpets (v. 24). The chapter activated all five of my senses! All through the narrative portions of God's Word these word pictures may be found.

Each festival reminded me of the coming Messiah, the sacrificial lamb of God. The first feast mentioned the Lord's Passover (v. 5) immediately before God would deliver His people from the Egyptians. Each family slayed a lamb (or goat) and spread its blood over the doorpost so the death angel would pass them by (Ex. 12:5–7), a picture of the later blood sacrifice by the Christ. Meanwhile the festival of trumpets (Lev. 23:24–25) reminded me of a future rejoicing in heaven as an angel blows his trumpet and Christ's kingdom appears in all its glory (Rev. 11:15–18).

Today in my morning reading from the poetic section of the Bible (Psalm 59 in particular), other word pictures appeared. I saw my enemies (v. 1). I smelled the bloodthirsty men (v. 2). I tasted the meat my enemies knew not of (v. 15). I heard the laughter of the Lord (v. 8). I touched His mighty shield (v. 11). Psalm 59 came alive! These kinds of word pictures leap off the pages of all the poetic books.

Pictures in the New Testament

Before I put down my Bible this morning, I also read from Jude, the final letter of the New Testament. Jude is only one chapter, but virtually every one of its twenty-five verses is crammed with word pictures. I heard the call of God (v. 1). I saw certain apostates creeping through the side door into the churches (v. 4). I touched the polluted garment (v. 23). I smelled the fire and brimstone destroying Sodom (v. 7). I tasted the food in the love feast (v. 12)!

The words of our Lord abound in word pictures. Hughes says that 75 percent of our Lord's teaching is in the form of word pictures.[8] His Sermon on the Mount is a huge source of graphic pictures. At least nineteen questions and 142 comparisons are found there. Arthurs says, "These metaphors, figures, and likenesses keep stabbing His listeners' minds and memories into constant alertness."[9]

The parables of Jesus are especially helpful in our understanding of the use of word pictures in the Bible. Mark tells us, "With many such parables he [Jesus] spoke the word to them, as they were able to hear it. He did not speak to them without a parable" (Mark 4:33–34). The common definition of a parable is "an earthly story with a heavenly meaning." The Greek word for parable is *parabolais*. Two words are combined: *ballo*, meaning "to throw" and *para*, meaning "alongside." Jesus used pictures from the visible world to teach truth about the invisible world. Abstract truth is made vivid and understandable by means of concrete pictures.

One-third or more of our Lord's teaching is contained in parables. Wiersbe points out that a parable is a picture that becomes a mirror and then a window.[10] As a picture, the parable begins with a picture taken from common life. The picture becomes a mirror by which we see ourselves. Then the parable is intended to be a window through which we see our world, God Himself, and His truth. Who cannot be captivated by His four-in-one parable in Luke 15? Who has not been thrilled by the lost sheep that was found by the Shepherd? Or who has not been intrigued and instructed by the parable of the lost coin? Or who has not been moved by the compassion of the loving father when the lost prodigal returned home? And, who has not been searched and challenged by the elder brother who was offended by the music and dancing at the younger brother's homecoming celebration?

Mark has an interesting notation about the audiences as they listened to our Lord's teaching. He says, "The great throng heard him gladly" (Mark 12:37). The NASB translates, "And the large crowd enjoyed listening to Him." Peterson paraphrases, "The large crowd was delighted with what they heard" (THE MESSAGE). The Greek word translated "gladly," *hedeos*, is interesting, meaning "with pleasure." The word comes from a root, *hēdús*, which means "sweet." The common people were pleased with the Lord's preaching because it appealed to their senses and was sweet to their souls.

There are several helpful books that catalogue the word pictures in the Bible. Warren Wiersbe's *Preaching and Teaching with Imagination*, has an entire section given to word pictures in Scripture.[11] The most extensive volume I have found is *Dictionary of Biblical Imagery*.[12]

Using Word Pictures in Your Sermons

Preaching is both a science and an art. It may be said that hermeneutics is a science that enables us to find out what a passage of Scripture is saying, what it means, and how it may be applied to life. Homiletics is the art of putting the factual data of a Scripture passage into a clear, understandable message. Ryken says, "Expositors tend to look on sermon or lesson preparation in terms of doing research for a lecture or paper. They should view it more like writing a story or poem."[13] This explains why some sermons put people to sleep and others keep them on the edge of their seats. By using word pictures in our preaching we can greatly enhance the likelihood that people will be attentive and responsive.

As you prepare your sermon, look for the word pictures in your passage. Then, pass them on to your listeners in graphic picture form. Be sure to use word pictures as you convey the great truths of Scripture. Take the word pictures from Scripture, place them on the easel of your imagination, and produce a vivid, colorful work of art.

Put your imagination to work on your passage. Ask yourself, "How can I put the truths found here into a clear, understandable form?" Make use of sensuous words. Note I didn't say, sensual—words that gratify carnal, especially sexual, appetites. Sensuous words are those that appeal to the senses, and their use achieves three welcome outcomes in preaching. First, you get the listeners' attention as your words appeal to both sides of the brain.

Second, they are better able to understand what you are saying. Third, words that paint pictures in the minds of your audience will aid them in taking the truths of Scripture home with them and into their daily lives.

Where to Find Word Pictures

Observing Daily Events

The question then arises, "How may I learn to preach utilizing word pictures?" Fortunately, there are ways for you to learn how to do this. As you read your Bible, look for the pictures there. In addition, you can develop the faculty of seeing the word pictures that are all around you, through ordinary, everyday experiences of your life. For example, you can paint pictures in your sermons from the behavior (or misbehavior!) of your children. In one of my messages I described one of my children's insistent but futile attempts to tie his own shoes. Finally, with tangled shoe strings my child tearfully came to me to untangle the mess he had created. I painted this picture to convey the truth that we get our lives all tangled up when we refuse the help of the Lord.

Observing Nature and Making Comparisons

The world of nature abounds with word pictures as well. You may not live near a nature preserve, but the vegetable garden or lone tree in your own backyard—even butterflies in spring—may bring friendly, easy illustrations for your message. These may lead to metaphors, similes, and analogies that are imaginative, even evocative for your Sunday listeners. In preaching about Enoch, I said his clean, godly life in his day was like "a lily on a dung heap." Train yourself to see illustrations and metaphors from the world all around you.

Jesus Himself regularly called on the sights and sounds of the outdoor world as He taught. In *Expository Preaching with Word Pictures*, Jack Hughes says of the Lord, "He found tongues in trees, sermons in stones, books in the running brooks and homiletic figures in everything."[14]

Reading in many fields is vital to good sermon artistry. Unfortunately, too many preachers confine their reading to biblical and theological books. This kind of reading alone can cause your preaching to become rather methodical, and yes, boring. Branch out! Read books about nature. Read fiction, drama, and poetry that contain descriptive passages. Such reading will enhance your skill in the art of sermon preparation. More than one fiction writer has helped me learn how to paint a picture of a Bible character. For example, I have found Charles Dickens's works very helpful in this regard. You can learn from his powers of description.

Reading Sermons by the Masters

One valuable approach is to read the sermons of those who were masters in the use of sensory appeal in their preaching. Charles H. Spurgeon is a case in point. Though his language may seem outdated to our modern eyes and ears, he can teach us much. Jeffery Arthurs helps us see this as he refers to a section in one of Spurgeon's messages:

> Notice the sensory appeal: "(sound) Our hearts are beating funeral marches to the tomb. (touch) The heart is very slippery. Yes. The heart is a fish that troubles all gospel fishermen to hold . . . slimy as an eel, it slippeth between your fingers. (taste) Suppose you tell me that honey is bitter. I reply, 'No, I am sure you cannot have tasted it; taste it and try.' (smell) So it is with the Holy Ghost. The precious perfume of the gospel must be poured forth."[15]

Wow. What vivid, sensuous preaching!

Study or listen to preachers who understand the art of the sermonic. Preachers of the past are helpful. I find the sermons of Frank W. Boreham always fire my imagination. Consider what he said about Isaiah 45:22, the text that was used to bring Spurgeon to Christ. Boreham says, "I look to my doctor to heal me when I am hurt; I look to my lawyer to advise me when I am perplexed; I look to my tradesmen to bring my daily supplies to my door; but there is only One to whom I can look when my soul cries out for deliverance. 'Look unto Me and be ye saved, all the ends of the earth!'"[16]

Beyond the parallelism and repetition, Boreham is asking us to see a doctor, lawyer, and blue collar workers skilled in key trades. These are pictures for our minds. Get the picture?

Preachers who are our contemporaries can stir our imaginative powers to create word pictures. One of the blessings I have received from my African American contemporaries is the vividness of their imaginations and the word pictures they paint. I will never forget what William Holmes Borders, pastor of Wheat Street Baptist Church in Atlanta, said about Jesus' word to the adulterous woman's accusers: "He that is without sin among you, let him first cast a stone at her" (John 8:7 KJV). Borders said, "If a one of 'em had cast a stone, the Lord would have turned its center to rubber, and it would have bounced back and bust their brains out!" Get the picture?

WORDSMITHING

If sermon development is art, and it is, then the preacher-artist must apply the finishing touches. For those who deal in words the current term is *wordsmithing*. A person who works with words, especially skillfully, is a word-smith. Thus, wordsmithing is the art of crafting words for maximum impact.

Crafting Words for a Winsome Sermon

I am using this concept with the idea that the preacher who has done the initial work of hermeneutics now uses various means to polish the sermon and make it clear and winsome to those who hear it. Exegesis, involving investigation, interpretation, and application of a Scripture passage, gives the initial broad strokes of a sermonic painting. The art of wordsmithing applies the finishing touches.

Wordsmithing also involves using the right words. Mark Twain's well-known statement is helpful: "The difference between the almost right word and the right word is a large matter—'tis the difference between the lightning bug and the lightning."[17] As you prepare your sermon for delivery, the importance of selecting vivid, clear, understandable words can't be overestimated. And, try to use words the people weren't expecting. Spurgeon said, "Brethren, take them at unawares. Let your thunderbolt drop out of a clear sky."[18]

A Personal Case Study

Wordsmithing an Introduction

I find it very helpful to wordsmith my introduction and conclusion. I always try to write out in full my sermon introduction. In 1987 I was asked to preach the main sermon at the annual meeting of the Southern Baptist Convention. We were in the midst of what has since been called the Conservative Resurgence. Those of us who were conservatives were seeking to restore our convention to its conservative roots. The pertinent issue was the inerrancy of Scripture. My message was entitled "A Baptist and His Bible." My Scripture passage was 2 Timothy 3:14–4:13. I was keenly aware of the crucial nature of the message. I began my message with this paragraph:

In beautiful human language resplendent with divine revelation Paul sets before us the Bible's doctrine concerning itself. He quickly takes us to the counseling room and shows us the intention of the Bible; the classroom and shows us the inspiration of the Bible; then the crisis room and shows us the implications of the Bible.

The paragraph had been carefully wordsmithed. Communication professors Carl L. Kell and L. Raymond Camp later wrote, "[Vines] spoke his memorized line to the gallery—everyone present knew this sermon was special."[19]

Wordsmithing a Conclusion

The conclusion of your message also needs some careful wordsmithing. Henry Wadsworth Longfellow said, "Great is the art of beginning, but greater the art of ending."[20] Again, in "A Baptist and His Bible," I carefully worded my conclusion. I used a simple illustration about an old farmer who placed a lighted bundle of pine branches into a young preacher's hand with these words, "It will see you home." Then, holding up my Bible I concluded, "Do you see this Book? . . . It will see you home!"

A variety of rhetorical tools may be used as you wordsmith your sermon. I confess my addiction to alliteration. For some reason, I seem to see it in many, many passages. I also confess that I have overused it through the years. If it works for you, fine; if not, don't use it. Wiersbe (who got me started using it!) says it is possible to provide an overdose of alliteration. He continues, "If a simple alliterative outline grows naturally out of the text, the preacher may be wise to use it; but he is unwise to waste precious hours searching through the dictionary for another word that starts with 'M' and means 'confidence.'"[21]

Metaphor and simile are very helpful in putting the finishing touches on your message. A metaphor simply states a comparison. In my "A Baptist and His Bible" sermon I compared rational opinion to a "tollgate" to which, we are told, the Bible must pay tribute. Similes use words *like* and *as* to make the comparisons. Again, I used simile in the message saying the Bible is "like a soft pillow" for a weary saint's deathbed.

My convention message also made use of personification. This is a figure of speech in which human qualities are given to ideas to make them come to life. I called destructive biblical criticism an old thief who had quietly entered our country, moved steadily down the East Coast to invade the Southern Baptist Convention. I talked about his heretical hammer, cynical saw, and critical crowbar.

THE GOAL: A CLEAR
MESSAGE FROM GOD'S WORD

By use of "sanctified imagination," good word pictures, and skilled word-smithing, your sermon can be extremely helpful in giving your listeners a clear message from God's Word.

Fortunately, those of us who preach and teach have a very good Helper. God has promised the Holy Spirit will assist us as we prepare messages for the people. The truth is, we can't develop a sermon by ourselves. We need to claim 1 Thessalonians 1:5, "Our gospel came to you not only in word, but also in power and in the Holy Spirit." More than a well-prepared sermon is necessary to communicate God's message. Only when the Word is preached in words anointed by the Holy Spirit is the power of God present.

This excerpt from an African American prayer for preachers uses vivid word pictures in a powerful prayer for the local pastor. It fittingly concludes this chapter:

> Lord God, this morning—
> Put his eye to the telescope of eternity,
> And let him look upon the paper walls of time.
> Lord, turpentine his imagination,
> Put perpetual motion in his arms,
> Fill him full of the dynamite of thy power,
> Anoint him all over with the oil of thy salvation,
> And set his tongue on fire.[22]

READING FOR PROGRESS

Blackwood, Rick. *The Power of Multi-Sensory Preaching and Teaching*. Grand Rapids: Zondervan, 2008.

Wiersbe, Warren. *Preaching and Teaching with Imagination*. Wheaton: Victor Books, 1994.

PART 3

DELIVERING THE SERMON

THE AWAKENING OF THE REVEREND VAN WINKLE

CULTURE, CLARITY, AND COMMUNICATION

Jerry Vines

The Reverend Van Winkle was rather satisfied with himself after a long, tiring Lord's Day. As the people sang the great hymns in the morning service, the organ was loud and the soloist was flat. The congregation grew drowsy only a time or two during his message. Not bad. His series in the book of Romans was being well received by the people; he had done a thorough exposition. The people followed along in their King James Bibles, and there was a good response during the invitation time.

Sunday night's service was well attended, the music was lively, and the people were tuned in to Rev. Winkle's evening message on Enoch in his Old Testament heroes series. It was 1979, a good year to be a Southern Baptist pastor in America. Adrian Rogers was the new conservative president.

Rev. Van Winkle was part of the remarkable conservative resurgence underway in the Southern Baptist Convention. Time for sleep.

Drowsily Pastor Van opened his eyes. They gradually focused. Surprise! His beard was much longer. The house looked older. "Bev?" he called to his faithful wife. No one answered. Then, a young man walked into the bedroom. "Who are you?" Rev. Van Winkle asked.

"I'm your son, Rev. Bo Winkle."

"Bo? How old are you? You were only six when I tucked you in last night."

Bo chuckled. "I know, Dad, but you have been asleep for thirty-two years. I'm thirty-eight and the pastor of the church now. We've been trying to wake you up, but we couldn't."[1]

"I've been asleep all those years? . . . Where's your mom?"

"She died last year," Pastor Bo said sadly. Through tears, his father asked, "And the church? How is it doing?"

Bo replied, "Well! Let's go see."

The ride to the church was a revelation. His son's car was sleek and shiny, with strange buttons and what looked like a small TV screen on the dashboard. As they headed for church Rev. Van Winkle saw new sights. "What's that Apple store? A new specialized grocery?"

"No, Dad," laughed Pastor Bo, "that's where you buy a smartphone."

"Smartphone? What's that?" asked Rev. Van Winkle.

"Well, you can see it in the cupholder. I can call people on it, but it does more. It's a virtual computer. I can get weather, news, ball scores, stock reports, and just about any kind of information from anywhere in the world."

"This happened while I was asleep?" asked Rev. Van Winkle as he began to check out the mobile phone.

"Yes, Dad. Wait until you see the church."

They stopped in front of a corporate-style building. "What's this?" Rev. Van Winkle asked.

"Our church. We relocated from the older building. Let's go inside."

Van Winkle's eyes widened. "What are those drums, guitars, and that funny looking keyboard for?"

"To back up the praise singers."

"Where's the pulpit?"

"We don't use one anymore. We use that Plexiglas lectern," Bo answered.

"Those big screens?" his father asked.

"Image magnification screens," Bo replied. "Words to the songs, Scripture references, and even my picture can be put up there."

"And all these changes have been made while I was asleep?" asked Van.

"Yes, Dad. Things are different. All is changed; inside and outside the church. But Dad, some things haven't changed. The Bible is still the Word of God. The Lord Jesus is still the Savior of the world. And, 'Whosoever shall call upon the name of the Lord shall be saved.'"

Washington Irving's Rip Van Winkle slept through the Revolutionary War. Rev. Van Winkle slept through something of a revolution in the culture and in his church. Not I—I have stayed awake to witness the drastic culture shifts. Seismic changes have taken place in our churches. I have also seen the need to progress in how I use my words to communicate the Word of God to our current culture. Let's talk about it.

PREACHING TO A CHANGING CULTURE

Perhaps you feel that you fell asleep and woke up in a strange new world. Your preaching doesn't seem as effective now. The culture has changed; you can't connect. Culture may be defined as the sum total of a people's religious beliefs, social structures, ethical standards, and moral behavior. American culture has changed. To communicate is tough, especially inside the church. To compound the problem, it's not monolithic. Zack Eswine says on any given Sunday the average preacher will have three cultures in his congregation. First, those who are connected to the church. Second, those who are unchurched. Third, those who were once-churched or in-between.[2]

Each of those cultural groups has its own language. The preacher faces many obstacles. Hughes says we must "come to grips with the fact that those we preach to are distracted from the sermon by legions of ideas floating around in their heads, by Satan and by their environment."[3]

To overcome the obstacles to adequate communication of God's Word, some preachers lean heavily upon contextualization. Contextualization is delivering the gospel in ways that today's audiences can understand, with clear language in their cultural context. To do this preachers often spend more time reading, watching, and studying the cultural context of their listeners than they do studying God's eternal, timeless truth. Jim Shaddix has a helpful word of caution: "Today we are told, 'Don't use terminology that is unfamiliar to people who might not have grown up in church. Communicate in the language of the culture.'"[4] He points out that taking this approach has resulted in the loss of many essential Bible terms. Don't sell out the words of Scripture in an attempt to be "relevant." People can be taught biblical truth by capable Bible exposition. Shaddix makes another telling point: "Christian worship, then, does not have to be adapted to the whims and preferences of the secular heart and mind in order to have evangelistic impact."[5]

To be sure, understanding and clearly speaking to the cultural context is important. But getting the message from God's Word right is primary. Getting it across to the people comes next. David Helm says, "Contextualization is a good dance partner, but she should never be allowed to lead. . . . The trouble is that too many of us push exegesis back in our preparation, and we clothe the message in a short red dress of contextualization by focusing on culture and our ability to connect with it."[6] He adds, "Some preachers use the Bible the way a drunk uses a lamp post . . . more for support than for illumination."[7]

Having given that word of caution, let me emphasize our need to communicate the message in such a way that our listeners will listen to, understand, and remember God's truth, so that they may apply it to their daily lives. Delivering content is primary. It's essential.

KEEPING OUR MESSAGE CLEAR

Because Bible truth is primary and crucial, clarity on our part is a must. As Paul writes: "If the bugle gives an indistinct sound, who will get ready for the battle? So with yourselves, if with your tongues you utter speech that is not intelligible, how will anyone know what is said? For you will be speaking into the air" (1 Cor. 14:8–9). If our preaching is not clear, what is the point of preaching in the first place? People can't be changed by what they do not understand.

Stating your passage theme in one brief, clear statement is a helpful exercise. The goal isn't to display the tools you used to get the message. Marvin R. Vincent wrote, "The man who buys a nugget of gold cares nothing for the dirt and rock through which the miner has worked his way. He wants the nugget simply. So congregations care nothing for processes; they want results."[8] Rather, the goal is to communicate its meaning to those who listen. Why preach thirty (or more!) minutes if people have no clue what you are saying? Haddon Robinson says, "A mist in the pulpit can easily become a fog in the pew."[9] A parishioner said of her pastor, "Six days he is invisible; one day he is incomprehensible."

Do you use Twitter? I love Twitter. I primarily use it for fun purposes and to encourage others. At the time of this writing, tweets can have only 140 characters. That's it. Exceed that and you have to send another one. Could I suggest you might try to state the purpose of your preaching paragraph in a 140-character tweet? Albert Einstein supposedly once said, "If you can't explain it simply, you don't understand it well enough."[10] Again, Paul is helpful: "Pray also for us. . . . that I may make it clear, which is how I ought to speak" (Col. 4:3–4).

I always considered it a compliment when some parent said to me, "Caroline understood everything you said this morning." Don't use many big words, unless you explain them. Keep the children in mind as you prepare your message. A dictionary should not be needed when you preach. Think about the unsaved people who may be in the congregation. They don't know the official language of Zion. But, you can teach it to them! With clear words!

A LITTLE COMMUNICATION THEORY

Ralph W. Emerson reportedly said, "All the great speakers were bad speakers at first." I'm not sure I totally agree with the statement. Yes, some speakers (or preachers) do seem to have natural gifts for speaking. They seem to have a natural flow of language and vividness of expression that are not the result of training. For most of us, however, we indeed start out as bad speakers. Hopefully, we can progress toward more clarity and effectiveness in the delivery of the message.

Are there any disciplines to assist us as we seek to speak clearly? Fortunately, there are. One of these is communication theory. Hershael York is helpful concerning communication theory and preaching. He defines communication as "the intentional transmission of a mutually meaningful concept between at least two individuals. There is the sender, the receiver and the message that is encoded in verbal and/or non-verbal signals."[11]

The Levels of Communication in Preaching

In Bible preaching, York argues, there are three distinct, necessary levels of communication:

- *Level one.* On the first level God is the *sender*, the authors of the Bible books are the *receivers*, and the words of Scripture, inspired by the Holy Spirit, are the *message*.

- *Level two.* On the second level the Bible authors and the Holy Spirit are the *senders*, those who read Scripture are the *receivers*, and the inspired words of Scripture are the *message*.

- *Level three.* On level three, the preacher is the *sender*, the listeners are the *receivers*, and the Word of God is the *message*, conveyed in the verbal and nonverbal communication of the preacher.[12]

The preacher may use nonverbal clues—a facial expression, movement of the body, or gesture in addition to the words he speaks. In turn, those who receive the message may respond with a verbal "Amen," or a nod or (God forbid!) a snore. The preacher initiates the "tick" that becomes the "tock" to the listener's ear.[13] By means of words that speak to the head and nonverbal means of communication that speak to the heart, we are to give God's Word to those who listen to us preach.

Storytelling, Nonverbal Signals, and Other Ways to Maintain Attention

There is also much to be learned from current studies in communication as to how the brain receives information.[14] Recent studies indicate that brain activity is most pronounced when it is processing a story. The story of the rich fool who lived for time instead of eternity and for the material instead of the spiritual is more interesting than lectures on the length of eternity and the dangers of materialism (Luke 12:16–21).

To hear something new and exciting causes dopamine, a chemical that is responsible for transmitting signals in between the brain's nerve cells (neurons), to be released in one's brain. This assists the brain in experiencing what is being presented in a more vivid manner. Thus memory is greatly aided.[15]

The correlation between your words and your nonverbal signals is also an area of fruitful study. Carmine Gallo says, "If your voice, gestures, and body language are incongruent with your words, your listeners will distrust your message.[16] But, if verbal and nonverbal messages are consistently received by the brain, the mental correlations are quite a bit stronger. Again Gallo says, "If you hear information, you are likely to remember about 10 percent of that information three days later. Add a picture, however, and your recall rate will soar to 65 percent."[17] This underscores the importance of using word pictures (see chapter 8).

A great deal is made of attention spans. Though accounts vary, there is abundant evidence that our visually, digitally conditioned audiences have shorter attention spans than ever before. The TED Talks, which feature experts speaking on education, business, technology, or creativity, limit speakers to just twenty minutes. Does this mean, then, that those of us who preach should only preach twenty minutes? No. To adequately expound a passage of

Scripture in twenty minutes is rather difficult. Actually, I now view this in a different way. Feature films and football games sometimes last two to three hours. People stay interested because what they are watching is engaging to them. A boring speech is boring, whether it is sixty or twenty minutes in length. The key is to make your message engaging. How may this be done? Read on.

Gallo says that if a talk is longer than twenty minutes, you need to build in "soft breaks" (stories, videos, demonstrations) every ten minutes.[18] Steve Jobs, cofounder of Apple, whose product presentations to analysts and the public are legendary, often spoke for over an hour. But he kept his audience guessing, utilized the famous "rule of three" (presenting the material with three points; thus the old preacher's use of "three points and a poem"), and worked in some kind of break at the ten-minute mark. The length is beside the point. Whatever the length, *make what you say so interesting the people can't help but listen.* Many years ago there was an old cigarette commercial with the slogan, "It's not how long you make it; it's how you make it long." That applies to a sermon!

Hershael York puts it quite succinctly: "You can preach as long as you hold their attention."[19] This is what the preacher must do. By use of the vocal variables, humor, telling a story, etc., you can keep the attention of your audience. Pay close attention to audience response. Know your audience. Watch them. The people will give you helpful feedback by their laughter, facial expressions, and their glazed-over look! Leonard Sweet says, "Preaching is a collaborative process between pulpit and pew. A sermon isn't a sermon until it is received, and its success is based not solely on the preacher but as much if not more on the congregation."[20]

RHETORIC

"It's just rhetoric." Ever heard that dismissive statement? I certainly have. As I wrote this chapter, the United States populace was being subjected to a presidential campaign in 2016. Between the two major parties, more than a score of candidates ran for the highest office in the land. In their campaign stops and televised debates, listeners heard many over-the-top, outlandish statements, claims, and promises! More than one time I heard people say, "Well, it's just rhetoric." The statement suggests that rhetoric consists of insincere words and at times is even manipulative. Clearly rhetoric seems to have fallen on hard times.

Rhetoric has been pretty much in disfavor in the field of homiletics as well. But, not so fast, my friend. Rhetoric needs to be given another look. In and of itself, rhetoric may be helpful to the preacher as he seeks to communicate God's Word to today's culture in clear, understandable, life-changing language. The definition of rhetoric is rather simple. Rhetoric is "the art or study of using language effectively and persuasively,"[21] or, as Adam Dooley writes, rhetoric is "any means that one might use to communicate truth."[22] Would this not be helpful to those of us who seek to convey God's eternal truth?

But what about Paul? Some argue that the apostle joined in the trashing of rhetoric. He wrote that in his preaching he "renounced the hidden things of dishonesty, not walking in craftiness," nor did he "[handle] the Word of God deceitfully; but by manifestation of the truth" (2 Cor. 4:2 KJV). Was he condemning the use of rhetorical devices? If so, he was condemning himself! All through the Spirit-inspired letters of Paul we find he used those devices most effectively. Paul was condemning illicit man-generated manipulation, not God-enabled persuasion.

Much could be said about the general usefulness of rhetoric to the preaching task. Let's just take a look at a few of the tools of rhetoric. In chapter 6 we mentioned the use of metaphor and simile. Other figures of speech may be used to "dress up" your message. Let's begin. *Alliteration*: words that begin or end with the same letter or sound. Oh me, alliteration! I have admitted my addiction to it. However, if not overworked, it may be helpful in the delivery of a message.

There are other tools. *Antithesis*: putting opposites together. In a message I used a quote from Karl Menninger where, speaking about those who deny the reality of human sin, he said they "flit through life like a bluebird upon a dung heap." *Anaphora*: the repetition of a word or phrase for emphasis. Martin Luther King's repetition of "I have a dream," has lodged itself in the psyche of America. *Asyndeton*: omitting conjunctions to pick up the pace and give emphasis. Julius Caesar's "I came, I saw, I conquered" is an example. There are many, many of these rhetorical devices. The preacher who desires to communicate his message effectively will do well to study rhetoric.

One more brief matter you may find helpful. In his analysis of Steve Jobs's presentations at Apple, Gallo notes that Steve Jobs kept his audience guessing. He says, "Frequently, but not always, he will leave the audience with 'just one more thing' before he ends a presentation."[23] I have found that sometimes this device is helpful in nailing down the thrust of your message. At the conclusion of a message on the book of Jonah, I stepped away from the pulpit, then back to it and said, "And remember, after you're through running from God and running into Him, be sure to run with Him!"

PERFORMANCE IN PREACHING

All kinds of pastors stride into our churches' pulpits each week. Schmit and Childers colorfully describe it:

> Preaching is a big tent with nearly as many kinds of preachers as there are people. High-wire artists, lion tamers, sideshow barkers, and ring-masters are only the beginning. In preaching's tent there are acrobats and dancers, strongmen, sequined ladies, and, of course, several kinds of clowns. . . . It goes without saying that this is a field where stand-up comedians and hams coexist with prophets and martyrs. How can homiletics help them all?[24]

Which brings me to performance in preaching. In *Power in the Pulpit* we deal with the preaching event as it relates to the techniques of drama. Not that the preacher is putting on an act. Rather, that many techniques of drama can be helpful to the preacher. The preacher is not only a scientist (hermeneutics); he is also an artist (homiletics). As the latter he may use certain techniques that will help him communicate the message in an attention getting, im-pactful way.[25] In the chapter on genre (chapter 5), I briefly touched on pas-sage pathos. Our delivery should accurately reflect the emotions presented in the passage. Utilizing insights from the dramatic arts can be very helpful in this regard.

One of the most effective preachers of all time was George Whitefield. His powers of oratory are legendary. He was able to move masses of people to the things of God by his Spirit-directed delivery. In a fascinating book, Harry S. Stout deals with Whitefield's skills in dramatic preaching. He recounts his early training in the theater and his later condemning of the same as the "devil's workshop." But Stout shows how this training in the "methods and ethos of acting . . . were never forgotten. His dramatic expressions as he preached utilized these dramatic skills." Stout continues, "Tears, passion, and consolation fused in Whitefield's sermons to produce a new and powerful form of preaching."[26] The tools of drama may be baptized into the river of the Holy Spirit's anointing and used for God's glory and the people's good.

The expositor may glean insights from research into the skills of the dramatic arts to find helpful tools for his sermon delivery. Leonard Sweet says, "Preachers need first to have the wonder-filled eyes of a child, the imaginative mind of an artist, the pilgrim devotion of a saint, and the serious humor of a comedian."[27] There is much to be learned from our African American preacher brethren in this regard. I have found this adage, often used by many preachers, helpful: "Start low, go slow; climb higher, strike fire. Then sit down in a storm." That's preaching performance, brothers!

PULPITS, MICS, AND TIES

Now I've come to the fun part—and the scary. Fools rush in where angels fear to tread. Matters such as whether to use a traditional pulpit and how the preacher should dress are much debated. But, first, let's touch on some less controversial areas relative to the preaching setting.

Lighting and Sound

In recent years lighting and sound have changed in many churches. Lighting may enhance and beautify the preaching setting. Keep in mind that in September 2017 I will be an eighty-year-old old-school preacher. I love the beautiful lighting. The strobe lights and smoke machines don't bless me too much. It smacks too much of the glitzy world for my taste. I move on quickly.

The newest sound technology is cool. When we built our new auditorium at First Baptist Church, Jacksonville, Florida, we spent several million dollars in state-of-the-art sound boards, mics (microphones), speakers, etc. I thought the sound was gorgeous. I was among the very first preachers in the country to use a headset mic. Placing it on my ear and at the corner of my mouth was an adjustment. I was really rather self-conscious about it. I was doing fairly well when, after a service one of our singles said to me, "Oh, trying to be Garth Brooks, are you?" His life was in danger. (Ironically, our brand was a Countryman mic.) But I soon discovered the segment of the congregation that liked it best was senior adults. Because it stayed at the corner of my mouth, they never missed a word.

In addition, many churches now use projection screens to great effect. The projected slides enlarge the print of songs and hymns; they also can show major points of the sermon, offer photographs and images to illustrate points, and display key Bible verses. Just don't let them keep the people from using their Bibles.

Pulpit, Lectern, or No Stand?

The trend seems to be away from the traditional pulpit. The only use of "pulpit" in Scripture is a reference to the platform upon which Ezra stood to teach God's Word to the people, in Nehemiah 8:4 (KJV). Indeed, in the NKJV, ESV, HCSB, and NIV Bibles, the verse is translated "wooden platform." I certainly don't feel it is mandated by Scripture that we must have a pulpit.

Some pastors choose not to use a traditional pulpit, but rather use a Plexiglas lectern—or nothing at all. The idea is that this brings the preacher closer to the people and enables him to preach with his whole body. Perhaps. I'm not convinced. There are other factors that might encourage one to continue to use a pulpit. A place for notes or a partial or full manuscript is one. A place to set your Bible if you don't want to carry it around as you gesture, and a place to keep a water bottle are others. Whether or not one speaks from a pulpit (or a certain type of pulpit) should not be an issue.

Medical doctor Richard Cox has an interesting take here. He says visible symbols in church are important.

> The brain stores visual photographs for future use. There may be a message here for churches that have no stained-glass windows; no architectural symbols, no outward signs of being a place of worship. . . . In forsaking symbolism such as . . . the pulpit, the large open Bible and other visual reminders (memory enhancers), much learning potential is lost. . . . Churches that have largely eliminated traditional symbols have elected to forsake many powerful messages.[28]

Jim Shaddix says, "If you take the symbols away, friend, make sure you replace them with other intentional efforts toward making the Bible visible in preaching and worship."[29] Something to think about.

As an old-school guy, here's why I like to use a pulpit on an elevated platform. Architectural symbolism is important. Coming from my Baptist tradition, we old-school preachers believe the pulpit where the Word is preached should be centrally located and elevated to indicate that preaching the Word is primary and that it is authoritative over all. The preaching of the Word, not the music, must be the focal point of the worship service. I'm not going to fight over it. Just think about it.

Open Collar, Tie, or Tie Plus Suit?

What about attire? When I was a teenager I loathed ties. I wanted a job where I didn't have to wear a tie and didn't have to attend funerals or weddings. Then the Lord called me to preach. Think the Lord has a sense of humor? Now I fear someone might dig up some old pictures of me preaching when I was a young preacher. When I went to a church in Mobile, Alabama, the manager of a leading suit factory tailored me a large number of suits and gave me shirts and ties to match. Every color and design in the rainbow was in that wardrobe. On Sundays I looked like a tablecloth in motion.

So, I want to be as kind and as understanding as I can be. How you dress is important. Styles in attire have greatly changed over the years. They will change again . . . and again. But, hear some counsel from an old-school preacher—and other notable voices as well.

In his book on Steve Jobs, Gallo writes, "Great leaders dress a little better than everyone else in the room. . . . If you're going to dress like a rebel, dress like a well-off rebel."[30] While he acknowledges Jobs's rather informal attire (black mock, blue jeans, and running shoes) in his Apple presentations, Gallo points out that such attire was the best that money could buy (St. Croix sweaters, no less). And when Jobs went to the bank to borrow money he wore an expensive suit and a tie.

I close this section with my own personal preference. I prefer to wear a suit and a tie when I preach in the church setting. I am an ambassador for the King of kings and Lord of lords. I want to represent Him well, even in my personal appearance. Of course, men's retreats, youth events, and other informal settings call for different attire. But, in God's house I am communicating in many different ways. I try to look my age in my Sunday-go-to-meeting best.

One final word before I beat a hasty retreat: Whatever you wear, for our sakes, be sure it is cleaned and pressed. And, don't try to dress younger than your age. I read in *Reader's Digest* many years ago: "Some women grow old gracefully; others wear stretch pants." Let me paraphrase: "Some preachers grow old gracefully; others wear skinny jeans." Whew, glad this section is over.

THE GREAT COMMUNICATOR

Fortunately for the preacher there is a third party in the communication process. There is the human instrument, the preacher. There is the human audience, the listeners. Then, there is the Great Communicator. No, not Ronald Reagan. We have the Holy Spirit who supernaturally communicates the message of God to the minds and hearts of the people. Like Paul, we should be able to say, "Our gospel came to you not only in word, but also in power and in the Holy Spirit" (1 Thess. 1:5).

Remember, you and I can't persuade anyone to do anything. Only the Holy Spirit can do that. However, we may claim His guidance and assistance in the preparation and delivery of our message. More than a century ago R. W. Dale, speaking at one of the colleges of Yale University, said, "While the preacher is speaking there is another voice than his, appealing to the hearts and consciences of men, the voice of the Divine Spirit."[31]

Are you fully awake now, Rev. Van Winkle?

READING FOR PROGRESS

Eswine, Zack. *Preaching to a Post-Everything World: Crafting Biblical Sermons that Connect with Our Culture.* Grand Rapids: Baker, 2008.

Gallo, Carmine. *Talk Like TED: The 9 Public-Speaking Secrets of the World's Top Minds.* New York: St. Martin's Press, 2014.

Helm, David R. *Expositional Preaching: How We Speak God's Word Today.* Wheaton: Crossway, 2014.

Hughes, Jack. *Expository Preaching with Word Pictures.* Ross-shire, Scotland: Christian Focus Publications, 2014.

Schmit, Clayton J., and Jana Childers. *Performance in Preaching: Bringing the Sermon to Life.* Grand Rapids: Baker, 2008.

Shaddix, Jim. *The Passion-Driven Sermon.* Nashville: Broadman and Holman, 2003.

10

"JUST AS I AM"

EXTENDING THE INVITATION

Jerry Vines

Scenes from a life. I am nine years old. At a friend's invitation I am attending the Sunday night service at Tabernacle Baptist Church in Carrollton, Georgia. Before the evening service my friend, Ray, and I go to see our pastor, Brother Ebb. He shares the gospel with us. We are now in the service. The music has been sung. Bro. Ebb has preached. The lights in the building highlight the tears rolling down his cheeks as he pleads with sinners to come to Jesus. We all stand. The choir and the congregation begin to sing,

> Just as I am, without one plea,
> But that Thy blood was shed for me,
> And that thou bidd'st me come to Thee,
> O Lamb of God, I come, I come.[1]

I step into the aisle from my second row seat. I walk toward Bro. Ebb. There is a big smile on his face. I give my hand to Brother Ebb and my heart to Jesus.

I am now sixteen years old. Recently called to preach the gospel, I am watching a fiery young evangelist preach on our tiny black and white TV. At the end of his message he issues an invitation for people to come to Christ. Behind him a youthful song leader leads a mammoth choir. They begin to softly sing "Just As I Am." People begin coming forward from all parts of the huge stadium. Billy Graham is the evangelist. Cliff Barrows is the song leader. They have called for people to come forward, making public decisions for Christ thousands of times in countries all over the world. Millions have responded.

I am an eighteen-year-old pastor. In my first church, Centralhatchee [meaning "between two creeks"] Baptist, Georgia, I preach the gospel as best I can. At the conclusion of the message I ask people to come forward to receive Christ as their personal Savior.

I am sixty-eight years old. I am retiring after twenty-four years as pastor of First Baptist Church, Jacksonville, Florida. With deep emotion I preach the gospel again. I transition from the message to a time of invitation. One more time I invite people to "Come to Jesus."

Such is my heritage as a Southern Baptist preacher of almost sixty-five years. I have extended a public gospel invitation for people to come to Christ throughout my ministry. As did W. A. Criswell, who pleaded, "While we sing this song, make your decision for Christ . . . a family—you . . . a couple—you . . . or just one, somebody—you." As did Adrian Rogers, who pled with arms outstretched, "Come to Jesus."

They, I, and thousands of faithful pastors have been preaching the gospel message and issuing the gospel invitation for "whosoever will" to come to Christ. L. R. Scarborough once wrote, "The invitation is the logical climax of the evangelistic sermon. Without it the message is incomplete and its effects unknown."[2] Invitation is at the heart of the gospel. Those who respond to the "Come" are to go and invite others. Yet many opponents question the need for an invitation at the conclusion of every sermon. So the question is, "Have I and thousands of other preachers like those mentioned above been in error to extend such a call for response?"

Before answering this question, let me first make sure we're using the same dictionary. I'm certainly aware that there's a variety of legitimate ways to call for a response to God's Word. Those ways include invitations for listeners to respond privately in their hearts at their seats, to come to the front of an auditorium, to stand at their seats or raise their hands, to make their way to some form of an "inquiry room," or simply to record their responses on a card. These and other approaches are valid and can be very effective. In our previous volume entitled *Power in the Pulpit*, Jim Shaddix and I deal extensively with multiple models of calling for response.[3] The information in that book relative to different aspects and forms can be extremely helpful.

But most of the time when I use the term *invitation* I have in mind what is traditionally referred to as an "altar call." I'm talking about inviting people to move from where they're seated to the front of the auditorium as a physical expression of their spiritual response to the preached Word. Personally, this is my preferred approach to calling for a response to the sermon. So in this chapter I'm arguing for the legitimacy of the traditional invitation, a method of calling for response that has fallen into disrepute in recent years. Furthermore, while I believe there is a need to call believers to respond to the preached Word as well, I'm specifically addressing here the responsibility we have to give unbelievers a way to say "yes" to the gospel. Whenever a sermon includes a presentation of the gospel or a reference to Christ's sacrifice at Calvary, an invitation to respond publicly is valid and preferred. In addition, after certain messages calling for surrender to Christ, it may be appropriate to invite people to come forward to respond with total commitment, surrender to full-time ministry, etc. I believe the public invitation is the clearest expression of our conviction that "we don't preach merely to hear ourselves talk or simply to convey information. We preach for a response. We are calling for a verdict."[4]

My intention in this chapter is not to rehash what we've written in *Power in the Pulpit*, but rather to look at the biblical and historical justification for continuing the public gospel invitation. Written material on the invitation is rather sparse. I will lean heavily on two wonderful works on the subject, R. Alan Streett's *The Effective Invitation* (Revell, 1984) and Roy Fish's *Coming to Jesus: Giving a Good Invitation,* 2nd ed. (CreateSpace, 2016).

OBJECTIONS TO THE INVITATION

There seems to have always been opposition to the traditional invitation. Some naysayers have suggested that the traditional altar call is tacking on something unnecessary and extraneous to preaching. These dissenting voices are somewhat louder at this point in our contemporary era. Other critics say the public invitation is unscriptural, manipulative, and a man-made ploy to get people to the front of the building to record a dubious "decision for Christ." Some would charge that it's just a way for the preacher to get another notch on his gospel gun.

Though the objections to extending a public, come-forward invitation are many, I will confine them to four primary categories. First, some objections are psychological in nature. Some see the appeal for people to come forward in a public manner as illegitimate manipulation. I have indeed witnessed invitations that were manipulative and extreme. But this need not be. Billy Graham said that a number of psychologists and psychiatrists wrote him through the years to tell him that his "method is psychologically sound."[5] There is a difference between manipulation and persuasion, as we shall see.

Second, others object on historical grounds. They maintain that the public invitation is of recent origin, dating back only 225 years in church history. They argue that the practice was initiated by evangelist Charles G. Finney (1792–1875). "Such an accusation is historically incorrect," Streett says, a contention that he documents in detail.[6] In the next section we will briefly survey the historical development of the public invitation.

Third, some object for theological reasons. This group, including some who are more Calvinistic in their theology, says the come-forward invitation gives people false hope that they are saved, contributes to spurious conversions, and fills churches with unregenerate members. I know of no sincere, Bible-believing, gospel-preaching minister who is not desirous that decisions for Christ be genuine, filled with gospel assurance and hope. Also, surely we would all want our churches to have a regenerate membership. I hasten to say that many brothers of the Calvinist persuasion believe in and offer public invitations. R. T. Kendall, who is a professed Calvinist, has written a strong defense of the public invitation.[7] John MacArthur Jr., the well-known Bible expositor who also embraces Calvinistic theology, says, "We see hundreds saved and baptized every year. We never have a service without an invitation, and we never have an invitation without people coming into our prayer rooms."[8]

Fourth, and more crucial, some object to the public, come-forward invitation on biblical grounds. The contention is that there is no biblical precedent for such an invitation, and therefore it is not to be used in churches today. I will maintain that there is ample reason and indeed, strong evidence that not to extend an invitation fails to model the biblical precedent.

I question in no way the sincerity of those who offer these and other objections. However, most of the objections seem to stem from having witnessed the abuses of a public invitation rather than proper uses of it. In the next section I will trace the history of the public invitation from the first century to the current era. Then I will examine in summary fashion the biblical basis for the public invitation.

HISTORICAL PRECEDENT
FOR THE INVITATION

Those who criticize the giving of an invitation after the preaching of the gospel say it is something that is of recent origin. They maintain that the practice originated with Charles G. Finney; yet Streett demonstrates that such a claim has no basis in historical fact. As we shall see in the next section, first-century gospel preachers publicly called for various expressions of public repentance, faith responses, and baptism. While all of those expressions didn't look exactly like our contemporary models, they reinforce the general idea of calling people to give some immediate, physical expression of response to their spiritual decisions.

Admittedly, there is not a consistent trail between the biblical and modern practices of the invitation. "It is correct to say that the invitation fell into disuse soon after the apostolic period and did not make a full comeback until modern times."[9] Streett and Fish both affirm that the discontinued physical response was due to infant baptism being initiated as a result of Christianity being declared the state religion of the Roman Empire by Constantine in AD 324. There is later record, however, of the Roman Catholic preacher, Bernard of Clairvaux (1093–1153), calling for a show of hands by those who wanted to be restored to God and the church. John Chrysostom (347–407) witnessed people rising from their seats as he preached.[10] The possibility is strong that groups outside the Roman Catholic Church did extend public invitations, though there is little additional historical record to confirm it.

During the Reformation era (1517–1648) the major reformers remained largely a part of the Roman Catholic Church and continued to baptize babies. Thus, no public invitation would have been considered necessary. My spiritual ancestors, the Anabaptists, seemed to extend a form of invitation at the conclusion of their gospel presentations. Among Anabaptist preachers who evidently did are Balthassar Hubmaier (1481–1520), Conrad Grebel (c. 1498–1526), and Felix Manz (c. 1498–1527).

The Role of the Great Awakening

Much of what we do today in the way of public invitations is rooted in the period of the Great Awakenings of the eighteenth century. In the First Great Awakening, Jonathan Edwards (1703–1758) did not call for people to come forward at the end of the sermon, but he did ask them to meet him privately. Another prominent preacher, George Whitefield (1714–1770), followed a similar pattern. Kendall has an interesting account of Eleazer Wheelock, founder of Dartmouth College, inviting people to come forward in his services. He records that Wheelock "called to the distressed, and desired them to gather themselves together below."[11]

In England John Wesley (1703–1791) carried the gospel to the common people. He always issued a public appeal, using a variety of methods, including personal workers among the listeners, a coming forward and even a mourner's bench. Streett writes, "On both sides of the Atlantic, the public invitation gained gradual acceptance and use."[12]

Certain features of the modern invitation seem to trace their origin to the camp meetings of the 1790s. Attended by thousands, these meetings crossed denominational lines and featured strong, fervent gospel preaching. Lorenzo Dow and others asked people who wanted to be prayed for to stand. Those who did so were urged to come forward and kneel at an altar that had been built in front of the pulpit.

The Examples of Finney, Spurgeon, and Moody in the Nineteenth Century

That brings us to Charles G. Finney. There is abundant evidence that Streett is correct that Finney did not originate the public invitation. I would agree with Kendall that it is more accurate to say that Finney "popularized and systematized a practice that had its roots in the preceding century when the Great Awakening in New England was at its peak."[13]

Though it may be surprising to some, C. H. Spurgeon used several forms of a public invitation. He did—as should we all—warn against the abusive use of a public invitation. But, he led evangelistic meetings and arranged for after-meetings with those under conviction. Though the architecture of the Metropolitan Tabernacle made it difficult for people to publicly come forward, on some occasions he even did it anyway. And he even would have "Just As I Am" sung![14]

Evangelist D. L. Moody (1837–1899) preached for Spurgeon on occasion. Spurgeon supported Moody's evangelistic work. In his meetings Moody would urge people who wanted to be saved to stand and say, "I will," if they wanted to receive Christ. They would then be asked to come forward and go to an inquiry room. There they would be led to Christ by a trained worker. There is no indication that Spurgeon disapproved of Moody's method of invitation. To the contrary, Spurgeon was once asked to comment on Moody's invitation methods. He said, "I believe that it is a great help in bringing people to a decision when Mr. Moody asks those to stand who wish to be prayed for. Anything that tends to separate you from the ungodly around you is good for you."[15] There is no evidence that either Spurgeon or Moody ever heard Finney preach or knew anything about his invitation methodologies. There is strong evidence that Spurgeon and Moody were influenced by one another in their invitational methods.

The Examples of Twentieth-Century Evangelists and Pastors

There is little need to discuss the use of the invitation in the modern era. Evangelists such as Sam Jones, Billy Sunday, and Billy Graham all used some form of a public invitation. Millions came to Christ in evangelistic meetings. Such notable pastors as W. A. Criswell, Adrian Rogers, O. S. Hawkins, and John MacArthur gave or give some form of public invitations for people to express their spiritual decisions. I for one rejoice in every attempt to publicly call people to come to Christ at the climax of faithful gospel proclamations. Tragic indeed will be efforts to cease the public invitation for men, women, teens, boys, and girls to come to Christ. I agree with Streett: "The twentieth century has witnessed the public invitation restored to its New Testament place of prominence. As Jesus called men to repent and believe in public fashion, so the modern evangelist follows in the steps of his Master by issuing the invitation."[16] Which brings us to an even more important question: is there a biblical basis for extending the gospel invitation?

BIBLICAL BASIS FOR THE INVITATION

The service at First Church of Corinth is beginning. The gathered saints sing several psalms and hymns and choruses. The singing is energetic and happy. After the singing a member of the staff makes a few announcements. The ladies trio, backed by the choir, sings a beautiful gospel number. The apostle Paul stands to preach an expository message from the book of Isaiah. He shares with the people that the Lord Jesus Christ fulfills all the prophecies of Isaiah concerning the coming Messiah. With great precision and passion he preaches the death, burial, resurrection, and appearances of the Lord Jesus, the Messiah.

An Invitation in the Early Church?

"Now," says Paul, "I want to plead with those of you who have never believed on Him, to do so this morning. We will pray, then stand while an invitation hymn is sung. Come to Jesus. I will be at the front to greet you." Several people come forward and Paul kneels with them in front of the pulpit.

Chapter? Verse? No need to look. What I have just described isn't there.

If you can't find in the Bible what I have described, then it isn't to be done in a worship service. Is that right? Should we have in our services just those elements that are specifically mentioned in the New Testament?

Regulative Versus Normative Principles in the Church

This takes us to a discussion of what has been called the regulative versus the normative principles of worship. What's the difference between them? The regulative principle of worship maintains that only those things that are specifically mentioned in Scripture are to be a part of our worship services. The normative principle, on the other hand, maintains that anything not expressly forbidden in the Bible is perfectly acceptable to be used in our worship services. Taken to extremes, the regulative principle would say there are to be no musical instruments used in worship. And, there can be no choirs, chairs, Sunday schools, nor offering plates. Using this as a guide also would eliminate any kind of invitation in the public services—and a benediction at the end of the service, for that matter. On the other hand, taken to extremes, the normative principle would say secular songs and the trappings of secular venues are acceptable in our worship services.

There are strengths in both positions. The regulative principle seeks to honor the Word of God. Focusing on the worship of God is another strength. The normative principle seeks to utilize the tasteful use of musical instruments and incorporates elements that enhance our worship of God and the study of His Word.

I would like to make a modest proposal for some middle ground in the whole matter. Let me put forth what I call the suggestive principle of worship. That is, look at the direct indications from Scripture relative to certain elements of worship. These directives would include the preaching of the Word, singing, and some other elements. Also, include those elements of worship that are suggested from principles that emerge from the words, examples, and patterns we find in Scripture. I believe the public invitation certainly fits into the category of the suggestive principle. As Fish writes, "True enough, we do not find an exact example of the modern evangelistic invitation in the Scriptures, but this fact does not condemn it as unscriptural."[17]

Before I briefly survey the biblical information that suggests the appropriateness of the public invitation, let me make this point. There are some matters that call for some sanctified common sense. Anything that helps us carry out the directions and suggestions of the Bible relative to the worship of God and bringing people to Christ surely may be used. Are we going to fight old battles, covering the same ground our forefathers did regarding principles of worship?

Principles of the Invitation in the Old and New Testaments

The principles of the invitation may be found in the Old Testament. God Himself invited Noah and his family into the ark of safety (see Gen. 7:1). Moses called the people back to God from the calf idol, saying, "Who is on the LORD's side? Come to me" (Ex. 32:26). Joshua called the people to "choose this day whom you will serve" (Josh. 24:15). Elijah publicly invited people to follow the Lord (see 1 Kings 18:21), as did Jonah (see Jonah 3:3–4).

In the New Testament, we find Jesus publicly calling people to follow Him. That invitation was extended to the disciples (e.g., Matt. 4:18–22; John 1:35–51). Among others, He called Zacchaeus (see Luke 19:5–10). Note that Zacchaeus was a sinner and that Jesus issued to him a public call. Zacchaeus, in full view of a large crowd, gave public testimony to a changed life and Jesus confirmed his salvation. Billy Graham has often said that every person Jesus called He called publicly.

The apostles extended some kind of call or invitation for people to repent of their sins and by faith, trust Christ as their personal Savior. Paul did so on numerous occasions. Notably, he invited the Philippian jailer to publicly testify to his faith in Christ by means of baptism (see Acts 16:27–34). Whitesell wrote of Paul, "If he did not use our methods of invitation, he must have used something akin to them."[18]

The day of Pentecost is especially instructive relative to the public invitation. The apostle Peter preached the gospel on the day of Pentecost, gave an invitation, and three thousand professed their faith in Christ by being baptized (see Acts 2:14–41). There is no longer any concern as to how that many people could be baptized in the city of Jerusalem. In the 1970s, numerous ritual pools were unearthed. These could easily have been used. There was some method used to arrive at the number three thousand (see also the five thousand in Acts 4:4). There had to be some kind of public, come-forward movement on the part of the converts. How did they get to the baptismal pools? Did they just stumble into them? We may reasonably surmise that this account indicates that a public invitation was extended and suggests that some practical means were used. Fish's words are telling: "How did those who were conducting the service and doing the baptizing know who to baptize out of the crowds who heard them? Some call for public declaration was essential."[19]

Four Key Principles

From these and many other Bible examples emerge certain principles that suggest the public invitation. First, certain Bible words carry within them the principle of invitation. "Come," used over and over in the Bible, is perhaps the greatest word of invitation of all. The Bible's opening and closing chapters contain the invitation to "come." The word is found in Genesis 7:1 (KJV), and then three times in the final invitation of Revelation 22:17. The word *exhort* is another Bible word of invitation. Occurring 108 times, the Greek word literally carries the idea "to call to the side." I have heard Southwestern Baptist Theological Seminary president Paige Patterson say, "I have frequently translated 'exhort' as 'Give an invitation.'" The word is used in describing what Peter did on Pentecost: "And with many other words he bore witness and continued to exhort them, saying, 'Save yourselves from this crooked generation'" (Acts 2:40). The word *persuade* is often used as well (e.g., Acts 13:43 KJV; 18:4, 13; 19:8; 2 Cor. 5:11), with the connotation of "seeking to win over."

Second, public, physical movement was common as people responded to the Lord and the preaching of the gospel. Zacchaeus came down from the tree. The converts moved to places where they were baptized. The worship service mentioned in 1 Corinthians 14:23–25 is most instructive, as well as suggestive. A lost sinner is pictured coming into a worship service. Though an unbeliever, he is "convicted by all." God reveals the secrets of his heart and he is "falling on his face," worshiping God. What does he do next? He reports that "God is really among you."

Third, the invitation is always preceded by gospel proclamation. An invitation is only given after there has been a clear presentation of the good news of how to be saved. Paul makes this abundantly clear when he says, "I declare unto you the gospel which I preached unto you, which also ye have received" (1 Cor. 15:1 KJV). This proclamation is made in the power of the Holy Spirit, working through the heart of the preacher and to the hearts of the unsaved who hear. Streett quotes Billy Graham: "I don't believe any man can come to Christ unless the Holy Spirit has prepared his heart. . . . My job is to proclaim the message."[20]

Fourth, the Bible gives credence to the note of urgency that must accompany the invitation. The words mentioned above (*come, exhort, persuade*) are like trumpets blowing, alarms ringing, sirens sounding. Paul gives this urgency voice when he says, "'In a favorable time I listened to you.' Behold, now is the favorable time; behold, now is the day of salvation" (2 Cor. 6:2). Paul was *helping* the Corinthians to respond to Christ. Feel the urgent, pleading invitation for sinners to come to Christ? In the Bible sinners are invited to be saved with a sense of urgency. Can we do any less?

Give an Invitation!

The Bible teaches us that some are gifted with the office of the evangelist (cf. Eph. 4:11–12). Church leaders would be wise to use these gifted men. God especially uses them in "drawing the net." But all believers, especially pastors, are to "do the work of an evangelist" (2 Tim. 4:5). Don't miss out on the blessing of extending an invitation after you preach and seeing people come to Christ. Give an invitation!

It's true that many of the messages in our churches primarily are addressing unbelievers. And when we preach those messages, I think we should call on believers to respond. But even then, we need to make sure we give unbelievers a chance to respond to the gospel as well. That's why when I give a public invitation, I like to use what I call "the evangelistic twist."[21] Every message may be turned to give a gospel appeal. If you are preaching on giving, you can say, "If you are not a believer, God isn't asking for your money. He is asking for you to give your life to Him. As Paul said in 2 Corinthians 8:5, the believers in Macedonia 'gave themselves first to the Lord.'" Give an invitation!

Ask people to ask Jesus to come into their hearts. Innately most people know the difference between the physical heart and the spiritual heart. Nevertheless, explain that with the "heart"—which means with our life, with our very being—we are to believe on Christ. In Romans 10:8–10, three times Paul refers to the spiritual meaning of "heart." Give an invitation!

Lead people in a sinner's prayer. Jesus told a parable about a man who prayed such a prayer. The publican—a sinner—prayed, "God, be merciful to me, a sinner," and then he went home a saved man (cf. Luke 18:13–14). Recall the various ways Spurgeon gave invitations. He primarily asked people to go to a lecture hall where workers would assist them. On occasion he would have people come forward in the service. He would even have the hymn "Just As I Am" be sung. And, he was even known to use a sinner's prayer! After preaching on the publican's prayer, Spurgeon closed with this plea: "Join with me while I put words in your mouths, and speak them on your behalf, 'Lord, I am guilty. I deserve thy wrath. Lord, I cannot save myself. Lord, I would have a new heart and a right spirit, but what can I do? Lord, I can do nothing, come and work in me to will and to do of thy good pleasure.'"[22] And there is promise to those who call upon God: Romans 10:13 says, "Everyone who calls on the name of the Lord will be saved." Does this not mean sinners? Is this not prayer? Surely God uses means to help poor, lost sinners to Jesus. Again, Spurgeon says, "Prayer and means go together."[23] Lead the people to pray a sinner's prayer. Give an invitation!

I am puzzled by some who object to all of the above. I appreciate their desire for a regenerated membership. I share that desire. I agree that we do not want to give anyone false hope. That's why I make it very clear in my public invitations that praying a prayer, walking down an aisle, nothing they can do will save them. Only Jesus saves. But if it is all predetermined, as some would say, none of those who will be saved will have any false hope. And if those who won't be saved do any of the above and have a false hope, nothing is changed. Kendall—again one who embraces Calvinism—says, "I know I am not going to lead savingly to Christ one of the non-elect . . . neither can I dislodge any of God's chosen."[24] What harm is actually done? Give an invitation!

I urge you to give an invitation after you preach the gospel. O. S. Hawkins says, "The public appeal has had a significant place in Christian commitment since the Lord's use of it almost 2,000 years ago. We need not excuse it nor apologize for it in our day."[25] Give an invitation!

One Sunday night Dwight L. Moody preached, and instead of giving a public invitation, told the people to take a week to think about what he had said. Tragically, many of them never saw another day. That night the great Chicago Fire raged, killing hundreds. Moody said, "What a mistake! I have never dared to give an audience a week to think of their salvation since. . . . I would rather have that right hand cut off than to give an audience now a week to decide what to do with Jesus."[26] Be wise like Moody and give an invitation!

READING FOR PROGRESS

Fish, Roy J. *Coming to Jesus: Giving a Good Invitation*. Fort Worth: Colter & Co., 2015.

Hawkins, O. S. *Drawing the Net*. Dallas: GuideStone, 2002.

Streett, Alan. *The Effective Invitation*. Old Tappan, NJ: Revell Company, 1984.

II

RISING ABOVE FOYER FEEDBACK

THE ART OF
OBJECTIVE SERMON EVALUATION

Jim Shaddix

Brother Shaddix will be standing at the back so you can speak to him as you leave." If I've heard those words once, I've heard them hundreds of times. Spoken from the lips of a well-meaning host pastor or staff member as he closes a worship service where I've been the guest preacher, those instructions reflect the long-standing tradition in many smaller churches where the pastor or guest preacher stands in the foyer and is greeted by every person in attendance as they exit.

To be perfectly honest, I've never been a big fan of this ritual. For starters, I'm normally worn out from preaching and desperately need to sit down. And the people (who usually have been sitting a long time listening to me preach!) are hungry and, therefore, anxious to get home or to the local restaurant for lunch. But maybe the most stressful part of this religious routine is the awkward conversation that takes place while it's unfolding.

"Good sermon, preacher." "I enjoyed your service." "Good job." "Thank you for your message." Those are some of the more common surface niceties articulated by parishioners as they file out. And seriously, how many creative ways can a preacher actually respond with "Thank you" and "To God be the glory"?

But even the awkwardness—and, honestly, the insincere nature—of these conversations isn't the worst part of this ceremonious procession. The most tragic reality is that this kind of well-intentioned but shallow interaction is the only kind of feedback that most preachers ever get about their sermons. And if it doesn't come from those little old ladies telling us we're going to be the next Billy Graham as they exit the church building, it comes from "that guy" who sends an email every week carping about our sermons and encouraging us to reevaluate our calling. The feedback we get often is limited to these two extremes—overindulgent compliments or unforgiving criticisms. Consequently, most foyer feedback and email evaluations aren't objective and don't provide much useful material that can help a preacher progress and improve in his preaching.

So how do we avoid these two extremes? How do we rise above the foyer feedback and get some objective input that will actually help us grow in our preaching? Through the course of my own journey as a preacher and a teacher of preaching, I've discovered some principles that have been helpful to me and other expositors. I have grouped these principles into some major categories. See if any of these suggestions will serve you well as you seek constructive criticism about the sermons you deliver.

HOW TO RECEIVE VALID AND OBJECTIVE FEEDBACK

Developing an Intentional Plan

Once you've decided that getting some feedback on your sermons will help you progress in your preaching, the first step is to develop a plan. General George S. Patton, one of America's most successful army generals of World War II, is accredited with the famous appeal, "Lead me, follow me, or get out of my way."[1] Those words reflect his conviction that everyone ought to at least do something to help the cause instead of just being in the way. The same is true with sermon evaluation. If you don't take the initiative to evaluate your sermons, you'll just be in the way of making progress in your preaching ministry. And the only feedback you'll get will be the foyer feedback and/or a negative email evaluation like "that guy" above.

So whatever you do, don't *not* do anything! Be proactive in finding somebody to help you get objective feedback. Here are some places to look to find help with evaluating your preaching.

Using Your Staff Team

Staff teams probably serve as the primary sermon feedback group for pastors in multi-staff churches. Healthy staff atmospheres can be fertile soil for preachers to grow in their calling and craft. When I served as a teaching pastor with David Platt at the Church at Brook Hills in Birmingham, Alabama, our Tuesday worship evaluations were some of the most beneficial times for me as a preacher. Listening to those brothers objectively pick apart the good and bad of our sermons provided much fodder for improvement. We followed a simple process that I've used in churches that I've pastored, as well as in classrooms where I've taught sermon delivery. We simply asked participants collectively to identify "Three Things to Keep" (strengths) and "Three Things to Throw Away" (weaknesses) from each sermon. This approach is reflected on the sermon evaluation form found in the appendix (and discussed in the section "Use a Good Instrument"). Such an approach ensures balance in the evaluation and helps prevent the group from camping out too long on any one particular element.

Be aware that using staff teams for sermon evaluation certainly has its challenges. First, a healthy atmosphere for evaluation usually is only developed over time and under good leadership. You will need to lovingly shepherd your staff to the place of giving helpful feedback. Second, staff members who are paid by the church and supervised by the senior (or lead) pastor often are hesitant to offer any negative criticism and prone to err on the side of telling the pastor what they think he wants to hear. You'll need to model objective evaluation for your team, be transparent with your own self-evaluation, and demonstrate a humble and teachable spirit.

Whatever you do, don't harbor ill feelings or resentment toward a team member who shares constructive criticism. That will cause you to forfeit your opportunity—and privilege—to shepherd that brother or sister under your care.

Third, other preachers and staff members have a tendency to "overanalyze" sermons. You'll need to give gentle guidance in keeping them from becoming too technical in their evaluation.

Using Your Church Members

The reality is many pastors don't have the luxury of multiple staff members to engage in the process of evaluation. And believe it or not, staff team discussions don't always make the *best* arenas for sermon feedback. There's much to be said for getting feedback from people who don't listen to our sermons through a "seminary lens" or other professional filter. Nonprofessionals are more inclined to receive our messages as words from God and then—at our invitation—offer feedback from the perspective of average people who are fleshing out the Christian life in the work-a-day world. The people who sit in our congregations voluntarily are better positioned to offer unbiased opinions about our sermons.

So don't limit your sermon evaluation to staff members even if you have them at your disposal. Try to involve some of your laypeople. Put together a group of your church members and give them a meaningful way to serve the body that they've probably never thought about before. This is much more effective than the brief, often awkward comments of church members after a worship service. Consider a small group of longtime members (five years or more) who are representative of different demographic groups and walks of life. You might try to include a student, a children's worker, a single parent, a parent of teenager(s), a senior adult, and other people who represent various segments of your flock. Their various perspectives and evaluative lenses will offer you valuable insight into how you can improve your communication to your entire congregation. As you lead them, be sure to foster an atmosphere of honesty and freedom. Do everything you can to develop in them qualities that inform objective feedback, which we'll discuss in the following section. We will suggest how to find them in the section "Finding Objective Evaluators" (page 171).

Using Your Colleagues

While we hope the situation would be rare, it's possible that you could find yourself in a situation where you don't have either of the above options available to you. You want to get some help improving as a preacher, but you don't have a staff team and you can't find any people in your congregation who are either ready or willing to help. Maybe you're planting a church and only have a handful of people, or maybe you just inherited a single-staff congregation that hasn't been discipled very well. So you simply don't have anybody that you feel can give you good feedback. Are you just out of luck when it comes to sermon evaluation?

Not in the least! Besides being intentional with self-evaluation, you can partner with some guys outside your congregation to get helpful input into your preaching ministry. Enlist a group of pastor friends or preaching buddies to be a part of a sermon feedback group. If they serve in churches close by, schedule a time to meet regularly and take turns critiquing one another's sermons. If they live and serve a long way off, use the Internet. It can serve you well at this point. YouTube, Vimeo, chat rooms, email, or any number of other online resources can enable you and your colleagues to share sermon videos and give one another feedback. Modern technology leaves most every preacher without excuse when it comes to doing beneficial sermon evaluation.

Adding Yourself—Or Going Solo

Regardless of which of these avenues you take to putting together a sermon feedback group, you should always be a part of that group. In other words, you should always participate in evaluating your own sermons. In fact, even if for some reason you can't find anyone else to help, you can still do some beneficial sermon critique of your own messages. After all, God may call you to a remote jungle where your only audience is a couple of natives who've never heard preaching before. Even in that context you ought to be able to do some degree of sermon evaluation simply because you're there. Today, it's possible to record your sermons by audio and video on just about any smartphone. If you don't have any other means for capturing your messages, you can set your smartphone on the pulpit or lectern (or tree branch!) and record enough of your sermon to enable you to engage in at least some element of evaluation.

Whether you have a team to help you or you're all by yourself in this endeavor, self-evaluation can be a bit of a challenge. Most of us don't like to listen to ourselves preach, much less critique our own sermons. The reality of viewing and/or listening to ourselves can be a painful experience! But pressing through the awkwardness can produce good fruit. No one knows you like you, so putting your eyes on your own preaching brings a perspective to the table that nobody else can bring. While I rarely will watch or listen to one of my sermons in its entirety, I do try to evaluate a segment of each one on a regular basis. And when I'm working with a sermon evaluation team, I always find that I notice some things that no one else notices. While we have to work hard to be objective about our own preaching, it's important for us to be a part of the process.

FINDING OBJECTIVE EVALUATORS

I've already suggested that one of the most important qualities of helpful feedback is that it's objective. The word *objective* suggests a willingness to not be influenced by personal feelings, interpretations, or prejudices. It speaks of being fair and not levying judgments that aren't based on facts. While it can take some work finding them, objective people are the kind of people you need speaking into your preaching ministry. So who are these objective evaluators and where do you find them?

Enlist People Who Are for You

All of us will have people in the congregations we preach to who could not care less whether we ever get better. If they give us feedback, it's only for the purpose of seeking a return compliment or actually taking a jab at us to make themselves feel knowledgeable or even superior to us. But there also are those in the congregation who love us, want good for us, and are genuinely interested in seeing us grow as preachers. Those are the people you want to enlist to help you evaluate your sermons.

I'm not talking about people who just tell you what you want to hear. Those people aren't really for you. Such listeners simply want to keep the peace or make you happy with the way you are. I'm talking about people who love you and want God's best for you. These are people who are willing to be graciously honest about the strengths and weaknesses of your preaching. They want to see you improve, and they're willing to help you get there. These people are most often discovered in relationship over time. You may need to "do life" with your people for a while before you're able to discern which ones really have your best interest in mind, but you will discover them over time.

Enlist "Critical" People

A critical thinker isn't the same thing as someone who's always critical. I've already noted that there's not a lot of value in the extreme feedback that comes from the person who trashes our sermons in weekly emails. A critical thinker isn't someone who has only negative things to say about our preaching. He or she is someone who is clear, rational, open-minded, and makes decisions that are informed by evidence.

So find some people who are perceptive, honest, and caring to help you critique your preaching. Some people stumble through life with their heads in the clouds, never processing what's going on around them on any more than a surface level. Those people won't be able to help you much when it comes to analyzing your sermons. You need people who are able to break down what they see and hear in such a way that they can identify the good and the bad. Find some people who can think critically about your preaching.

Enlist Godly People

Preaching is a spiritual event—or at least it ought to be! We're dealing with the supernatural Word of God and the Holy Spirit who inspired it. We're representing the Creator of the universe and telling people what He's actually saying to them. We're proclaiming the gospel that is His power for salvation. We're equipping the church to be the bride of Christ for all eternity. Every time we preach, something otherworldly is taking place. There's a heavenly mystery that's unfolding. Consequently, the last thing you want to do is limit the feedback you get about your sermons to people who are living in the flesh! You need some people who think and walk in the Spirit to be speaking into this lofty endeavor for which you're responsible.

You don't have to have a group of people who are at exactly the same place spiritually. In fact, it can be beneficial to have a mix of folks who are at different stages of spiritual maturity. But they should all be people whose faith is vibrant and who are on an upward trajectory in their spiritual journeys. These people are best positioned to offer insight into both your content and delivery. They can help assess whether or not you've handled the text rightly as well as whether or not you've maintained good eye contact with your audience. They can discern if the Spirit appeared to attend your message while at the same time identify any distracting gestures you employed. Entrust the improvement of your preaching to people who walk closely with the One who called you to the task.

Enlist Faithful People

Years ago, while serving as dean of the chapel at New Orleans Baptist Theological Seminary, one of my responsibilities was to invite guest preachers to speak in our chapel. Needless to say, sugar-stick sermons were regular fare, just like they are in most chapel and conference venues. In contexts like those, many preachers like to pull out their favorite message and something with which they're very comfortable and confident. When given the opportunity, however, I would always encourage pastors who preached in our chapel to preach something that was indicative of what they did in their church week-to-week. Those sermons were better representations of the pastor's preaching ministry and usually better examples for our students.

A similar thing is true in reverse when it comes to sermon evaluation. People are best positioned to give us objective feedback when they hear what we do on a regular basis. I don't put near as much stock in the critique of the person who shows up once a month to hear me preach as I do the one who's present week in and week out. People who pop in and out may catch me on the day I strike out or they may catch me on the day when I get a couple of base hits. Either way their evaluation will be skewed. Faithful church members, on the other hand, see my whole game. They have a consistent view of the breadth of my pastoral preaching ministry and, therefore, are able to weigh the strengths and weaknesses together to arrive at balanced conclusions. Their feedback is formulated from broader and more realistic observation.

So when you're putting together a team of people to give you feedback on your preaching, look for people who can evaluate it in context. Enlist people who are faithful to the weekly worship of your congregation and who hear you preach on a regular basis.

Enlist Teachable People

One of the questions I ask when I'm looking for young men to disciple and mentor is, "Is he teachable?" I'm really not concerned about how much Bible or pastoral ministry he knows, or about how much natural ability he has. I just want to know if he has a spirit of humility and is open to someone else speaking into his life. Pride—especially *spiritual* pride—is one of the greatest hindrances to discipleship. The term *disciple* suggests a learner. A person has to be willing to learn if they're going to be of service to the kingdom.

The sermon evaluation process is a discipleship opportunity. Obviously it's an opportunity for you the preacher to learn because that's the primary goal. But it's also an opportunity to disciple some people in your church. You'll have the opportunity to explore God's Word in your preaching texts on a deeper level with this specific group of people. You'll have the chance to teach them some things about the noble task of preaching and its crucial place in the community of faith. Because you'll need to teach them to use some kind of sermon evaluation tool, you'll be able to help them improve their own communication skills in public speaking. Sermon evaluation groups can be great arenas for training more and better Bible teachers in your church. So look for people who are open to learning themselves just as they are helping you learn.

FOSTERING A GOOD ATTITUDE

Once you've found a team to help you with sermon evaluation, you'll need to equip them to do it well. Healthy sermon critique begins with attitude, something that's a challenge for us preachers when it comes to listening to preaching. One of the reasons most of us don't like to solicit feedback on our sermons is that we're afraid people will evaluate us the same way we evaluate other preachers. And typically we're not very objective when we listen to other preachers. We normally start with a cynical attitude and end with a hypercritical analysis. Why? Let's be honest: the easiest way to build ourselves up is to tear others down. Being overly critical about other preachers always makes us look and sound a little better.

Sadly, this expression of depravity is common among the fraternal order of preachers. The fact that this attitude is common, however, doesn't make it right. We have to rise above this work of the flesh and learn to listen to preaching in a more spiritual posture, especially if we're going to help others learn how to evaluate preaching well. In fact, the people we enlist and train to be part of our sermon evaluation process likely will take their cue from us and adopt our demeanor as sermon evaluators. So consider the following guidelines for helping you and your team members approach sermon evaluation with a more Christlike attitude.

Listen First for a Word from God

I remember a formative conversation with my dad shortly after I had responded to God's call to preach. I was confused about some high-profile preachers who had been caught in scandalous sin. Some of them were men who I knew had been used of God to do some very good things. And yet it had been determined that all the while they were living in secret sin. That didn't make sense to me, so I asked my dad how it could be. I'll never forget his answer. He said, "Son, don't ever forget that God uses us in spite of ourselves." That's been an encouraging truth for me throughout my ministry, especially when I'm frequently reminded of the wickedness of my own heart.

It's also an important truth to remember when you're on the receiving end of the sermon. Don't ever forget that God can use that preacher to speak to you even if he doesn't do everything exactly right or even the way you would do it. When you listen to preaching, don't let your first thought be toward evaluation, critique, and analysis. Lend your ear to the voice of God before you assess the presentation of the preacher. Ask not how you would preach the sermon differently; ask how the sermon needs to make you different. Let your first concern be to hear a word from God before you begin analyzing the sermon.

Desire Your Own Improvement

Always have a basic desire to improve your own effectiveness in proclaiming the gospel even when you're helping someone else improve theirs. In other words, maintain a humble posture and teachable spirit that enables you to see every point of the critique of someone else's sermon as information that can be helpful in your own preaching. Every time you hear a sermon, three things ought to take place. First, you hear a word from God as we discussed above. Second, you see and hear things that cause you to assess your own preaching. Third, given the proper context, you discern constructive criticism that you can pass along to the preacher in order to help him progress in his preaching

Here's how this might look. I'm listening to someone else preach with the intent of giving them some feedback. I notice that the preacher's volume isn't always consistent with his content. He's kind of loud, even when what he's saying doesn't call for it. As I process that criticism, I should always think first about my own preaching. Is this something of which I'm conscious in my own delivery? Is my volume consistent with my content? Does it vary with the nature of what I'm saying at any given point in my sermons? This is a place in which maintaining a "me first" mentality can be a good thing. I need to be a learner before I'm a teacher. Additionally, if you view every sermon you hear as a learning laboratory for your own preaching, it will guard you from being overly critical about the one who's preaching and enable you to be more balanced in your analysis.

Identify Strengths and Weaknesses

One of the most important things in helpful sermon evaluation is balance—addressing the good and the bad. Focusing only on one aspect of someone's preaching is not only dishonest, but it leaves him with either a false sense of security or an undue sense of discouragement. We always want to identify some things the preacher does well in addition to things to which he needs to give attention. No preacher is terrible at every aspect of preaching, and neither is any preacher a master of all. All of us do some things effectively, and all of us have some areas in which we need to improve.

As mentioned earlier, one practice that I've found helpful is to encourage evaluators to identify "three things to keep and three things to throw away." Things to keep obviously are qualities of a preacher's content and delivery that he does well and needs to continue to incorporate into his preaching. Things to throw away are characteristics of his preaching that need to be eliminated, altered, or improved in some way. Identifying some things in each of these categories does two things. One, it helps us maintain balance in the evaluation so that we don't send false messages. Two, it forces us to look and listen closer when the sermon is being preached because we know we're going to need to find three elements in each category.

Be Helpful, Not Hurtful

Sermon analysis is a kingdom enterprise. Our ultimate goal is to advance the gospel and see Christ exalted. That means we need to see other preachers as co-laborers in kingdom work, fellow soldiers in the cosmic battle. So our intent in giving one another feedback should be to help them and not hurt them. We should always purpose to be constructive in what we say or write about someone else's preaching as opposed to being destructive in our criticism. We want to build them up instead of tear them down. We want them to be encouraged and motivated to improve, instead of being devastated to the point of wanting to quit.

As we suggested above, this doesn't mean we give only positive feedback when we're evaluating the preaching of others. But it does mean that we communicate both a positive and negative critique with the spirit of Christ, which has the preacher's best interest at heart. We should always have a sincere desire to see the preacher become as effective in his preaching as he can possibly be. We want to see him reach his full potential according to the measure of Christ's gift in his life. That means our feedback should be edifying and not paralyzing. Make sure every time you critique someone's preaching you desire to be helpful and not hurtful.

Exercise Christian Courtesy and Grace

Always approach sermon evaluation with the kindness and grace exemplified by our Lord. Jesus taught His followers to treat one another with mutual respect and accountability. He said things like, "Whatever you wish that others would do to you, do also to them" (Matt. 7:12). He said, "If your brother sins against you, go and tell him his fault, between you and him alone" (Matt. 18:15). The apostle Paul encouraged the same kind of attitudes. He told the Ephesians to "be kind to one another, tenderhearted, forgiving one another, as God in Christ forgave you" (Eph. 4:32). To the Galatians he exhorted, "Brothers, if anyone is caught in any transgression, you who are spiritual should restore him in a spirit of gentleness. Keep watch on yourself, lest you too be tempted" (Gal. 6:1).

While these expressions of Christian ethics have their own specific contexts, they all reflect a heartbeat that is important for healthy sermon evaluation. You should always give feedback the way you want it to be given to you. And you shouldn't articulate what you're not willing to say personally to the preacher. Never write on a written evaluation what you're not willing to say to him face-to-face. And always keep the gospel in mind when you evaluate others. Grant the same kind of grace to other preachers that Jesus gave you on the cross. And always be gentle in your critique, remembering that you're susceptible to the same preaching mistakes that you identify in others. Being gracious, courteous, and just exercising good manners will go a long way in fostering healthy sermon evaluation.

Don't Question Second-Order Doctrine

Nothing will derail good sermon critique quicker than getting sidetracked by something that is of secondary importance. No place is this more frequent than with doctrinal issues that aren't top-tier components of the Christian faith. We preachers especially have a tendency to bristle up when we hear another preacher articulate something that's different from our own belief or conviction. But when we get bogged down with issues that great men of faith have debated for centuries, we likely undermine ripe opportunities to be helpful when evaluating the preaching of other pastors, our brothers in Christ. So it's important to choose our battles well and pick our spots purposefully when it comes to the doctrinal issues we raise in sermon evaluation.

My cardinal rule is to only question first-order doctrinal issues when critiquing sermons. I would never suggest that we shouldn't push back on first-order doctrines. Doing so is crucial when evaluating sermons. If someone is preaching heresy, it should be noted and duly addressed. That's definitely something he needs to throw away! But if his view on the rapture is different than yours, or we find ourselves in different places when it comes to election and predestination, I don't think hashing those things out as part of sermon feedback is helpful to anyone. Plus, doing so consumes precious time that could be given to helping a brother improve in his preaching ministry. And that's what we're after in objective sermon evaluation. So save discussions about second-level doctrines for another time.

Pray for the Preachers You Critique

It's difficult to become unduly critical of people for whom you're praying. It's hard to talk to God about someone and then rip that person apart. So pray for the preacher that you're about to evaluate; this will help you approach your evaluation in a healthy manner. If you're critiquing someone's sermon spontaneously, take a moment to pray for them under your breath. Or if you know you're going to be listening to someone preach at a conference or in a worship gathering, spend some time calling their name and their assignment before our Lord. Doing so will build some fences around your assessment of their preaching.

If you're part of a sermon evaluation team, approach your responsibility prayerfully. Prior to the time you will be listening to a sermon, spend time on your knees crying out to God on behalf of the preacher. Pray for him as he prepares his sermon. Pray that he would be able to preach the gospel in a clear and compelling way. Pray for yourself and other evaluators to have ears to hear what the Holy Spirit is saying to you as team members, as well as to have His help in evaluating the sermon with integrity. And don't forget to pray that others who hear the message would respond in faith and obedience. Any preacher who understands the gravity and responsibility of rightly dividing God's Word will cherish these kinds of prayers, especially from people who are on a journey with him to help him get better.[2]

DOING HOLISTIC EVALUATION

Once you have an evaluation team that has a healthy attitude, you will need to equip them with the nuts and bolts of sermon assessment. The approach you teach them needs to be holistic in nature—all-inclusive in its ability and intent to measure every aspect of your preaching. That way you have the best chance of not overlooking important pieces of the preaching puzzle. Just as you need to be intentional about doing sermon evaluation, you need to be intentional in preparing for the evaluation. I encourage you and your evaluators to do two things in particular. First, use some kind of good evaluation tool to help guide the process. Second, learn to ask good questions so you can offer helpful insights in response to the sermons you critique.

Use a Good Instrument

A good evaluation tool will be very helpful for those recording their assessment and providing the preacher with usable information. The evaluating instrument should possess several important qualities that will yield a holistic evaluation, including the following:

1. *The instrument is listener-oriented.* Think about evaluation from a listener's perspective, not a speaker's. In other words, as much as possible, your tool should reflect terminology and values that are familiar to the average person sitting in a congregation, not those shared by a group of seminary students in a classroom. It's the ears of people who regularly listen to our sermons that should be our greatest concern.

2. *The instrument is two-dimensional.* Your instrument should help you critique both dimensions of preaching: content and delivery. Sometimes sermon evaluation is limited to aspects of physical presentation and, therefore, is lacking in a complete view of the preaching task. Daniel "Danny" L. Akin, president of Southeastern Baptist Theological Seminary, says, "What you say is more important than how you say it, but how you say it has never been more important."[3] His words are wise, and they remind us that we need to give first attention to the substance of our sermons, but we must not neglect the way we deliver them. Both content and delivery are crucial in holistic sermon evaluation.

3. *The instrument is user-friendly.* Your tool should be relatively simple, easily understood, and able to be completed in a reasonably short period of time. You don't want evaluators to get overwhelmed or discouraged by the complexity and length of your instrument.

The appendix contains a "Sermon Presentation Feedback Guide" that I've used for a number of years. While this tool contains a couple of technical elements, the vast majority of it meets the criteria above. Feel free to adapt it for your own use, or start with a blank page and develop one that's unique to how you think and how you want to train your people. But be sure to give your evaluators some kind of helpful tool that will guide them in intentional evaluation so they can assist you in growing in your preaching ministry.

Ask Good Questions

The most helpful sermon evaluations (and corresponding measurement tools) are those that encourage evaluators to make comments as opposed to simply checking boxes or circling options. Comments help the preacher to understand why an evaluator assessed him a certain way in various elements of the evaluation. So it's important for evaluators to learn to think critically about every part of the sermon so they can offer insightful remarks.

One of the best ways to formulate comments that will be helpful to the preacher is to ask good questions while evaluating the sermon. Asking and answering the right questions can help evaluators intentionally focus on aspects of the preaching event that can and should be improved. Aristotle is helpful at this point. His three famous rhetorical means of persuasion—*ethos, logos,* and *pathos*—found in his *Art of Rhetoric* can be helpful in organizing good questions in the evaluator's mind. Paige Patterson says, "Although there are a number of good methods to assess the value of a sermon, my thesis is that, from the point of view of simplicity and yet sufficient comprehension to cover the matter, these three canons of rhetoric, though born in a pagan context, are both adequate and remarkably serviceable."[4] Consider asking some important questions in each of Aristotle's three categories.[5]

Ethos

Ethos speaks of the credibility or moral character of the speaker. Aristotle said that when a speaker delivers a speech in a way that breeds confidence in him, his impact is greater than all the other aspects of his message put together.[6] To help you evaluate the preacher's credibility, you can ask these questions:

1. Does the speaker appear to have paid the price of preparing to preach this sermon?
2. Does his background and preparation make me confident in his message?
3. Is his appearance and demeanor such that I'm inclined to trust him?
4. Do I get the impression that he's a real man of God?
5. Does he give evidence of being genuinely knowledgeable about his subject?
6. Is he believable?
7. Do I get the feeling that he's actually talking to me and not just delivering a speech?

Logos

Logos deals with the content of the speaker's message, or the sermon itself. It includes the sermon's logical quality and biblical content, as well as its theology and gospel orientation. To help assess the preacher's content, ask these questions:

1. Is the message coherent? Does it make sense to me?
2. What is the preacher actually saying, and what does he actually mean?
3. Does his subject really matter to begin with? Is it an important issue or doctrine?
4. Is the message profoundly biblical? Does it cast light on the biblical passage?
5. Does the message reflect Christ and the gospel?
6. Is it significant enough to foster a change in my life?
7. Does it teach me something about my spiritual life?

Pathos

Pathos concerns the preacher's passion. It's essentially his drive, his evident motivation as dictated by the gospel, and his calling to proclaim the gospel. Patterson rightly observes,

> The preacher is not simply making a speech. He is not making a living. If there were no compensation, he would still preach because "woe is me if I do not preach the gospel" (1 Cor. 9:16). The eternal destinies of men and women are at stake every time he preaches. The ability to cope with life and to find meaning and happiness constitutes the fabric of his preaching; and he is driven, knowing the difference that obedience to the truth of God can generate.[7]

To help evaluate the preacher's pathos, ask:

1. Is the message in the preacher's soul or just in his brain?
2. Is it something he knows but doesn't seem to really care about?
3. Do I get the impression that this message is profoundly important to the preacher?
4. Does the message have gravity? Does it have a prophetic cutting edge?
5. Am I essentially bored, amused? Am I unmoved, moved, or greatly moved by the sermon?
6. Does the preacher appear to have spent serious time with God in preparation for this sermon?
7. Does the preacher communicate genuine concern for his listeners?

As evaluators ask and answer these questions as part of their assessment, they will be able to formulate specific insights to go along with more objective measurements. These descriptive comments will give the preacher better handles on which to hold. Combined with objective measurements, these more subjective observations should help the preacher identify aspects of his preaching to which he can give attention on the road to preaching improvement.

READING FOR PROGRESS

Collier, Keith. "How to Evaluate Your Pastor's Sermons," June 18, 2015, https://9marks.org/article/how-to-evaluate-your-pastors-sermons-2.

Dever, Mark, and Greg Gilbert. *Preach*. Nashville: B&H, 2012.

Jones, R. Clifford. "Evaluating the Sermon: Ten Elements to Consider After You Preach," March 1, 2005, http://www.preaching.com/author/r-clifford-jones.

TEACHING ABOUT PREACHING

HELPING PEOPLE WORSHIP THROUGH THE SERMON

Jim Shaddix

My late-night flight landed at Atlanta International Airport and our plane began taxiing toward the terminal. As we turned toward the gate several fire trucks with flashing red lights approached the plane. Once there, the fire engines began spraying it with water!

The man next to me nervously asked, "What do you think that's about?" Another passenger across the aisle excitedly asked, "Is the plane on fire?"

But I was calm through it all. In fact, I was enjoying the moment! Why? Because before we departed, the gate agent had informed some of us that this was the captain's final flight. He was retiring after thirty-four years of flying, and it was customary for the fire crews to shower the plane in salute when it reached its final destination.

Some of us who knew what was going on were enjoying the celebration! Awareness was the difference between panic and a party.

I think most congregations come to the preaching event like the passengers on my flight who were unaware of the fire trucks' ultimate purpose. Because they are uninformed about what preaching is about, they formulate preconceived ideas that cause them to totally miss the experience, or at least approach it in a guarded way. Many come to church wondering what all the commotion is about. Some think it's where the preacher tells everybody they're destined for a fiery hell. Others think it's where the preacher puts out the fires in their lives. Whatever their impression, many people keep the sermon at arm's length and miss the joy of the experience.

What they need is a "gate agent"—someone in the know to let them in on what's going on so they can experience all that God intended in the preaching event. And pastors need to be those gate agents. We need to help educate people to God's design for preaching so they know what to expect and what their role is in this important part of the church's life. Consider some suggestions for why we need to teach people about preaching, what we ought to teach them, and how we can go about doing it.

WHY WE SHOULD TEACH
OUR PEOPLE ABOUT PREACHING

Several years ago I was preaching at a conference for people who lead in musical worship. At this amazing event some of the country's best musicians and vocal artists led several thousand in wonderful times of praise to our Lord. In one particular service a three-hundred-voice choir, a praise team and band, and numerous other leaders guided the crowd in high praise. People in the congregation were raising their hands, singing at the top of their lungs, and some were even weeping. You could truly sense the presence of our Lord in that place! I remember it well.

But I also remember an unsettling sight when the musical portion of the service came to a close. As I made my way to the stage to preach, my eyes scanned the mass of men and women on the platform and in the choir loft who were settling in for the sermon. But something was glaringly absent—I didn't see a single Bible in anyone's possession on the stage or in the choir loft. Out of the three-hundred-plus worship leaders, not one had a Bible!

I wish I could say that was an isolated incident, but the truth is that the scenario has repeated itself numerous times in my ministry. We're part of a Christian culture today that has mistakenly made the word *worship* a synonym for *music*. So we have worship pastors, worship songs, and worship sets. Without thinking, we've limited our understanding of worship to music. Consequently, many so-called "worship leaders" don't put the same emphasis on the preaching of the Bible as they do the playing of their instruments and singing of praises.

To be fair, the same is true in reverse for many preachers. I grew up watching many pastors stand on the platform during the musical worship, but instead of participating in the singing, they were reviewing their notes!

Preaching As an Act of Worship

All of us have a tendency to think our part of the service is the most important. The truth is, however, that true worship can only take place when God reveals Himself. And He's chosen to record His revelation of Himself in His Word, the Bible. That reality alone makes the preaching event an act of worship among God's people. John Stott says,

> Thus Word and worship belong indissolubly to each other. All worship is an intelligent and loving response to the revelation of God, because it is the adoration of his Name. Therefore acceptable worship is impossible without preaching. For preaching is making known the Name of the Lord, and worship is praising the Name of the Lord made known. Far from being an alien intrusion into worship, the reading and preaching of the Word are actually indispensable to it. The two cannot be divorced.[1]

The great leader of the Reformation, Martin Luther, put it this way: "The highest worship of God is the preaching of the Word; because thereby are praised and celebrated the name and the benefits of Christ."[2]

When the preacher preaches a text of God's inspired Word, he's leading in worship. And when the people hear, receive, and obey the message from God's Word, they are worshiping. That makes the preacher a worship leader, and it makes the people who listen to preaching worshipers. Although we could give many reasons for teaching our people about preaching, this is the most important: the preaching event is an act of worship in the community of faith. And we need to teach our people how to worship!

Worship through Bible Reading in Ezra's Day

Make no mistake about it, worship includes music, but it's not limited to music. When the children of Israel returned to their homeland after being in exile, they were hungry to hear from God. Amidst the rubble of the destroyed temple they found the Book of God, to which they hadn't had access for many years. So they gathered together, and this is what happened:

And all the people gathered as one man into the square before the Water Gate. And they told Ezra the scribe to bring the Book of the Law of Moses that the LORD had commanded Israel. So Ezra the priest brought the Law before the assembly, both men and women and all who could understand what they heard, on the first day of the seventh month. And he read from it facing the square before the Water Gate from early morning until midday, in the presence of the men and the women and those who could understand. And the ears of all the people were attentive to the Book of the Law. And Ezra the scribe stood on a wooden platform that they had made for the purpose. . . . . And Ezra opened the book in the sight of all the people, for he was above all the people, and as he opened it all the people stood. And Ezra blessed the LORD, the great God, and all the people answered, "Amen, Amen," lifting up their hands. And they bowed their heads and worshiped the LORD with their faces to the ground. Also Jeshua, Bani, Sherebiah, Jamin, Akkub, Shabbethai, Hodiah, Maaseiah, Kelita, Azariah, Jozabad, Hanan, Pelaiah, the Levites, helped the people to understand the Law, while the people remained in their places. They read from the book, from the Law of God, clearly, and they gave the sense, so that the people understood the reading. (Nehemiah 8:1–8)

I love this narrative for many reasons. First, the people were unified around hearing God's Word. The text says they were gathered together "as one man." Second, the people "told Ezra the scribe to bring the Book of the Law of Moses." They wanted to hear God's Word. That's what I want my people to do. I want them to expect, and even demand, that those who mount their pulpit bring them the Book of God—nothing else! Third, the leaders read from the Book a long time, early morning until noon. And the people listened for a long time! They didn't get in a hurry with God's Word. Fourth, they set up the place in such a way that God's Word would be the focal point and that everyone could hear it. They even had a platform similar to the design of most of our church buildings. Fifth, the leaders read the Book and explained it to the people. "They gave the sense, so that the people understood" (v. 8). They did expository preaching.

But there's one more thing I love about this story. Did you notice the ways the people responded when God's Word was read? They stood, they blessed the Lord, they said "Amen," they raised their hands, they bowed their heads, they put their faces to the ground, and they worshiped God (v. 6). That's incredible! Isn't it true that most of those expressions are expressions that we often associate with other forms of worship, such as music and prayer? But notice, they did all of this in response to the preaching of God's Word! Why? Because they didn't make a big distinction between God and His Word. When God's Word was read and taught, they were prompted to worship Him.

Worship in the Psalms when Hearing God's Words

The writers of the Psalms made the same connection:

> In God, whose word I praise, in God I trust; I shall not be afraid. What can flesh do to me? (Ps. 56:4)

> I will lift up my hands toward your commandments, which I love, and I will meditate on your statutes. (Ps. 119:48)

> I wait for the LORD, my soul waits, and in his word I hope. (Ps. 130:5)

> I bow down toward your holy temple and give thanks to your name for your steadfast love and your faithfulness, for you have exalted above all things your name and your word. (Ps. 138:2)

God makes little distinction between His own nature and His own Word. This truth should compel us to teach our people to engage God's Word in the preaching event as an expression of authentic corporate worship.

WORSHIP WHILE HEARING GOD'S WORD

So how can people who listen to preaching engage God's Word in the sermon as an expression of worship? Let me offer just a few practical suggestions of things you can teach your people to do in order to worship their God as they listen to you preach.

First, teach your congregation to bring their Bibles and to follow the passage as you preach. Following along enables the listener to interact with God's voice. As long as we live in a country where we can still own Bibles, I think we should bring them to worship! I don't care whether it's a print copy or an electronic version. Just encourage your people to bring a copy and open it up or turn it on. For those who don't have one, make copies available either as they come in or at their seats. Lead them to *see* God's Word as they *hear* God's Word. Remind your people often that you're not a good enough speaker to hold their attention simply with your oratory skills.

What about projecting the Bible verse or passage on a screen? There are advantages, yet I would encourage otherwise. People will get lazy and stop bringing their Bibles. Use the screen(s) for your major points and maybe for cross-references, but do not include your primary preaching text. Teach your people to bring their Bibles and follow you on the journey through the text.

Second, teach your congregation to still their hearts. Probably the thing most preachers want their people to do while they're preaching is to be quiet. We all hope that the sermon can be delivered without distraction. But we need to teach our people that their silence can be more than just an act of courtesy while the preacher is preaching. Looking upon the Scriptures in their hands can focus their attention and calm their hearts. In fact, often people will be overwhelmed by God's voice and they can't do anything else but be quiet. Let your people know that—as God's Word grips them—their quietness is an expression of their awe of Him. Even silence can be a sincere act of worship to our God. God often engulfs us with His truth and all we can do is sit silently in awe before Him.

A third way your people can worship while listening to God's Word is for them to say something in response. Vocalization can be a legitimate act of worship when driven by our God-given passions. God created us as emotional beings, so God's people should honor Him with their emotions when prompted by His voice. That's what they did in Nehemiah 8. God's Word stirred them, so they responded with their voices and even their bodies sometimes.

Teach your people that being emotional isn't the same thing as emotionalism. They don't need to be a distraction during worship. You don't need your worship service to become a circus. Corporate worship should be done decently and orderly (cf. 1 Cor. 14:40). But your people need to be encouraged to worship God in the preaching event with their whole being. Teach them not to be inhibited when He stirs their heart to agree vocally. There may be a time when a Bible verse or biblical truth proclaimed from the pulpit moves someone, and you can encourage them to feel free to add an "Amen!" or a "That's right!" or even to clap as expressions of agreement. Sometimes the Holy Spirit may convict them to bow before Him even while the Word is still being preached. At other times God's Word may cause individuals to tremble like Isaiah said: "Hear the word of the LORD, you who tremble at his word" (Isa. 66:5). Free up your people to express what they're feeling when they hear God's Word preached.

God's voice—heard directly through the Scriptures and indirectly through the preacher who proclaims its words, meaning, and application—deserves to be revisited. Taking notes during the sermon seems to be the most logical way to make this happen. People can record insights while you're preaching or fill in blanks in a listening guide. They can also write down any insights, important truths, and their feelings as the Word is preached. Later they can go back and review what they wrote. They can be reminded of what they heard, and even discuss the truths with others.

At the same time, there's much to be said for encouraging people not to take many notes during the sermon, as they focus on the Word being spoken. Some truth may be missed when one is trying to listen and write at the same time. There's something mysterious about the preaching moment, and you may do well to encourage your people to give their undivided attention to what you're saying so they don't miss anything. So remind them only an occasional note is necessary. Many churches today record sermons on disc and/or stream them online as "podcasts" afterwards; many listeners can add notes as they listen to the message again.

Whether they take notes or not during the sermon, teach your people to reflect on what they heard and experienced after the worship event is over. Teach them to revisit the message, meditate on it, and soak it in.

WHAT WE SHOULD TEACH ABOUT PREACHING

Because preaching is an act of worship, it naturally brings glory to God when it's done right. Paul talked about this reality in 1 Corinthians 1 when he said the message of the cross "is the power of God for salvation" (Rom. 1:16), which is totally contrary to the thinking of the world (see 1 Cor. 1:18–21). In fact, the apostle said it's foolish and offensive to the world. God chose a seemingly foolish message of atonement, namely the cross. And He chose the "foolish" method of preaching to advance that message (see v. 21). And if that were not enough, He chose foolish men to proclaim it!

Why did God set it up this way? God's intent in doing this is articulated in two purpose clauses in 1 Corinthians 1:29 and 31. Paul said it was "so that no human being might boast in the presence of God . . . so that, as it is written, 'Let the one who boasts, boast in the Lord.'" God set all this up for one reason—His glory. The whole deal is rigged so that when He does otherworldly stuff through the work of the gospel, He alone will get the glory!

The break between 1 Corinthians 1 and 2 is one of the places in our English Bibles that the chapter divisions do us a disservice. Those chapter and verse divisions weren't there when the Holy Spirit inspired the Bible. In

1 Corinthians 2, Paul immediately began to talk about preaching, a subject which can't be disassociated with the discussion in chapter 1. We can't deal in 1 Corinthians 1 with the cross as God's power for salvation to the end that He may glorified, and then stop. We have to keep going.

When we do, we find Paul telling the Corinthians in verses 1–5 how he preached when he was with them so that God alone would get the glory. In fact, 1 Corinthians 2:5 even bookends the thought with another purpose clause: "so that your faith might not rest in the wisdom of men but in the power of God." Paul preached in such a way that only God would get the glory, which culminated with the Corinthians putting their faith in God's power and not in Paul's wisdom. Do you know what that says about preaching? The reason Paul preached, and the reason he preached the way he preached, was so God would get the glory.

Sandwiched between those purpose clauses in 1 Corinthians 1:31 and 2:5 that instruct us to glorify God and not ourselves are three characteristics of the preaching event. Each ensures that God receives glory instead of the preacher or the congregation. Pastor, teach your people what you do as a preacher to ensure that the following things happen, and teach them what they can do to help.

Effective Preaching Focuses an Audience on God's Word

God's Word deserves that people pay attention when it's preached. If that's going to happen, distractions need to be minimized. Paul told the Corinthians, "When I came to you, brothers, [I] did not come proclaiming to you the testimony of God with lofty speech or wisdom" (1 Cor. 2:1). The word *lofty* in 1 Corinthians 2:1 means "rising out above" and carries the idea of having preeminence or superiority.[3] It refers both to the way the message is presented —"speech"—and the way in which the mind organizes the message— "wisdom." Paul wasn't saying he refused to use good speech or healthy thought processes. He simply said he refused to allow those things to overshadow—or *rise out above*—his message when it was presented.[4] In other words, he did everything he could to make sure that nothing distracted attention away from God's Word when it was preached.

As preachers, we're compelled to make sure that nothing we do or say distracts from God's Word in the sermon. We can't make God's Word more powerful than it already is. But if we're not careful, we can distract from it and hinder its supernatural power from impacting our people. When I teach sermon delivery courses I tell preachers that it's not about us becoming more polished orators, as if we could make God's Word more powerful. But it's about us learning how to minimize things we say and do that can derail its power. Paul said as much when he wrote he didn't come with "lofty speech or wisdom" (1 Cor. 2:1).

What this means is that the preacher must evaluate everything he does and says in the sermon to make sure he is not distracting from God's Word. This requires brutal honesty, keen discernment, and careful interrogation. Is my outline so flowery that it impresses the listeners but doesn't help the journey through the text? Are any of my illustrations so emotionally charged that people might get caught up in them and miss the truth they're trying to illustrate? Concerning outward appearances, is my attire conducive for the preaching event in my context, or might it be a distraction to some listeners? Does the way my platform is set up call attention to the Word or overshadow it? Do my graphics prop the Word up, or do they just wow the people?

Those are just some of the kinds of questions we need to ask to make sure we're not distracting from God's Word. Teach your people that you're committed to this kind of sermon assessment in order to ensure God's glory.

But what about our people? What can they do to make sure God's Word has their undivided attention when it's preached. Here are five ways you can encourage your people to maximize their focus during the preaching event.

1. *Pray for the message in advance.* All week long God's people should be asking Him to show up, to talk directly to them, to anoint their preachers, to change their lives, and to save lost people. As the preacher, think of creative ways to use social media, email, and printed materials to remind your people to pray for the preaching event.

2. *Plan for the preaching event in their schedules.* Teach your people to make the preaching event a priority, not an afterthought. Encourage them not to plan their week out and then decide to come to church just because they have some time left over. Stanfield described preaching as "giving the Bible a voice."[5] If the Bible is God's Word to men and women, and preaching is putting that in audible form, we can remind our people to come each week in order to hear wisdom and hope from God.

3. *Prepare their hearts for the message.* Encourage your people to think ahead about the preaching event, to anticipate it. Teach them to ask God to prepare them for it. Talk to your people about going to bed

early enough on Saturday night so they're rested and alert. Help them plan ahead to stay tuned in during the sermon and not to depend on your oratorical ability to keep them awake.

4. *Participate in it every week.* Teach your people to engage in the preaching event instead of being a spectator. Instruct them to open their Bibles and follow along in their worship notes. Challenge them not to multitask on their phones or tablets. If you're using a fill-in-the-blank listening guide, tell them not to check out when the last blank is filled in. The Scriptures are still being preached! They need to stay engaged instead of gathering their stuff to go home.

5. *Process it when it's over.* Encourage your people to revisit the text of Scripture in the coming week. They can review their notes, discuss the message with their families or small groups, and even tell an unbeliever what they learned. They can use it to start a spiritual conversation that can lead to a gospel presentation.

6. *Practice it in their lives.* Exhort your people to obey what God says. Challenge them to give the sermon feet by putting it into practice. Caution them about letting it fall by the wayside as an academic exercise. God's Word always demands a response. Paul assumed as much when he wrote, "That your faith might not rest in the wisdom of men but in the power of God" (1 Cor. 2:5).

As your people begin to participate actively in the preaching event, they will take more ownership of it. The value they place on the sermon will rise, and you will gain new partners in making sure the Word is lifted up and God is glorified. And when that happens, the community of faith will ascend to new heights in worship.

Effective Preaching Gives the Audience a Gospel Focus

The second element of effective preaching is the message centered on the gospel. As Paul wrote to the Corinthian believers, "I decided to know nothing among you except Jesus Christ and him crucified" (1 Cor. 2:2). Paul determined that God was glorified when he magnified the message of the gospel in his preaching.

He didn't merely present Jesus as the perfect teacher, the perfect example, or the perfect man. He proclaimed Him as the divine Savior and Lord who has the right to lay claim on every person's life. Now we're not to conclude from Paul's statement that all he did was preach evangelistic messages in Corinth and call people to be saved. The word *crucified* in the language of the New Testament is in a tense that indicates that Christ not only was crucified, but He continues in the character of the crucified One. In other words, He was crucified at a point and time in the past, but the implications of His death continue into the present. That means the effect and nature of the crucified Christ still have bearing on every person's life today, both believers and unbelievers (cf. Luke 9:23–24; 2 Cor. 4:10; Phil. 3:10–11).

Pastors and preachers, this truth suggests that the content of our preaching primarily should be about the crucified Christ and the call on our lives to be conformed to His death. That means crucifying our fleshly desires and dying to self every day. Much of the "felt needs" and "life application" preaching today runs contrary to this truth. While claiming to have Christ as its theme, it offers practical help for dealing with the human situation without ever demanding that we crucify our flesh. It addresses felt needs but never beckons people to die to their worldly desires. People often leave the preaching event with practical help for life situations, but with no desire to lose their lives for Christ's sake. They go away from the sermon understanding more about themselves but no more about the crucified Christ.

The message of the cross and the crucified life will surface regularly if we preach expositorily, laying open the Spirit's intended meaning in every text. Teach your people that this is your resolve in your sermons, as well as for their lives.

So how can our people help keep the gospel central in the preaching event? Essentially, you need to change their worldview and expectations when it comes to the sermon. They need to be helped to think differently about what's happening when the Word is preached. Consider teaching them these five ways they should engage the preaching event in order to magnify the gospel:

1. *Listen for the crucified Lord in every sermon.* Invite your people to hold you accountable for exalting Christ and the cross in every sermon. Tell them to let you know when they don't hear it. Challenge them to listen to see how the gospel is featured. Ask them to join you in not just giving and receiving moralistic life lessons that would be equally at home in a Jewish synagogue or a Muslim mosque.

2. *Look for the crucified life in every sermon.* As they hear about the crucified Christ, teach them to look for what it demands of them. Tell them to ask, "What in my life today needs to be crucified by this

truth? What fleshly desire or characteristic or habit needs to die today because of who Christ is and what He's done? And what character of Christ needs to replace it?" Even when you—as the preacher—don't provide specific application to everyone's life, they can be making application themselves.

3. *Expect the sermon to re-create, not merely rehabilitate.* No doubt, the Bible will do some rehabilitation in your people's lives, but God wants far more. He wants to make them look like Jesus. Teach your people that something intangible is always going on when the Word is preached rightly and obeyed promptly. It's a supernatural thing that isn't always discernable in pragmatic application. Remind your people often that they should expect God to do this glorious work in them through the preaching event.

4. *Expect the sermon to foster godliness, not just give guidance.* To be sure, the Bible gives a lot of guidance about a lot of stuff in life. But God is more concerned about giving your people the divine guidance of the Holy Spirit to empower His nature and life inside them. Teach them to think about how the sermon calls them to godliness instead of how it merely gives them guidance for the daily events in their lives.

5. *Expect the sermon to provide transformation, not just information.* The Bible is filled with a lot of good, interesting information. But that information isn't intended to fill our people's minds with knowledge. It's intended to change them into new people. Encourage your people to evaluate the sermon, not on the basis of whether or not it was interesting and kept them awake, but on the basis of whether it made their lives different than they were before they heard it.

As the gospel transforms your people to look like Jesus, as it develops God's life inside of them, and as it transforms them into new men and women, they'll discover answers to a whole lot more of their questions and find guidance for a whole lot more of their life issues. So be intentional about changing their perspective when it comes to the preaching event.

Effective Preaching Reminds
Both Preacher and Audience of Their Human Weakness

The third quality of effective preaching is harder for us to get our arms around because it's so contrary to what our culture teaches. It's God's seemingly twisted approach of manifesting His power through our weakness.

There is power for us when we let God work through us, writes Paul in 1 Corinthians 2:3–4. When the apostle arrived in Corinth, he wasn't much to see or hear by Corinthian standards. Some accounts say he was short, bald, bowlegged, had only one eyebrow, and probably had a black eye. He was a poor and run-down figure indeed! Why? His "weakness" in verse 3 likely was because he had been in prison in Philippi, driven out of Thessalonica and Berea, and basically ignored in Athens. He was drained physically and emotionally. His "fear" and "trembling" likely was due to his burden for the gospel to take root in an unpromising place like Corinth. While the audiences of Corinth liked polished oratory and philosophic presentation, neither Paul's "speech" nor "message" contained "plausible words of wisdom" (v. 4). His word choice and delivery weren't very enticing and persuasive by cultural standards. Yet His preaching was done "in demonstration of the Spirit and of power." The one thing Paul had was the power of God's Spirit, and he was okay with that!

Like Paul, our human weakness and condition gives us the perfect way to demonstrate the mighty hand of God so He gets the glory instead of us. Since the beginning of history God has operated with this weird economy (cf. 1 Sam. 16:7; Zech. 4:6; 2 Cor. 4:7; 12:9–10). To ensure that nobody steals His glory, He's worked within a set of rules that seems so twisted to the world. While the world thinks power comes through power, God demonstrates power through weakness.

In His economy, if you want to be first, you have to be last.

If you want to be a leader, you have to be a servant.

If you want to be exalted, you have to be humbled.

If you want to live, you have to die.

That seems messed up! But that's the way God works. So be encouraged! God uses weak and powerless men through whom to release the supernatural power of the preached Word.

When you sense your weaknesses as a preacher of God's Word, you can respond these ways:

1. *Embrace God's "twisted" economy when you feel weak.* When you are at your weakest point and in your most difficult circumstances, you may have your greatest opportunity to experience God's power. Don't be in a hurry to get out of a tough ministry situation and find a "better" church. Stop when you're in that valley and remember that it has been in times and places like yours that God has shown Himself strongest to His preachers!

2. *Celebrate your weaknesses as a preacher of the gospel.* If you desire God's Spirit to move in your preaching, then adopt a different view of preaching talent. Stop measuring effectiveness by smooth oratory, dynamic personality, skillful delivery, attractive appearance, and theological education. Certainly be thankful for the variety of gifts God has given you as a preacher, and never cease being a lifelong learner. But don't celebrate those things. Instead, celebrate your human weakness as it yields to God's Spirit, knowing that's where you're most likely to find God's power!

3. *Come to the message of the cross with your weaknesses.* If preaching Christ involves bringing the cross to bear on our fleshly and worldly desires, then bring your weaknesses and failures and surrender them to the cross. Let the cross of Christ slay them every week, regardless of the cost. "It is highly unlikely that any man will ever know the Spirit's power until he is willing to confess before God, 'If You must hurt me to make me a suitable channel of Your power, then do so.'"[6] If you find yourself in a position of weakness, desire God's power so much that you're willing to endure it. And if you're in a position of strength, don't hesitate to ask God to mess it up if that's the only way you can experience His power!

The people of faith in your congregation also can help glorify God by celebrating His power through weakness. But be aware that it's an uphill battle to get them to do so. Not only does everything in our sinful nature pull against this reality, but everything in our culture programs Christians to view preachers the same way we do movies stars and concert artists—choosing favorites and criticizing others. That's exactly what was going on in Corinth. The purpose clause in 1 Corinthians 2:5 essentially is tied to the beginning of chapter 1 where Paul rebukes the Corinthians for attaching themselves to preachers the same way they followed Greek orators and philosophers.

The Corinthians listened to orators and philosophers for entertainment, much like we go to theatres and concerts. When the gospel came to Corinth, the church suddenly had its own version of orators and philosophers. They called them preachers! And some of the believers began to apply their secular entertainment values on the church's 'high profile' figures. While the preachers listed in 1:12—Paul, Apollos, and Cephas—didn't have conflicting theologies or different messages, they certainly had differing personalities, styles, and even levels of giftedness. So the church developed its own version of groupies and fan clubs. That's why Paul wrote, "There is quarreling among you, my brothers. What I mean is that each one of you says, 'I follow Paul,' or 'I follow Apollos,' or 'I follow Cephas,' or 'I follow Christ'" (1 Cor. 1:11–12).

Paul apparently thought some of the Corinthians were putting their trust in the wrong place, even placing entertainment values on to the preaching event. That's why he preached as he did, "so that your faith might not rest in the wisdom of men but in the power of God" (1 Cor. 2:5). Note this, preacher: People will put their faith in whatever they consider most important in the preaching event. And that's why it's important for us to teach them how to lean into God's economy of power through weakness so He gets the glory when they put their faith in the right place.

Here are some things you'll want to shepherd them to do:

1. *Resist the Christian 'Rock Star' culture.* I remember listening to an interview with John Piper in which he was asked about a young preacher who was growing in popularity. The interviewer described the young man as a "rock star" in evangelicalism. With a troubled expression and tone, Piper responded: "Let's not be the ones who use that terminology." If we're not careful, we'll become like the Corinthians who simply transferred the economy of contemporary entertainment and wisdom onto the preaching event in church. While tragically some preachers pursue such accolades, others are not seeking the limelight. But many Christians thrust it on them. We need to educate our people to this disconnect and compel them to avoid it.

2. *Affirm faithful pastors of local churches.* Our podcast and social media culture has birthed wonderful benefits and opportunities for gospel advancement. But it's also bittersweet in that those media have created a seedbed for unhealthy ecclesiology. Some Christians have replaced involvement in the local church with their favorite downloadable preacher, and they've undermined the value of local church pastors by making unhealthy comparisons. It's unhealthy and unfair when believers start comparing their own pastors with the preachers who write books and preach at conferences and have available podcasts. There are many shepherds of local churches who are faithfully preaching this same message of the gospel every week, yet who may not have the same level of giftedness, style, personality, or resources as

a higher profile preacher. Pastor, while it may be awkward for you to address with your own people, exhort them not to compare preachers with larger platforms with those who faithfully and consistently assume the platform in our local churches every week. Encourage them to affirm and encourage their pastors with their words, notes, service, and faithfulness.

3. *Credit the message, not the messengers.* When God does supernatural stuff in our lives, it makes sense that we should give Him credit. When He saves us, heals our bodies, restores our marriages, delivers us, and otherwise shows Himself strong to us, then we should thank and praise Him as opposed to His servants. Encourage your people to give credit where credit is due. Tactfully and gracefully train them not to say things like, "Pastor Jim taught me this truth," or "Pastor Tony changed my life." Instead, encourage them to say things like "The Bible says," or "God did this in my life," or "The gospel radically changed me." While we always want our people to encourage us in our work, we need to help them give the credit to God and His gospel instead of one of His messengers.

James Spurgeon was the grandfather of Charles H. Spurgeon, the famed British pastor known as "The Prince of Preachers." The elder Spurgeon also was a pastor, and equally committed to elevating the gospel message above the popularity of the preacher. On one occasion Charles, already a well-known figure, had been announced to preach at a church in Suffolk, but was late in arriving. So his grandfather started the service. When Charles still didn't show up, his grandfather began to preach a sermon "By Grace You Are Saved" from Ephesians 2. After a while, a disturbance at the door made it apparent that the distinguished Spurgeon had finally arrived. So the elder Spurgeon said to the congregation, "Here comes my grandson. He can preach the Gospel better than I can." Then in mid-sentence he turned to address his grandson coming down the aisle: "But you cannot preach a better Gospel, can you, Charles?"[7]

The gospel doesn't increase in quality or effectiveness based on the oratory, wisdom, or giftedness of the preacher. One preacher may be able to preach better than another, but he can never preach a better gospel! Let's intentionally teach our people how to approach the preaching event so that God alone gets all the glory.

HOW WE CAN TEACH PREACHING

All of us have our own particular ways we like to enter into spiritual conversations with strangers that we meet. One of my favorites is to ask people what they do for a living. Usually, after they've told me what they do, they'll ask me what I do. My answer is always the same: "I have the hardest job in the world. I'm responsible for teaching Baptist preachers how to preach without being obnoxious." The responses I get to that answer are always similar. "Man, that is hard!" someone will exclaim. "How do you do that?"

Possibly you're thinking the same thing about this subject of teaching preaching to your congregation. Maybe you find yourself saying, "Okay, I can see the value of educating my people about preaching. But how do I do that?"

Great question. I'm glad you asked. Here are some ways I've found helpful in teaching a congregation how to value and engage the preaching event so they can worship our Lord and bring glory to Him.

Preach about Preaching

One of my pet peeves in preaching is when a pastor uses the preaching event to do something other than preach, especially without clarifying or qualifying it with his congregation. I feel uncomfortable when a pastor presents an annual "state of the church" address during his weekly preaching time without prefacing it with something like, "I'm not going to preach today." I've seen others address particular cultural issues that the Bible doesn't address, but couch those discourses in sermonic form and deliver them in the weekly time allocated for preaching.

When we do that, we abdicate the preaching event to something that it was never intended to be, and that's hearing from God. Even worse, we unwittingly teach our people that anything and everything is preaching.

Similarly a pastor should surrender his preaching time to teach his people about preaching. Do so and you will send a wrong message that will be counterproductive to what you actually want to do. However, that doesn't mean that you can't sometimes "kill two birds with one stone" by teaching people about preaching *while* you're preaching. How? By preaching about preaching! When we preach on the subject of preaching we are capitalizing on the best of both worlds—addressing a subject through the medium for which that subject was intended. On top of that, when we preach about preaching we are able to do it with confidence that the Holy Spirit is attending our effort with otherworldly power!

Even though the Bible was never intended to be a homiletics textbook, God actually does address the preaching event directly in a number of places. We've already noted a couple of them in this chapter as we considered the events of Nehemiah 8. Verses 1–12 offer a wonderful text on the worship of God's people driven by the reading, explanation, and application of Holy Scriptures. Some form of the word *understand* appears five times in those twelve verses, underscoring the importance of biblical exposition in the life of the community of faith. Similarly, Paul forthrightly addressed how he preached for God's glory in 1 Corinthians 2:1–5.

But there are other passages describing the preaching event, including Paul's words to Timothy, a young preacher. First Timothy 4:11–16 reveals the preaching pattern of pastors in the early church who read the Scriptures publicly, and then explained and applied them to people's lives. And in 2 Timothy 4:1–5, the apostle Paul speaks to the preaching event straight up when he exhorts the young pastor to "preach the word" (v. 2).

So let me encourage you to preach periodically on the subject of preaching from appropriate and relevant passages. Sometimes you can do that as you come to those texts in systematic exposition series. When you do, no one can ever accuse you of just preaching on your favorite subject or magnifying your particular role in the church. Instead, your people will be helped to see this important subject in the context of God's redemptive plan. At other times you will want to address the subject of preaching in a stand-alone message here and there. The texts mentioned above—as well as many others—can serve you well in those times, with implications for both the preacher and the congregation. You might even do a short series on the role of preaching in the life of the church in which you expound one of those passages in each message. In addition to passages that speak directly to the preaching event, a plethora of biblical texts have implications for preaching (e.g., Pss. 19 and 119; Luke 24:13–49; 2 Tim. 3:10–17). When you're preaching those passages, you'll want to be careful not to make the subject of preaching the primary focus. But you can still include the subject and make relevant application to you and your people.

Teach about Preaching

In addition to preaching about preaching, be intentional about inserting shorter "teaching segments" that will help educate your people. I like to think of these deposits as "preaching infomercials." Again, you'll want to be sure that you don't give these shorter segments as substitutes or replacements for your preaching time; however, they can be used to preface or conclude a sermon, or even to be a feature at some other point in a worship gathering.

As a pastor, I have often prefaced a sermon by saying something like, "Before I read our text this morning I want to take a moment to remind you why we do what we do at this point in our worship times." And then I will take no more than about five minutes to give some explanation and exhortation about preaching. I might talk to the people about why we study through books of the Bible, why we treat individual texts expositionally, or why I ask them to open their Bibles and follow along. At other times I might give them some practical suggestions for listening to the sermon, taking notes (or not taking notes!), or how to involve their children in the sermon for that week. The previous discussions in this chapter may provide you with other ideas of things you can use in short teaching times like this.

Another way to teach your people about preaching is periodically to offer a class or even a training course on the subject during your church's discipleship training program or adult Bible classes on Sunday mornings. Go back and locate your notes from your Bible college or seminary course, or your notes from the last conference on preaching that you attended. But be careful not to just dump that information on your people and overwhelm them with technical details and approaches to sermon development. While that information may be helpful for other preachers and Bible teachers in your congregation, the majority of your people will be better served by instruction on how they are involved in the preaching event. So think about things like we've already discussed in this chapter, specifically those subjects that help them understand the preaching event in the church, stuff that helps them think differently about it and be involved in it. Give them a new worldview about preaching. Include information about the congregation's role in the preaching event, and how they can prepare to be meaningfully engaged in it. You will be surprised about the interest your people take in such instruction.

Write about Preaching

Shepherding a congregation in part through writing has been an aspect of pastoral ministry for many years. Since the inception of public mail service pastors have been writing columns in church newsletters and sending all-church mail-outs to communicate important information and provide their people with helpful guidance. Additionally, brief exhortations from the pastor in weekly church bulletins have been regular fare for numerous congregations. More recently, emails and brief electronic newsletters have joined the mix. These media have provided effective ways to give congregations guidance and encouragement outside of the pulpit.

Such forms of mass communication can be used to teach people about preaching. If you're using any of these means to communicate with your people, consider making preaching and its role in the congregation the subject of some of the main articles. These brief preaching "news flashes" can make important contributions to your people's understanding of and value on the preaching ministry. Many pastors write church columns in series as well, packaging a number of weekly installments under the same topic. Doing one of these series each year on the subject of preaching can go a long way toward educating your people about the crucial role of the public proclamation of God's Word.

Obviously, modern technology, including mass emails and church websites, have taken opportunities to shepherd through writing to a new level. Pastor's columns are now posted on church websites and can be included in emails that are sent to every member of the congregation. Other pastors are using online blogs—in written, audio, and video forms—to make additional deposits in their people's spiritual growth. Facebook and Instagram posts are serving as still other means to reach large numbers in our congregations with teaching, instruction, and encouragement that extends far beyond the weekly sermon.

There are even those tweets. Sent out on Twitter, they can reach massive audiences on an almost instant and immediate basis. So why not make a periodic deposit of 140 characters (or less) about preaching in the hearing of your people, especially when you know it's going to be retweeted to an even larger number of people? Likewise you can send a Facebook posting on the ministry of the Word that will be "liked" and linked to multiple conversations. The host of mindless and meaningless ways these mediums often are used can be redeemed to help shape our people's understanding of the weighty and eternal ramifications of the preaching event. Don't sleep through the revolution of mass and social media when it can actually be used to inform and shape your people in healthy ways.

Practice Faithful Preaching

"Preach the Gospel at all times. Use words if necessary." This quote is often attributed to St. Francis of Assisi, the founder of the Franciscan Order. The only problem is there's no record that dear Francis ever said it![8] Yet numerous people have used it to suggest that proclaiming the gospel by example is better than actually using your voice. Even if the great monk did say it, I think I would still have to push back. Not only does the suggestion create a useless dichotomy between speech and action, it also implies that preaching is something other than it is—an oral communication event.

At the same time, the suggestion that "actions speak louder than words" is appropriate in some contexts. And teaching preaching may be one of them. Without question, the most important and effective way to teach your people about preaching is to model it before them every week. When you faithfully proclaim God's Word, you not only teach your people God's truth, but you teach them how to study the Bible with integrity. They eventually begin to apply your hermeneutical and exegetical lens to their own personal study of the Scriptures. They develop a high view of the Bible and its proclamation merely by listening to you teach and preach it with passion. They grow to hunger for God's Word, and they long to hear it preached. They say as the returned exiles said to Ezra, "Bring us the Book!" (see Neh. 8:1).

But they also learn some other things. They learn that the preaching event is important because of the time and energy you spend in preparing to do it. They are encouraged to interact with it as you take them on a journey characterized by a combination of your oral speech as you verbalize instruction, and their own vision as you prompt them to look at particular verses, words, or phrases in their Bibles. The more they witness transformation taking place in their lives and the lives of their family members and friends, the more they find themselves praying for you and your preaching. Soon they begin to ask God to help them as they hear, receive, and obey His Word. They begin to glorify God more and more as they see the powerful attendance of God's Spirit on their pastor, even amidst all of his weaknesses and inabilities. They learn about preaching by watching and listening to you.

Pastor, in all your teaching and preaching, teach your people about preaching by practicing it faithfully every time you stand before them!

READING FOR PROGRESS

Azurdia, Arturo, III. *Spirit Empowered Preaching*. Ross-shire, Great Britain: Mentor, 1998.

Shaddix, Jim. *The Passion-Driven Sermon*. Nashville: Broadman & Holman, 2003.

Thompson, James W. *Preaching like Paul*. Louisville: Westminster John Knox, 2001.

CONCLUSION

CONSTRUCTION IN PROGRESS

Jerry Vines

Anumber of years ago, as we still often do, Janet and I were riding on an off-the-beaten-path country road. We always enjoy the beautiful scenery and unexpected places we find. As we drove along the winding mountain road we came upon a sign that said: "Caution: Construction in Progress."

For the next mile or so we found a bumpy road with delays, construction equipment, dust, and narrow stretches of road. The inconveniences and delays challenged our patience. I have often thought about that road with the sign "Caution: Construction in Progress" in relation to preaching. Those who listen to us preach may feel some of the same discomfort I felt that day. I fear in too many of my messages I have led hosts of weary listeners on some winding, bumpy, dusty roads of sermonic journey!

As we preach, our preaching remains a work in progress. As Jim pointed out in the previous chapter, God works through weak human vessels so the glory may be His (1 Cor. 2:3–5). Hopefully we are making progress so that our hearers are themselves making progress in their spiritual journey.

John Bunyan vividly traces the journey in *The Pilgrim's Progress*. Our messages should lead sinners through the Wicket Gate to the cross where they may lay their heavy burden down. And our sermons should lead believers up Difficulty Hill, to the Palace Beautiful, through Vanity Fair, etc., and prepare them to go across the Dark River to the Celestial City.

We should never think we have "arrived" in our preaching preparation or proclamation. E. M. Bounds said, "Preaching is not the performance of an hour. It is the outflow of a life. It takes twenty years to make the man. The true sermon is a thing of life. The sermon grows because the man grows."[1] So, as with our life, our messages are very much under construction. We must never think we have "arrived" in our Christian life, nor in our preaching. Your best sermon is yet to be prepared. Your most effective sermon is yet to be delivered.

I remember quite well the morning I awoke after my final message as pastor of First Baptist Church, Jacksonville, Florida. I had preached there for almost twenty-four years. In all I had been preparing and preaching messages for over fifty years. That morning there was no sermon to prepare for the next Sunday. I was not engaged in a systematic exposition of any Bible book. What was my plan? There has to be a plan. If not, retirement can be very frustrating and boring.

So I had a plan. I decided to put myself through seminary again. I laid out a course of study. I would read church history, go back through my Hebrew and Greek grammars, study biblical introductions and surveys, read constantly in the field of homiletics, etc. I would prepare messages for my itinerant schedule during my "fourth quarter" ministry. As I have done for many years, I continue to give my mornings to study. I am not content to coast to the finish line. I intend to keep making progress as a preacher until then.

Whether you're retired from the pastorate or you're still in the thick of a vocational or bi-vocational preaching ministry, you're still a work under construction. And, therefore, you still need to be progressing in your pulpit work. There are so many new, helpful tools available to preachers today. I try to read the newest offerings in a wide field of biblical, theological, and practical ministry studies. I am learning to utilize the astonishing new technology now available to preachers. Let me encourage you to take advantage of all the new resources you can get your hands on, and continue to read and learn in a variety of fields that shape you as a Christian and as a preacher. Marshall Goldsmith challenges his readers to picture themselves at ninety-five years of age facing imminent death. He says to imagine you can go back in time and talk to yourself at your current age. What advice, warnings, and encouragements would you give to yourself?[2] I pray that all of us would tell ourselves, "Be a life-long learner."

Ruth and Billy Graham were driving on a mountain road some years ago. They found themselves on a similar road construction as Janet and I did. The road was difficult to navigate. There was much construction underway with the same kind of inconveniences Janet and I encountered. Then Ruth saw a sign. She exclaimed, "That's what I want on my tombstone!" If you visit her grave at the Billy Graham Library in Charlotte, NC, you will find this epitaph on her tombstone: *End of Construction—Thank you for your patience.* Hopefully, what she said about her life can be said of ours.

Over time, we continue to grow in patience and all the other fruit of the Spirit. And God is continuing to use us in our weaknesses, for His glory. And one day our preaching will have come to the end of the road. Then, all of us who preach can say, "Construction Ended: Thank You for Your Patience."

NOTES

Introduction: "He Will Have to Do Better than That!"

1. Charles H. Spurgeon, *Lectures to My Students* (London: Marshall, Morgan and Scott, 1973), 207.
2. Ibid., 209.
3. John R. W. Stott, *The Message of I Timothy and Titus* (Downers Grove, IL: InterVarsity, 1996), 122.
4. Ibid., 123.
5. Johnson Oatman Jr., "Higher Ground," verse 1 (Chicago: Hope Publishing, 1957), 357. In public domain.

Chapter 1: "Gentlemen, This Is a Sermon!"

1. "'Gentlemen, This Is a Football,'" Packerville USA blog post, May 30, 2010 at http://packerville.blogspot.com/2010/05/gentlemen-this-is-football.html; also "Lombardi's 'This Is a Football,'" http://www.joelbieber.com/2012/06/lombardis-this-is-a-football/.
2. The terms *Bible, Scripture,* and *Word* (capitalized) are used synonymously and interchangeably by the author.
3. John A. Broadus, *A Treatise on the Preparation and Delivery of Sermons*, 4th ed., revised by Vernon L. Stanfield (San Francisco: Harper and Row Publishers, 1979), 19.
4. Ibid.
5. James D. Hernando, *Dictionary of Hermeneutics* (Springfield, MO: Gospel Publishing House, 2005), 26. See also Stanley Grenz, David Guretzki, and Cherith Fee Nordling, *Pocket Dictionary of Theological Terms* (Downers Grove, IL: InterVarsity, 1999), 66; and Millard Erickson, *Christian Theology*, 2d ed. (Grand Rapids: Baker, 1999), 199.
6. Merrill F. Unger, *Principles of Expository Preaching* (Grand Rapids: Zondervan, 1955), 18.
7. H. C. Brown, Jr., *A Quest for Reformation in Preaching* (Nashville: Broadman, 1968), 88.
8. Jim Shaddix, *The Passion-Driven Sermon: Changing the Way Pastors Preach and Congregations Listen* (Nashville: Broadman & Holman, 2003), 71–72.
9. David L. Allen, *Hebrews* (Nashville: Broadman & Holman, 2010), 104.
10. Hernando, *Dictionary of Hermeneutics*, 36.
11. Ibid., 15.
12. Bryan Chapell, *Christ-Centered Preaching: Redeeming the Expository Sermon* (Grand Rapids: Baker, 1994), 270.
13. John A. Broadus, *A Treatise on the Preparation and Delivery of Sermons* (Philadelphia: Smith, English, & Co., 1873), 145.
14. Steven W. Smith, *Recapturing the Voice of God: Shaping Sermons Like Scripture* (Nashville: Broadman & Holman, 2015), 1.
15. Ibid., 1–2.
16. Jerry Vines and Jim Shaddix, *Power in the Pulpit,* rev. ed. (Chicago: Moody, 2017), 34.
17. John R. W. Stott, *Between Two Worlds* (1982; reprint, Grand Rapids: Eerdmans, 2000), 96.
18. Shaddix, *Passion-Driven Sermon*, 278–79.
19. Stott, *Between Two Worlds,* 96.

Chapter 2: A Holy Man of God

1. Jerry Vines and Jim Shaddix, *Power in the Pulpit: How to Prepare and Deliver Expository Sermons*, rev. ed. (Chicago: Moody, 2017).
2. C. H. Spurgeon, *Lectures to My Students* (London: Morgan and Scott, 1973), 18.

3. Ibid., 17.
4. Jack Hughes, *Expository Preaching with Word Pictures* (Fearn, Scotland, UK: Christian Focus Publications, 2001), 28.
5. As cited in Stephen F. Olford and David L. Olford, *Anointed Expository Preaching* (Nashville: Broadman and Holman, 1998), 44.
6. Spurgeon, *Lectures*, 44.
7. The books include *My Utmost for His Highest* by Oswald Chambers; *Streams in the Desert*, *Springs in the Valley*, and other devotionals by Mrs. Charles E. Cowman; and the two volume set *For the Love of God* by D. A. Carson.
8. s.v. "plagarism," https://en.oxforddictionaries.com/definition/plagiarism.
9. For a deeper discussion of the anointing of the Spirit, see Vines and Shaddix, *Power in the Pulpit*, 78–79.
10. Olford and Olford, *Anointed Expository Preaching*, 217.
11. James M. Garretson, *Princeton and Preaching* (Edinburgh: The Banner of Truth Trust, 2005), 207.
12. Ibid.
13. Ibid., 115.
14. Jana Childers and Clayton J. Schmit, *Performance in Preaching: Bringing the Sermon to Life* (Grand Rapids: Baker Publishing Group, 2008), Kindle loc. 3220.
15. Jerry Vines and Jim Shaddix, *Power in the Pulpit* (Chicago: Moody, 2017), 78–79.
16. Jim Shaddix, *The Passion-Driven Sermon* (Nashville: Broadman and Holman, 2003), 39.

Chapter 3: Never Without a Word
1. Originally presented in Jim Shaddix, *The Passion-Driven Sermon* (Nashville: Broadman & Holman, 2003), 9.
2. Shaddix, *Passion-Driven Sermon*, 69–70.
3. Stephen Rummage, "Planning Your Preaching," *Preaching Source* (blog), September 5, 2016, http://preachingsource.com/ blog/planning-your-preaching-2/.
4. Brandon Cox, "4 Reasons to Plan a Year of Preaching," Pastors.com, December 23, 2015, http://pastors.com/4-reasons-plan-year-preaching/.
5. Ibid.
6. See also Jerry Vines and Jim Shaddix, *Power in the Pulpit: How to Prepare and Deliver Expository Sermons*, rev. ed. (Chicago: Moody, 2017), 37–38, 145–49, 159–61.
7. F. B. Meyer, *Expository Preaching* (Grand Rapids: Baker, 1974), 32.
8. Vines and Shaddix, *Power in the Pulpit*, 51–55.
9. John Piper, *Doctrine Matters* (Minneapolis: Desiring God, 2014), iv.
10. Stephen Rummage, "Planning Your Preaching." See also Stephen Nelson Rummage, *Planning Your Preaching: A Step-by-Step Guide for Developing a One-Year Preaching Calendar* (Grand Rapids: Kregel, 2002).

Chapter 4: Pulpit Discipleship
1. See Matthew 28:18–20; Mark 16:14–16; Luke 24:33–35, 44–49; Acts 1:8, 12–13.
2. E. M. Bounds, *Power Through Prayer* (Grand Rapids: Christian Classics Ethereal Library, n.d.), 37.
3. Jim Shaddix, *The Passion-Driven Sermon*: Nashville: Broadman & Holman, 2003), 117–18.
4. Ibid., 113.
5. Ibid., 118.
6. James W. Thompson, *Preaching Like Paul* (Louisville: Westminster John Knox, 2001), 93–94.
7. Ibid., 98–99.

Chapter 5: King James, Prince, and Merle

1. Northrop Frye, *The Great Code: The Bible and Literature* (New York: Harcourt Brace Jovanovich, 1982), xvi.
2. Norman L. Geisler and William E. Nix, *A General Introduction to the Bible*, rev. ed. (Chicago: Moody Press, 1986), 493.
3. Frye, *The Great Code*, 4.
4. Daniel L. Akin, David L. Allen, and Ned Mathews, *Text-Driven Preaching,* (Nashville: B&H, 2010), 129.
5. Leland Ryken, *The Legacy of the King James Bible*, (Wheaton: Crossway Books, 2011), 149.
6. Gustavus S. Paine, *The Men Behind the King James Version* (n.p: Thomas V. Crowell, 1959; repr. Grand Rapids: Baker, 1977), 172.
7. Ryken, *The Legacy,* 14.
8. Ibid., 232.
9. Paine, *The Men Behind the King James Version*, 125.
10. Jerry Vines and Jim Shaddix, *Power in the Pulpit: How to Prepare and Deliver Expository Sermons*, rev. ed. (Chicago: Moody, 2017), 150–53.
11. For an excellent article on poetic and wisdom literature, see "Introduction to the Poetic and Wisdom Literature," ESV Study Bible (Wheaton: Crossway, 2008), especially page 866, which notes the overlap of Psalms and Proverbs into both genres.
12. Steven W. Smith, *Recapturing the Voice of God* (Nashville: B&H, 2015), 27.
13. Jeffery Arthurs, *Preaching with Variety: How to Re-create the Dynamics of Biblical Genres*, (Grand Rapids: Kregel, 2007), 22.
14. Smith, *Recapturing the Voice of God*, 28.
15. Barry McCarty, "The Power and Peril of the Parables" (lecture, Southwestern Baptist Theological Seminary, Fort Worth, TX, March 2016).
16. Arthurs, *Preaching with Variety*, 603–605.
17. *The Prince of Egypt*, directed by Brenda Chapman, Stephen Hickner, and Simon Wells (Dream Works, 1998); DVD, DreamWorks Animation.
18. Arthurs, *Preaching with Variety*, 756.
19. David Buttrick, *Homiletic Moves and Structures*, (Minneapolis: Fortress Press, 1987), 245.
20. Abraham Kuruvilla, *A Vision for Preaching: Understanding the Heart of Pastoral Ministry*, (Grand Rapids: Baker, 2015), 81.
21. Akin, Allen, and Mathews, *Text-Driven Preaching,* 104.
22. Zack Eswine, *Preaching to a Post-Everything World: Crafting Biblical Sermons That Connect with Our Culture* (Grand Rapids: Baker, 2008), 67.
23. Steven Horst, *The Stanford Encyclopedia of Philosophy*, Spring 2011 Edition, s.v. "The Computational Theory of Mind."
24. Carmine Gallo, *Talk Like TED: The 9 Public-Speaking Secrets of the World's Top Minds* (New York: St. Martin's Press, 2014), 193–94.
25. Ibid., 194.
26. Carmine Gallo, *The Presentation Secrets of Steve Jobs* (New York: McGraw-Hill, 2010), 51.
27. Steven Smith, personal email response sent to author on August 29, 2016.
28. Jerry Vines and Jim Shaddix, *Power in the Pulpit*, rev. ed. (Chicago: Moody, 2017), 279, 281.
29. Adam B. Dooley and Jerry Vines, "Delivering a Text-Driven Sermon," in *Text-Driven Preaching*, Daniel L. Akin, David L. Allen, and Ned L. Matthews, eds. (Nashville: B&H, 2010), 249.
30. Bryan Chapell, *Christ-Centered Preaching:* (Grand Rapids: Baker, 1994), 93, as quoted in Dooley and Vines, "Delivering a Text-Driven Sermon," in *Text-Driven Preaching*.
31. Dooley, "Delivering a Text-Driven Sermon," 264.

Chapter 6: We Deal in Words, My Friend

1. Albert Mohler, "A Giant Has Fallen: The Death of Justice Antonin Scalia and the Future of Constitutional Government," February 14, 2016, www.albertmohler.com/2016/02/14/a-giant-has-fallen-the-death-of-justice-antonin-scalia-and-the-future-of-constitutional-government/.

2. Lauren Leatherby, "'Jiggery-Pokery': The Justices Have a Punny Way with Words," June 30, 2015, National Public Radio, http://www.npr.org/sections/itsallpolitics/2015/06/30/418645881/jiggery-pokery-the-justices-have-a-punny-way-with-words.

3. Walter C. Kaiser Jr., *Preaching and Teaching from the Old Testament* (Grand Rapids: Baker, 2003), 11.

4. Jerry Vines, "A Baptist and His Bible," Southern Baptist Annual Convention, June 16, 1987, St. Louis, MO.

5. Philip P. Bliss, "Wonderful Words of Life," *The Baptist Hymnal* (Nashville: Convention Press, 1991), 261. In public domain.

6. See Jerry Vines and Jim Shaddix, *Power in the Pulpit*, rev. ed. (Chicago: Moody, 2017), 140, 156, 173–76, chap. 5.

7. Marvin R. Vincent, *The Expositor in the Pulpit* (New York: Randolph, 1884), 7.

8. Daniel L. Akin, David L. Allen, and Ned L. Mathews, eds., *Text-Driven Preaching* (Nashville: B&H, 2010), 8.

9. As quoted in Jack Hughes, *Expository Preaching with Word Pictures* (Geanies House, UK: Christian Focus Publications, 2014), 20.

10. Kaiser Jr., *Preaching and Teaching from the Old Testament,* 10.

11. Akin, Allen, and Matthews, *Text-Driven Preaching,* 4.

12. I am indebted to David Allen for many of the definitions in this section. See David Allen, "Crash Course in Linguistics for Text-Driven Preaching," February 8, 2016, drdavidlallen.com/preaching/crash-course-in-linguistics-for-text-driven-preaching/.

13. David Alan Black, *Linguistics for Students of New Testament Greek* (Grand Rapids: Baker, 1995), ix.

14. As cited in Constantine R. Campbell, *Advances in the Study of Greek: New Insights for Reading the New Testament* (Grand Rapids: Zondervan, 2015), 40.

15. D. A. Carson, *Exegetical Fallacies,* 2nd ed. (Grand Rapids: Baker, 1996), 115. Also in chap. 4, no. 16 of *Power in the Pulpit.*

16. Campbell, *Advances in the Study of Greek*, 180.

17. Ibid.

18. Black, *Linguistics for Students*, 98.

19. Campbell, *Advances in the Study of Greek*, 23.

20. Ibid., 34.

21. Ibid., 35.

22. Black, *Linguistics for Students*, 2.

23. Carson, *Exegetical Fallacies*, 128.

24. Andreas Köstenberger, Benjamin Merkle, and Robert Plummer, *Going Deeper with New Testament Greek* (Nashville: B&H, 2016), 461.

25. Ibid., 475.

26. Ibid., 475–76.

27. Carson, *Exegetical Fallacies*, 27.

28. Moisés Silva, *Biblical Words and Their Meaning: An Introduction to Lexical Semantic,* (Grand Rapids: Zondervan, 1994), 10.

29. D. A. Carson, "Word-Study Fallacies," Silva, *Biblical Words and Their Meaning,* 70.

30. Silva, *Biblical Words and Their Meaning*, 38.

31. Carson, *Exegetical Fallacies*, 70.

32. Köstenberger, *Going Deeper with New Testament Greek*, 488.

33. David Allen, "Discourse Analysis and Preaching," The Northcutt Preaching Lectures, Southwestern Baptist Theological Seminary, Fort Worth, August 29, 2004.

Chapter 7: Is a Beeline the Best Line?

1. Christian George, blog, "6 Things Spurgeon Didn't Say," August 24, 2016, http://center .spurgeon.org/2016/08/24/six-things-spurgeon-didnt-say.
2. See also Matthew 5:18–19; Luke 4:20–21.
3. George H. Guthrie, "Hebrews" in *Commentary on the New Testament Use of the Old Testament*, ed. G. K. Beale and D. A. Carson (Grand Rapids: Baker, 2007), 919.
4. Bruce Ware, *Father, Son, and Holy Spirit: Relationships, Roles, and Relevance* (Wheaton: Crossway, 2005), 110.
5. Arturo Azurdia III, *Spirit Empowered Preaching* (Ross-Shire, England: Christian Focus Publications, 1998), 52.
6. Christopher J. H. Wright, *Knowing Jesus Through the Old Testament* (Downers Grove, IL: InterVarsity, 1995), 2.
7. "The Baptist Faith and Message," available online at http://www.sbc.net/ bfm2000/ bfm2000.asp.
8. Albert Mohler, "Charles Haddon Spurgeon—A Passion for Preaching," Part 3, http:// www.albertmohler.com/2004/09/22/charles-haddon-spurgeon-a-passion-for-preaching-part-three.
9. Thabiti Anyabwile, "About that Beeline to the Cross . . . ," http://thefrontporch .org/2016/02/ about-that-beeline-to-the-cross.
10. Ibid.
11. Ibid.
12. Tony Merida, *The Christ-Centered Expositor* (Nashville: B&H, 2016), 33.
13. Daniel Block, "Daniel Block on Christ-Centered Hermeneutics," in *Christ-Centered Teaching and Preaching,* ed. Ed Stetzer (Adobe PDF eBook; Nashville: Lifeway, 2013), 6.
14. Merida, *Christ-Centered Expositor*, 35.
15. Ibid., 36.
16. Norman L. Geisler, *Christ: The Theme of the Bible* (Chicago: Moody, 1968), 7.
17. Jeramie Rinne, "Biblical Theology and Gospel Proclamation," 9Marks, August 20, 2014, http://9marks.org/article/biblical-theology-and-gospel-proclamation/.
18. David Murray, "David Murray on Christ-Centered Hermeneutics," in *Christ-Centered Teaching and Preaching,* ed. Ed Stetzer (Adobe PDF eBook; Nashville: Lifeway, 2013), 10.
19. Sidney Greidanus, *Preaching Christ from the Old Testament* (Grand Rapids: Eerdmans, 1999), 227.
20. David Edward Prince, "The Necessity of a Christocentric Kingdom-Focused Model of Expository Preaching" (PhD diss., The Southern Baptist Theological Seminary, 2011), 81. Prince cites Enns' article "Apostolic Hermeneutics and an Evangelical Doctrine of Scripture: Moving Beyond a Modernist Impasse" in *Westminster Theological Journal* 65, (2003): 263–87. There Enns writes, "The term I prefer to use to describe this herme-neutic is *Christotelic*." This article very well may be the earliest appearance of the term in print.
21. Peter Enns, *Inspiration and Incarnation: Evangelicals and the Problem of the Old Testament* (Grand Rapids: Baker, 2005), 154.
22. Daniel Block, "Daniel Block on Christ-Centered Hermeneutics," 6.
23. Abraham Kuruvilla, *Privilege the Text! A Theological Hermeneutic for Preaching* (Chicago: Moody, 2013), 212.
24. Ibid., 117.
25. Bryan Chapell, *Christ-Centered Preaching*, 2nd ed. (Grand Rapids: Baker, 2005), 50.
26. Rinne, "Biblical Theology and Gospel Proclamation."
27. *New Dictionary of Biblical Theology*, ed. T. Desmond Alexander et al. (Downers Grove, IL: InterVarsity, 2000), 284.
28. Rick Warren, "How to Preach Like Jesus (Part 3): Keep It Interesting and Simple," July 24, 2015, http://pastors.com/preach-like-jesus-3.

29. Justin Taylor, "Carson: People Don't Learn What I Teach Them; They Learn What I'm Excited About"; an interview with D. A. Carson, November 19, 2010. This blog posting is available at http://www.blogs. thegospelcoalition.org/ justintaylor/2010/11/19/carson-people-don't-learn-what-i-teach-them-they-learn-what-im-excited-about/

30. Michael A. G. Haykin, ed., *The Revived Puritan: The Spirituality of George Whitefield* (Ontario: Joshua Press, 2000), 35–37.

Chapter 8: "Turpentine" the Imagination

1. As quoted in Warren Wiersbe, *Preaching and Teaching with Imagination* (Wheaton: Victor Books, 1994), 288.
2. Ibid., 288.
3. Ibid., 25.
4. W. Macneile Dixon, *The Human Situation*, (London: Longmans, Green, & Company, 1937), 65.
5. A. T. Robertson, *Word Pictures in the New Testament* (Nashville: Broadman Press, 1933), 205.
6. Arthur W. Hunt III, *The Vanishing Word* (Wheaton: Crossway, 2003).
7. Jack Hughes, *Expository Preaching with Word Pictures* (Dublin, Ireland: Mentor, 2014), 33.
8. Ibid., 123.
9. Jeffery Arthurs, *Preaching with Variety: How to Re-create the Dynamics of Bible Genre* (Grand Rapids: Kregel, 2007), 23.
10. Wiersbe, *Preaching and Teaching with Imagination*, 164.
11. Ibid., 89–198.
12. Leland Ryken, James C. Wilhoit, and Temper Longman III, *Dictionary of Biblical Imagery*, (Downers Grove, IL: InterVarsity, 1998).
13. As quoted in Wiersbe, *Preaching and Teaching with Imagination,* 50.
14. Hughes, *Expository Preaching with Word Pictures*, Kindle loc. 2254.
15. Arthurs, *Preaching with Variety*, 51.
16. F. W. Boreham, *A Bunch of Everlastings* (New York: The Abingdon Press, 1920), 149.
17. http://www.bartleby.com/73/540.html, as cited in George Bainton, *The Art of Authorship* (1890), 87–88.
18. Charles Spurgeon, *Lectures to My Students* (Grand Rapids: Zondervan, 1954), 138.
19. Carl L. Kell and L. Raymond Camp, *In the Name of the Father: The Rhetoric of the New Southern Baptist Convention* (Carbondale, IL: Southern Illinois University Press, 1999), 57. A recording of this message (in CD and DVD) is available at the store of www.jerryvines.com.
20. As cited in G. Robert Jacks, *Just Say the Word! Writing for the Ear* (Grand Rapids: Eerdmans, 1996), 140.
21. Wiersbe, *Preaching and Teaching with Imagination*, 234.
22. James Weldon Johnson, from "Listen, Lord—A Prayer" in *God's Trombones: Seven Negro Sermons in Verse* (New York: Penguin, 2008), 12.

Chapter 9: The Awakening of the Reverend Van Winkle

1. Van Winkle's extended sleep lasted "only" twenty years in Irving's classic tale, "Rip Van Winkle." In this adaptation we have extended his slumber to thirty-two years.
2. Zack Eswine, *Preaching to a Post-Everything World: Crafting Biblical Sermons That Connect with Our Culture* (Grand Rapids: Baker, 2008), 108.
3. Jack Hughes, *Expository Preaching with Word Pictures* (Geanies House, UK: Christian Focus Publications, 2014), Kindle loc. 957-958.
4. Jim Shaddix, *The Passion-Driven Sermon* (Nashville: Broadman and Holman, 2003), 118.
5. Ibid., 142.

6. David R. Helm, *Expositional Preaching: How We Speak God's Word Today* (Wheaton: Crossway, 2014), 40.
7. Ibid., 24.
8. Marvin R. Vincent, *The Expositor in the Pulpit* (New York: Randolph and Company, 1884), 15.
9. Haddon Robinson, *Biblical Preaching: The Development and Delivery of Expository Messages,* 3rd ed. (Grand Rapids: Baker, 2014), 101.
10. As quoted in Carmine Gallo, *Talk Like TED: The 9 Public-Speaking Secrets of the World's Top Minds* (New York: St. Martin's Press, 2014), 190.
11. Hershael York, "Communication Theory and Text-Driven Preaching," in *Text-Driven Preaching,* ed. Daniel L. Akin, David L. Allen, and Ned L. Mathews (Nashville: B&H, 2010), 226.
12. Ibid., 228–32.
13. Ian Stackhouse, *Text Message: The Centrality of Scripture in Preaching* (Eugene, OR: Pickwick Publications, 2014), 206.
14. The website www.ted.com is a goldmine of the latest information in this area. Look under the drop-down menu discover/topics/communication.
15. Gallo, *Talk Like TED,* 117.
16. Ibid., 76.
17. Ibid., 213.
18. Ibid., 187.
19. Hershael York, "The Long and Short of Sermons," January 2, 2016, *Pastor Well* (blog), http://www.pastorwell.com/blog/2016/1/2/preaching-points-the-long-and-short-of-sermons.
20. Leonard Sweet, *Giving Blood: A Fresh Paradigm for Preaching* (Grand Rapids: Zondervan, 2014), 51–52.
21. "Rhetoric," *The American Heritage Dictionary of the English Language,* 4th ed. (Boston: Houghton Mifflin, 2006).
22. Adam Dooley, "Delivering a Text-Driven Sermon" in *Text-Driven Preaching,* ed. Daniel L. Akin, David L. Allen, and Ned L. Mathews (Nashville: B&H, 2010), 246.
23. Carmine Gallo, *The Presentation Secrets of Steve Jobs* (New York: McGraw-Hill, 2010), 215.
24. Clayton J. Schmit and Jana Childers, *Performance in Preaching: Bringing the Sermon to Life* (Grand Rapids: Baker, 2008), 13–14.
25. Jerry Vines and Jim Shaddix, *Power in the Pulpit,* 2nd ed. (Chicago: Moody, 2017), 198–99, 268–76.
26. Harry S. Stout, *The Divine Dramatist: George Whitefield and the Rise of Modern Evangelicalism* (Grand Rapids: Eerdmans, 1991), xix.
27. Sweet, *Giving Blood,* 38.
28. Richard H. Cox, *Rewiring Your Preaching: How the Brain Processes Sermons* (Downers Grove, IL: InterVarsity, 2013), 44.
29. Shaddix, *The Passion-Driven Sermon,* 155.
30. Gallo, *The Presentation Secrets of Steve Jobs,* 198.
31. Robert W. Dale, *Nine Lectures on Preaching* (1878; repr. as *Nine Lectures on Preaching* [Charleston, SC: BiblioLife, 2009], 36).

Chapter 10: "Just As I Am"

1. Charlotte Elliott, "Just As I Am," *Worship and Service Hymnal* (Chicago: Hope, 1968), 198. In public domain.
2. L. R. Scarborough, *With Christ After the Lost,* rev. and exp. E. D. Head (Nashville: Broadman, 1952), 146.
3. See Jerry Vines and Jim Shaddix, *Power in the Pulpit,* rev. ed. (Chicago: Moody, 2017), 382–85.
4. Ibid., 246.

5. Roy J. Fish, *Coming to Jesus: Giving a Good Invitation* (Fort Worth: CreateSpace, 2016), 25.

6. R. Alan Streett, *The Effective Invitation* (Old Tappan, NJ: Revell, 1984; repr. Grand Rapids: Kregel, 2004), 181ff.

7. R. T. Kendall, *Stand Up and Be Counted* (Grand Rapids: Zondervan, 1984).

8. Quoted in R. Allen Streett, "The Public Invitation and Calvinism," in *Whosoever Will*, David L. Allen and Steve W. Lemke, eds. (Nashville: B&H, 2010), 246.

9. Streett, "The Public Invitation and Calvinism," 241–42.

10. Streett, *Effective Invitation*, 84.

11. Kendall, *Stand Up*, 47.

12. Streett, *Effective Invitation*, 93.

13. Kendall, *Stand Up*, 12.

14. Bob L. Ross, "Spurgeon and Altar Calls," June 19, 2010, www.reformedflyswatter .blogspot.com/ 2010_06_01_archive.html.

15. As quoted in Streett, *Effective Invitation*, 97.

16. Ibid., 107.

17. Fish, *Coming to Jesus*, 1.

18. Faris Whitesell, *Sixty-Five Ways to Give Evangelistic Invitations* (Grand Rapids: Zondervan, 1945), 12.

19. Fish, *Coming to Jesus*, 11.

20. Streett, *Effective Invitation*, 124.

21. Vines and Shaddix, *Power in the Pulpit*, 387.

22. Charles Spurgeon, "A Free Grace Promise" from the Metropolitan Tabernacle Pulpit, http://www.spurgeon.org/sermons/2082.php.

23. As quoted in Streett, *Effective Invitation*, 167.

24. Kendall, *Stand Up*, 71.

25. O. S. Hawkins, *Drawing the Net* (Dallas: GuideStone, 2002), 70.

26. William R. Moody, *The Life of Dwight L. Moody* (Murfreesboro, TN: The Sword of the Lord, n.d.), 145.

Chapter 11: Rising above Foyer Feedback

1. "11 Quotes that Show the Great Leadership of General George Patton," December 21, 2015, http://www.businessinsider.com/11-quotes-that-show-the-great-leadership-of-general-george-patton-2015-11/#1-a-pint-of-sweat-will-save-a-gallon-of-blood-1.

2. Keith Collier, "How to Evaluate Your Pastor's Sermons," June 18, 2015, https://9marks .org/article/how-to-evaluate-your-pastors-sermons-2/.

3. Daniel L. Akin, Bill Curtis, and Stephen Rummage, *Engaging Exposition* (Nashville: B&H, 2011), 4.

4. Paige Patterson, "Ancient Rhetoric: A Model for Text-Driven Preachers," in David L. Allen, Daniel L. Akin, and Ned Mathews, *Text-Driven Preaching* (Nashville: B&H, 2010), 17.

5. The questions in each category are adapted from Paige Patterson, "How to Evaluate a Sermon," https://www.youtube.com/watch?v=52XE6QCP0yU.

6. J. H. Freese, *Aristotle XXII; Art of Rhetoric* (Cambridge, MA: Harvard University Press, 1926), 17.

7. Patterson, "Ancient Rhetoric," 30–31.

Chapter 12: Teaching about Preaching

1. John Stott, *Between Two Worlds: The Art of Preaching in the Twentieth Century* (1982; Grand Rapids: Eerdmans; repr., 2000), 82.

2. Martin Luther, *A Manual of the Book of Psalms: or, The Subjects-Contents of All the Psalms* (London: Seeley and Burnside, 1837; repr. n.p.: BiblioBazar, 2009), 336.

3. Gordon D. Fee, *First Epistle to the Corinthians,* rev. ed., The New International Commentary on the New Testament (Grand Rapids: Eerdmans, 2014), 95.

4. Jim Shaddix, *The Passion-Driven Sermon: Changing the Way Pastors Preach and Congregations Listen* (Nashville: Broadman & Holman, 2003), 30.

5. John A. Broadus, *On the Preparation and Delivery of Sermons*, 4th ed., rev. Vernon L. Stanfield (San Francisco: Harper and Row, 1979), 19.

6. Arturo Azurdia III, *Spirit-Empowered Preaching: Involving the Holy Spirit in Your Ministry* (Ross-shire, Great Britain: Mentor, 1998), 145.

7. E. Y. Fullerton, *Charles Haddon Spurgeon: A Biography*, chap. 1, "The Spurgeon Country: 1965–1769," http://www.spurgeon.org/misc/bio1.php.

8. See Glenn Stanton, "Fact Checker: Misquoting Francis of Assisi," July 10, 2012, at https://www.thegospelcoalition.org/article/factchecker-misquoting-francis-of-assisi.

Conclusion: Construction in Progress

1. E. M. Bounds, *Power through Prayer* (London: Marshall, Morgan and Scott, n. d.), 11.

2. See Marshall Goldsmith, *What Got You Here Won't Get You There: How Successful People Become Even More Successful* (New York: Hyperion, 2007), 221–24.

APPENDIX

SERMON PRESENTATION FEEDBACK GUIDE

Preacher: _____ Evaluator: _____ Date:_____

CONSTRUCTION AND CONTENT

1. What did you **hear** to be the:
   Text of the Sermon:

   Theme/Subject of the Sermon:

2. Circle all of the following terms that describe your **Reaction** to the overall sermon content:

   Really enjoyed   Helpful   Interesting/Informative   Thought-provoking

   Touched me   Offended me   Over my head   Not that interesting

3. Circle all of the following terms that describe the sermon **Structure/Organization**, and jot down the **Main Points**:

   Easily understood   Mostly clear   Sometimes clear

   Not clear   Confusing   Tedious

4. Rate and comment on the following **Formal, Functional, and Expositional Elements**:

	Poor	Needs Attention	Satisfactory	Excellent	Comments
Introduction	1	2	3	4	
Explanation	1	2	3	4	
Application	1	2	3	4	
Illustration	1	2	3	4	
Argumentation	1	2	3	4	
Summation/Conclusion	1	2	3	4	
Integrity of Exposition	1	2	3	4	
Clarity of Development	1	2	3	4	
Transitions	1	2	3	4	
Christ-Centered?	1	2	3	4	
Gospel-Driven?	1	2	3	4	

VOICE

	Poor	Needs Attention	Satisfactory	Excellent	Comments
Volume	1	2	3	4	
Rate	1	2	3	4	
Articulation	1	2	3	4	
Oral Interpretation[1]	1	2	3	4	

1. Oral interpretation is the art of revealing meaning by virtue of the way the text is read aloud (e.g., inflection, emphasis, clarity, etc.).

BODY & DELIVERY

	Poor	Needs Attention	Satisfactory	Excellent	Comments
Eye Contact	1	2	3	4	
Facial Expressions	1	2	3	4	
Gestures	1	2	3	4	
Body Movement	1	2	3	4	
Overall Presence	1	2	3	4	
Use of Notes	1	2	3	4	

OTHER

1. Did you notice any distracting **Mannerisms** (unusual pacing, fidgeting with clothes, holding on to the podium, looking at the floor, hands in pockets, etc.) that are not addressed above? If so, what?

2. If applicable, describe the preacher's **Use of Objects** and/or **Media** in **one or more** of the following terms:

Effective	Added interest	Helped understanding
Had problems	Distracting	Didn't help

RECOMMENDATIONS

Three things to keep . . .   **Three things to throw away . . .**

1.   1.

2.   2.

3.   3.

RECOMMENDED
RESOURCES

Theology and Philosophy

Adam, Peter. *Speaking God's Words*. Vancouver: Regent College, 2004.

Allen, David L., Daniel L. Akin, and Ned Mathews. *Text-Driven Preaching: God's Word at the Heart of Every Sermon*. Nashville: B&H, 2010.

Begg, Alistair, *Preaching for God's Glory*. Wheaton: Crossway, 2010.

Goldsworthy, Graeme. *Preaching the Whole Bible as Christian Scripture: The Application of Biblical Theology to Expository Preaching*. Grand Rapids: Eerdmans, 2000.

Johnson, Dennis E. *Him We Proclaim: Preaching Christ for All the Scriptures*. Phillipsburg, NJ: P&R, 2007.

Lloyd-Jones, D. Martyn. *Preaching and Preachers*. Grand Rapids: Zondervan, 1971.

Meyer, Jason. *Preaching: A Biblical Theology*. Wheaton: Crossway, 2013.

Mohler, Albert. *He Is Not Silent*. Chicago: Moody, 2008.

Piper, John. *The Supremacy of God in Preaching*. Grand Rapids: Baker, 2004.

Shaddix, Jim. *The Passion-Driven Sermon: Changing the Way Pastors Preach and Congregations Listen*. Nashville: Broadman & Holman, 2003.

Stott, John R. W. *Between Two Worlds: The Art of Preaching in the Twentieth Century*. Grand Rapids: Eerdmans, 1982.

Prayer and the Holy Spirit

Azurdia, Arturo G. III. *Spirit Empowered Preaching*. Ross-shire, Scotland: Christian Focus Publications, 1998.

Bounds, E. M. *Power Through Prayer*. N.d. Reprint. Grand Rapids: Baker, 1991.

Heisler, Greg. *Spirit-Led Preaching*. Nashville: B&H, 2007.

Sargent, Tony. *The Sacred Anointing: The Preaching of Dr. Martyn Lloyd-Jones*. Wheaton: Crossway, 1994.

Interpretation (Hermeneutics)

Duvall, J. Scott, and J. Daniel Hays. *Grasping God's Word: A Hands-On Approach to Reading, Interpreting, and Applying the Bible*, 3rd ed. Grand Rapids: Zondervan, 2012.

Fee, Gordon D., and Douglas Stuart. *How to Read the Bible for All Its Worth: A Guide to Understanding the Bible*, 4th ed. Grand Rapids: Zondervan, 2014.

Greidanus, Sidney. *Preaching Christ from the Old Testament: A Contemporary Hermeneutical Method*. Grand Rapids: Eerdmans, 1999.

Hendricks, Howard, and William Hendricks. *Living by the Book: The Art and Science of Reading the Bible*, rev. ed. Chicago: Moody, 2007.

Plummer, Robert L. *40 Questions about Interpreting the Bible*. Grand Rapids: Kregel, 2010.

Preparation (Homiletics)

Akin, Daniel L., Bill Curtis, and Stephen Rummage. *Engaging Exposition*. Nashville: B&H, 2011.

Broadus, John A. *On the Preparation and Delivery of Sermons*, 4th ed., revised by Vernon L. Stanfield. San Francisco: Harper and Row Publishers, 1979.

Chapell, Bryan. *Christ-Centered Preaching: Redeeming the Expository Sermon*. Grand Rapids: Baker, 2005.

MacArthur, John F. *Preaching: How to Preach Biblically*, ed. Richard L. Mayhue. Nashville: Thomas Nelson, 2005.

Merida, Tony. *The Christ-Centered Expositor*. Nashville: B&H, 2016.

Richard, Ramesh. *Preparing Expository Sermons: A Seven-Step Method for Biblical Preaching*. Grand Rapids: Baker, 2001.

Robinson, Haddon W. *Biblical Preaching: The Development and Delivery of Expository Messages*, 2nd ed. Grand Rapids: Baker, 2001.

Rummage, Stephen Nelson. *Planning Your Preaching: A Step-by-Step Guide for Developing a One-Year Preaching Calendar*. Grand Rapids: Kregel, 2002.

Vines, Jerry, and Jim Shaddix. *Power in the Pulpit: How to Prepare and Deliver Expository Sermons*, 2nd ed. Chicago: Moody, 2017.

Communication (Delivery)

Ellsworth, Wilbur. *The Power of Speaking God's Word*. Scotland: Mentor, 2001.

Fasol, Al. *A Complete Guide to Sermon Delivery*. Nashville: Broadman & Holman, 1996.

Gordon, T. David. *Why Johnny Can't Preach: The Media Have Shaped the Messengers*. Phillipsburg, NJ: P&R, 2009.

McDill, Wayne. *The Moment of Truth: A Guide to Effective Sermon Delivery*. Nashville: Broadman and Holman, 1999.

Miller, Gary, and Phil Campbell. *Saving Eutychus: How to Preach God's Word and Keep People Awake*. Kingsford, Australia: Matthias Media, 2013.

Resources

bestcommentaries.com

Building a Theological Library (access at danielakin.com)

legacy.tms.edu/pdf/850Books.pdf

pastorscenter.sebts.edu/

preachingsource.com

ACKNOWLEDGMENTS

None of us makes progress in preaching—or in any other aspect of the Christian life and ministry—without the help of others. This project is no exception. It has come to fruition only because of the efforts of numerous other co-laborers who have helped us. Here we can only name a few . . .

Thank you, Lord Jesus Christ, for saving us and calling us to Your service. We've been helped by Your example of progressing "in wisdom and in stature and in favor with God and man" (Luke 2:52). So both of us say with the apostle Paul, "I thank him who has given me strength, Christ Jesus our Lord, because he judged me faithful, appointing me to his service" (1 Tim. 1:12).

Thank you, Janet and Debra, for walking beside us as partners in life and ministry for so many years. Without your patience and encouragement, these two preachers of the gospel would have never made any progress.

Thank you, Paige Patterson and Danny Akin, for your guidance and friendship. Dr. Patterson, your original encouragement in 1984 to write books on sermon preparation and delivery birthed a journey that has helped many preachers. Dr. Akin, your support on projects like this has challenged many pastors to be expository preachers and lifelong learners.

Thank you, Randall Payleitner and Jim Vincent at Moody Publishers, for partnering with us to help pastors grow in their preaching. You and your teams have kept these two preachers from hurting themselves at so many points.

Thank you—Michael, Neil, Clay, Ethan, and Quentin—for taking time out of your graduate studies to put your gifted eyes on our work. We're grateful for your partnership in the gospel, your progress as preachers, and your love for teaching others about this high calling.

INDEXES

SCRIPTURE INDEX

SUBJECT INDEX

IF EVER THERE WAS AN ENCYCLOPEDIA FOR PREACHING, THIS IS IT

"It is hard to improve a classic. Some would say it is impossible. I must beg to differ when it comes to the updated and revised version of Power in the Pulpit. *A really good book on preaching is now a really great book on preaching."*

DANIEL L. AKIN,

president, Southeastern Baptist
Theological Seminary, Wake Forest, NC

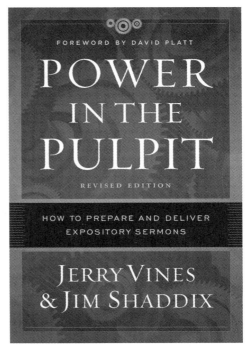

TAKE YOUR PREACHING TO THE NEXT LEVEL

"I enthusiastically recommend this helpful work."

STEVE GAINES,

pastor, Bellevue Baptist Church, Memphis, TN;
president, Southern Baptist Convention

MOODY
Publishers®

*From the Word **to Life**®*

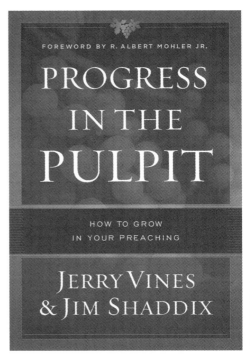

978-0-8024-1557-8

978-0-8024-1530-1

ALSO AVAILABLE AS EBOOKS